PAUL NEWMAN

By the same author:

Film Forum: Thirty-Five Top Filmmakers Discuss Their Craft
Sam Shepard: The Life and Work of an American Dreamer
Movies for a Desert Isle

PAUL NEWMAN

Elena Oumano

ROBERT HALE · LONDON

Copyright © 1989 by Elena Oumano
First published in Great Britain 1990

Robert Hale Limited
Clerkenwell House
Clerkenwell Green
London EC1R 0HT

British Library Cataloguing in Publication Data
Oumano, Elena
  Paul Newman.
  1. Cinema films. Acting. Newman, Paul, 1925–
  biographies
  I. Title
  791.43′028′0924

  ISBN 0-7090-3926-3

Printed in Great Britain by
St Edmundsbury Press Limited, Bury St Edmunds, Suffolk
and bound by WBC Bookbinders

LIST OF ILLUSTRATIONS

PICTURE CREDITS

The following photographs have been reproduced by kind permission of: Warner Brothers: 1; Twentieth Century-Fox: 2, 3, 5, 9; Orion Pictures: 4; Phototeque: 6, 7, 8, 10, 12, 13, 14, 15; Cineplex-Odeon: 11; Universal and The Memory Shop: 16

1

INTRODUCTION

"I'm really a very ordinary guy," Paul Newman has protested for almost forty years to anyone who would listen. Though he has long reigned as the epitome of true male glamour, we are finally coming to accept that, in many ways, Paul Newman really is just a regular guy. That, in itself, is part of what makes him extraordinary. Paul Newman is the first of the Hollywood paradoxes. His screen image is synonymous with the quintessential rebel, the misunderstood loner whose deepest instincts render him unfit to live within the strictures of society. Yet he's the son of an upper-middle-class Jewish businessman, the college-educated product of a wealthy Ohio suburb. Newman's conventional upbringing and his stable family life as a responsible husband and father are hardly the stuff of romantic legends. Or so it would seem. For Newman's heroic appeal has, if anything, grown stronger as the integrity of the man has shone over the years as brightly as his startling physical presence.

Paul Newman has been married to the same woman, actress and director Joanne Woodward, for thirty years, and he enjoys positive and productive relationships with his five daughters. Not only is he an award-winning actor and director, and a lifetime activist, but since age forty-seven he has become a champion car racer, and since the early eighties, with the establishment of his food company, Newman's Own, he has become an entrepreneur and philanthropist on a grand scale. How did this essentially modest son of America's bourgeoisie, a man whose humble pleasures are family, car racing, and working through a case of beers with a few good buddies, end up a screen legend, a member of America's royal family, a Hollywood king whose stroll onstage at the Pantages Theater to present the 1987 Best Actress Oscar Award brought his peers in the audience to their feet? The answer lies partially in the blessings heaped upon Paul Newman at birth—rare good looks reminiscent of Michelangelo's *David*—and partially in the lessons he has learned through life. With a sharp and insightful intelligence and a complex but sterling character, Newman is driven by an intense fear of failure and a need to succeed through the efforts of his own brain and hands.

Almost despite himself he created another persona, another Paul Newman, one painted larger than life, with the lights and shadows of moving pictures. The major struggle of his life has been to disentangle the real Paul from that illusory image. How close or far apart is, or was, Newman from that cinematic construct?

Before antiestablishment stances were the postures of the day, Paul Newman was the first of a generation of movie stars to eschew the glitter and glamour of the celluloid myths of the West Coast for the stability of family life on the East Coast and the grown-up responsibilities of world citizenship. He has always said what he wanted on any issue he considered important, dressed in the informal manner he prefers, and perched comfortably on shaky political limbs. Newman has insisted on marching to the beat of his own drummer without regard for the ever present risk to his career. In these respects at least, his lack of obeisance to the reigning studio nobility and to popular notions of movie-star lifestyles have made him a brother to his screen persona. He may have been a rebel in the eyes of the Hollywood and Washington establishments, but his rebellion was not the blind defiance often displayed by his less conscious screen characters. Newman has always been balanced within his own reality, though his reality may not have been the same as that of many of his contemporaries. Applying traditional values to arrive at often unorthodox conclusions, Newman's disagreements with the status quo have always been characterized by shrewd assessments and an ability to learn from experience, to take the best from the past and use it in the present.

Not much frightens Paul Newman, but he has always been terrified by the prospect of being fed through the Hollywood meat grinder and emerging at the other end as a plastic-wrapped piece of homogenized, soulless Tinseltown beefcake, packaged for mass public consumption. He has refused to suffer this fate, and this is largely why Newman has always been hypersensitive to praise of his looks, and has steadfastly ignored the advice of local pundits to coast on the appeal of his blue eyes and smooth muscles. In fact, Newman has professed puzzlement, along with consternation, at being the object of a tidal wave of sexual desire. He has refused to acknowledge that his movie-star image was and perhaps still is the hook for a mass projection of sexual fantasy. In the early years of his career, he continually agitated to be cast against type in interesting, challenging projects. Even when he was already a huge star at the box office, Newman accepted bit roles for the chance to disguise his masculine beauty under makeup, wigs, and beards. He wanted to prove that he could act and that there was more to him than just a pretty face.

Until relatively recently, Newman has had to fight just to hang on to the essential Paul that had nothing to do with being imprinted on celluloid or reflecting anyone's image of him. As soon as he was able, he bought out his studio contract and began controlling his film projects in productorial partnerships with people he knew had no interest in marketing a movie star but in creating something meaningful. Once he was no longer beholden to studio bosses, Newman's independence also translated to his private life, which he sought vigorously to keep out of the gossip columns. After a hard struggle of many years, he seems to have finally convinced the press that his home life is much too boring for the scandal mills. Yet Newman's presence remains as powerful in the eighties as it was in the fifties and sixties. Because in certain key ways he has acted out in his personal life a wonderful image of what a man can be, he has transcended his own considerable sex appeal and come to define a modernist, almost spiritual notion of the heroic male.

The emotional turmoil that often accompanies Newman's public appearances is an endless source of bewilderment and embarrassment to him. "I don't think Paul Newman really thinks he's Paul Newman in his head," says screenwriter William Goldman, who wrote *Harper* and *Butch Cassidy and the Sundance Kid*. Newman refuses to sign autographs, partially because of his need to separate the private Paul Newman from the public commodity and partially because of his natural inclination to guard his privacy. As

Westport neighbor, buddy, and business partner A. E. Hotchner (who is also the official biographer and adaptor of Ernest Hemingway's work) says, "He is the most private man I've ever known. He has a moat and a drawbridge, which he lets down only occasionally."

Gore Vidal, onetime fiancé of Joanne Woodward and longtime friend of the couple, was walking down Fifth Avenue in Manhattan with Newman one afternoon when the movie star lifted his gaze from its usual focus on the sidewalk and was recognized by an enormous woman lumbering toward them. "She gave a gasp as he looked up," Vidal recalled for *Time* magazine. "We kept going and we heard a terrible sound, and Paul said, 'My God, she's fainted. Let's keep moving.'" Susan, his oldest daughter, recalls that when they were younger, she and the other children found the commotion surrounding her father confusing and later annoying. "It was pretty bewildering when we'd go out to dinner and three hundred crazed women would approach our table." Even as far away as the countryside of Italy, she adds, a visit from Paul and the fields would ring with women's cries, "Paul-o Newman!" "It wears you down," says Susan. "It's tiring."

Though Newman refuses to sign autographs and is a notoriously poor interview subject given to long, far-off blue stares followed by monosyllabic answers or inaudible mumbles, he respects his public and acknowledges his responsibility, as a performer, to give his best. On occasion he has left the screen for the greater risk of performing in front of a live audience for Equity scale pay, and he all but forsook screen acting when he was at his peak at the box office, to begin a new career as a director with the award-winning *Rachel, Rachel.*

Newman claims to be a regular Joe with the irregular luck of having parlayed great looks and natural charisma into becoming a world-class legend, a private man whose public persona romanticizes certain aspects of what is basically a meat-and-potatoes nature, and if legendom signifies debauchery, sordid secrets, and titillating scandal, then Newman is right. He's not very romantic according to those standards. But if will, determination, and a powerful sense of purpose can be defined as romantic, then Newman the private citizen is almost as heroic as the public imagination would have him. He may have been raised a nice suburban boy, but he is a true maverick. The leonine courage and daring that color his screen persona are also expressed in his real life, with his progressive social and political views, his philanthropy, and his career as a car racer.

Acting has been only one of Newman's careers. Always seeking out new fields to conquer, endeavors that would appeal to his grandeur-loving side, after only ten years on the screen the restless Newman was already looking for something more. While his performances of the past few years have been those of a master, of one whose long apprenticeship has finally borne the desired fruit, it is in his original theatrical ambition to be a director that Newman's talents find their most suitable outlet. It is as director and actress that Newman and Woodward have found their most successful working arrangement. Newman has often commented that he enjoys the elaborate preparation for a role more than actually getting up in front of the camera, and this gift for constructing motivation and behavior does, in fact, seem to lie more in the realm of the director. "He feels less inhibited behind the camera," a friend has commented. "The deep, sensitive, creative, delicate side of him comes out as a director; as an actor up front, he seems almost ashamed to show it; it makes for an odd personality split, artistically."

Newman had already directed a twenty-five-minute film based on a short story by Chekhov, when in 1968 he directed his first feature-length film, *Rachel, Rachel,* and won the New York Film Critics Prize for Best Director. In 1970 he directed, coproduced, and starred in *Sometimes a Great Notion*, and in 1972 he again directed Joanne Woodward in *The Effect of Gamma Rays on Man-in-the-Moon Marigolds*, also to critical acclaim. In 1979 he directed a teleplay, *The Shadow Box*, which starred his wife and was produced by his daughter Susan. *Harry and Son* (1980) found Newman not only starring, producing, and directing, but also cowriting the screenplay. In 1987 he directed an intelligent and appropriately respectful film adaptation of Tennessee Williams's classic, *The Glass Menagerie*.

One of several production companies Newman has formed over the years, the Newman-Foreman company, packaged a film about car racing in 1968 called *Winning*. Never was preparation for a role more enjoyable for Newman. From earliest childhood he had craved recognition as an athlete but had always failed to realize that particular dream. At age forty-four he enrolled in a school for racers—ostensibly just to ready himself for the role—and ended up apprenticing for three years before becoming a professional racer in 1972, at the age of forty-seven. Newman now limits his acting to the winter months, the racing circuit's off-season. Springs and summers Newman is totally occupied with this relatively new career, one he now says he would have preferred to that of movie star if he had begun a few years earlier. By 1985 he had set ten new track records; he has won four national and five divisional autoracing titles driving a 2,550 steel-and-fiberglass monster, a turbo-charged Datsun 300ZX that tears up the raceway at speeds up to 191 mph.

"I enjoy the precision of racing, harnessing something as huge and powerful as a car and putting it as close to where you want it as you can," Newman explains. "Besides, it's a kick in the ass." Even his wife, initially horrified by her husband's passion for what she considered a reckless and dangerous sport, has come to share his enjoyment. "These people on the racetrack know what they're doing," Joanne Woodward told television's *Rich and Famous.* "I think it's very exciting. People should do what they want to do. I think it's wonderful that at the age of forty-seven, he decided to become a race driver. It's marvelous. It's what everyone should do."

Veteran driver Sam Posey considers Newman to be "one of the finest endurance racers in the world today. He has a born talent for getting the most out of a car without hurting it."

Perhaps Newman's most outstanding quality is the interesting contrast between his craving for challenge and change and his equally strong desire for security and traditional, even conservative values, most evidenced in his long marriage to Joanne Woodward. But what seems a conflict of impulses—a maverick exterior masking the soul of a conservative—most likely constitutes a balance. Newman's strong family life gives him a solid foundation from which to exercise his daredevil side. Then again, holding together a marriage in which not only one, but both partners are movie stars is a valiant enterprise in itself, an accomplishment one friend attributes to Newman's and Woodward's innate conservatism. "They are traditionalists. You make a commitment, it's a commitment. But it's a marriage like every other marriage. It's no different from any other. The only difference is that they both decided somewhere along the line that this is a commitment. And I think Paul did even more than Joanne. In that sense, he is extremely conservative."

In the mid-seventies Newman told writer Charles Hamblett, "If impermanence works for some people, fine. But speaking for myself, I can't imagine my life without Joanne and the kids. Everywhere you look you see signs of rapid change, built-in obsolescence, a sense of impermanence. There's too much fragmentation of ideas, ideals, family. . . . I'll settle for what we've got."

The Newmans have long made their home in the wealthy bedroom community of Westport, an artful re-creation of New England only one hour away from their Manhattan pied à terre. While they raised their three children, the couple lived in a converted carriage house that is now available to their grown daughters when they come for a visit. Mom and Dad now live almost directly across the road in a converted farmhouse surrounded by fields and woods. The Aspetuck River rounds through their property, and in the winter Newman breaks the ice for a skin-tightening splash after his ritualistic morning sauna. The Newmans have filled their home with all the paraphernalia of the normal American household: cats, dogs, piano, plus Newman's oil paintings and Woodward's needlepoints. They own a nearby stable where Joanne is pursuing her newfound hobby of horseback riding; Paul can frequently be found at a garage in a neighboring town, where the Sharp-Newman Racing Team coddles its 2,550-pound baby. When Newman isn't acting or racing his Datsun, he enjoys tennis, swimming, bridge, reading, and executing caricatures. Rather than drive a typical Hollywood star vehicle such as a Ferrari or a Rolls Royce, Newman used to negotiate Manhattan's congested streets on a plebian motor scooter, and, later, after injuring his hand in an accident, in a souped-up Volkswagen Beetle. For a long time, their front gate bore the sign: 'Please—they have moved—the Piersons.'" But by now, local delis, vegetable stands, and neighbors have learned to treat Newman as just another citizen. Those who dared, long ago, to ask for an autograph were quickly warned off by the foreboding Newman frown.

Much has been made in the press over the Newmans differing interests—his supermasculine pursuit of car racing and her passion for ballet and literature—as if husbands and wives had to share careers, interests, and hobbies to have a successful marriage. Perhaps the prescription for marital harmony lies not in total compatibility between a man and a woman, but in their ability to allow each other the space to be separate within their union, an agreement the Newmans seem to have made. "We have a deal," Newman says. "I trade her a couple of ballets for a couple of races."

"I've repeatedly said that for people with as little in common as Joanne and myself, we have an uncommonly good marriage," Newman told Hamblett. "We are actors. We make pictures—and that's about *all* we have in common. Maybe that's enough. Wives *shouldn't* feel obligated to accompany their husbands to a ball game, husbands *do* look a bit silly attending morning coffee breaks with the neighborhood wives when most men are out at work. Husbands and wives *should* have separate interests, cultivate different sets of friends—and not impose on the other. . . . You can't spend a lifetime breathing down each other's necks."

Paul Newman may be a traditional man living within the welcome shackles of a conventional marriage, but there is romance in his soul, and Joanne Woodward apparently brings it out. In 1980, when he was filming the potboiler *When Time Ran Out* in Hawaii, Newman surprised his wife on their anniversary with a beautiful gown. When she had dressed, they flew to a deserted golf course to enjoy a gourmet dinner *à deux* by the sea, serenaded by a string quartet no doubt blindfolded with white silk scarfs.

Like any successful marriage, the Newmans' has been one of accommodation, with Woodward's early decision to subordinate her career to that of her husband's in order to care for their growing family. Not only did Newman and Woodward have three children of their own—Elinor Theresa, Melissa Steward, and Claire Olivia—but when she married, Woodward became stepmother to one son and

two daughters, Scott, Susan, and Stephanie, whom Newman had fathered with his first wife, Jackie Witte. Though
Paul Newman is now enjoying a close relationship with his
five daughters, the children have over the years displayed
the sort of rebellion expected of the offspring of living legends. This has been exacerbated by Newman's tendency to
be withdrawn, even with friends and family members. Newman has been a good father "in flashes," he says, admitting
that, at times, his children "almost had to say a password"
to test his approachability.

The burden of being Paul Newman's son did not rest
easily on the broad shoulders of his firstborn child and only
son, Scott, a tall, green-eyed young man as handsome as
one would expect. Scott died tragically in 1978 at age
twenty-eight from a lethal combination of drugs and alcohol, just when he seemed on the verge of making peace
with his father and coming into his own. The loss was particularly painful for Newman, who had always kept the
specter of Hollywood brats before him. In his attempt to
give his children a normal life, Newman raised them in "the
most conventional manner imaginable," says a close friend.
"In fact, the only thing that is remarkable is how unre-
markable a father he is. He's very dedicated, traditional,
conventional, very strict, as befitting a half-Jewish, half-
Catholic, coming out of Ohio."

But Newman could well understand his son's problems
with liquor and drugs. The actor has publicly admitted to
difficulty in controlling his liquor intake in the past, particularly in the fifties when the conventional source of comfort
as well as the popular idea of a good time was to get drunk.
Toward the end of that decade, Newman was agonizing
over his career and over whether or not to leave his family
and marry Joanne Woodward. Unable to make a decision,
he turned to alcohol to relieve the stress. Age and a good
marriage seem to have remedied the problem, and though

Newman is famous for his love of brew, drinking is no longer a problem.

Despite their close bonds, Newman and Woodward's early screen couplings were surprisingly unsuccessful, but when Newman directed his wife in *Rachel, Rachel* in 1968, though, they seemed to find their ideal means of working together. Newman was initially reluctant to direct his wife, whose acting talent awes him, but he says now that he loves it. "Given the right parts, she is a great actress. She can find so many different facets of herself to play. That is magic." Though they haven't exactly set the screen on fire when they have appeared together, Newman takes great pleasure in acting with Woodward. "When we work together, we both know we can't get away with any old tricks, because the other one is sitting there nodding his head knowingly and saying, 'Yes, I seem to remember your doing that on the twenty-eighth page of *The Helen Morgan Story*.'"

Of the two, Woodward seems to be the more combustible. In the kitchen of their Manhattan apartment hangs a sampler embroidered by Newman that pictures a lit bulb and an exploding cannon underscored by the caption, "I will regulate my life. JWN." Evidently a reminder of a vow once made while Woodward was involved in a personal-growth program called Actualizations, a spinoff of EST, which may have helped Woodward overcome her Mrs. Newman complex, but whose New Age jargon drove Mr. Newman up the wall.

Not only has Newman remained constant to his thirty-year-old marriage, but his tastes and inclinations have remained virtually the same in other areas, both trivial and profound, throughout his life. From his earliest days as a hot new star of the fifties, screen magazines informed readers that beer and popcorn were Paul Newman's favorite foods. It was hardly surprising to those who know him that Newman decided to market his own salad dressing. He has

long been proud of his special celery salad creation, which
has been listed on the menu of a prominent Beverly Hills
restaurant since the beginning of his career. Newman has
also long been known for taking his restaurant salads into
the men's room for a thorough washing and then asking for
the ingredients to concoct his own recipe.

Another of his more endearing eccentricities is the peculiar brand of Newman humor, which seems to have sta-
bilized and fixed at around age fourteen, leavening his
serious side with a love of complex and outrageous practical jokes and a taste for risqué limericks. Constantly
queried by the press as to the secret of his enduring youth,
Newman has claimed to don a snorkel and mask and soak
his head in ice water for twenty minutes every day.
Whether or not one believes that depends on how well one
can follow the twists and bends of a quirky sense of fun and
an almost awesome willingness to go to any lengths for a
good laugh. These characteristics once prompted him to fill
Robert Altman's trailer with three hundred live chicks during filming of *Buffalo Bill and the Indians,* and to present
the director with a baby goat, saying, "Here, now you can
have your own vineyard." Newman claimed the white wine
Altman served tasted like "goat piss." He once sawed director George Roy Hill's desk in half and then did the same
to Hill's brand new sports car. He had Robert Redford's
face printed on every sheet of 150 cartons of toilet paper,
intending to send them to the star, but he then thought it
over and decided not to go through with it.

More significant is Newman's unswerving dedication to
lifelong activism for a wide variety of political and social
causes that began long before the klieg light shone on him.
Though he never liked that spotlight, as soon as he had a
public name Newman was willing to wield the power of ce-
lebritydom for the common good. A lifelong liberal, Newman marched for civil rights in the South in the early

demonstrations of the sixties and narrated the award-winning 1970 documentary made by Joseph Mankiewicz and Sidney Lumet, *King: A Filmed Record . . . Montgomery to Memphis.*

In 1968 Newman served as a Connecticut delegate to the Democratic National Convention in Chicago and campaigned tirelessly that year for presidential candidate Eugene McCarthy. In the seventies, Newman was a member of the U.S. delegation to the special United Nations session on disarmament. Newman and Woodward also supported the "No Such Foundation" of the Center for the Study of Democratic Institutions at Santa Barbara, dedicated to harnessing the best minds in various fields for planning positive changes in society. Other patrons who had the right to show up at the seminars, on subjects such as education, behavioral science, gerontology, and mathematics, were Kirk Douglas, Steve Allen, Dinah Shore and Jack Lemmon.

After Newman's son's death, he and Woodward formed the Scott Newman Foundation to create and support anti-drug films and television programs; and in recent years Newman's Own has turned into a multimillion-dollar corporation whose profits are turned over in their entirety to a variety of worthy causes, including an eight-million-dollar summer camp Newman has established for children who are seriously ill. The camp is called The Hole in the Wall Gang, after Newman and Redford's group of train robbers in *Butch Cassidy and the Sundance Kid.*

Though he has no use for the usual trappings of stardom and has avoided public appearances connected with his acting career, Newman will speak out on any issue that concerns him, from the need for a nuclear freeze to gay rights, projecting his message with a simple intensity far more persuasive than any rhetorician's bag of tricks. In the early eighties Newman debated on television with conservative

actor Charlton Heston; he was skeptical about his effec-
tiveness. Unlike Heston, who had honed his skills reading
the Bible on the Ed Sullivan Show, intoning the Holy Book
as if he himself had inscribed the words, the self-effacing
Newman typically delivered his opinions in an unaffective,
no-nonsense manner that he suspected was less persuasive
to the gullible than Heston's theatrics. "I've done better
and I've done worse," he concluded after the telecast, "but
in the final analysis, it was better than not doing anything at
all."

Those words might well be taken as a credo for what has
been an exemplary life of honor. Now in his maturity, and
relatively free of the sexual image he has found so con-
stricting and demeaning, Newman's persona, both on the
screen and in real life, has taken on the aura of an elder
statesman, a wise and experienced man who is too established to be afraid of anyone or anything.

An incident in 1968, when Newman was campaigning
McCarthy, clearly illustrates this intensely private man's
ability to reach out to the public with sensitivity when communication rises above the absurdities of gushing reporters
and fans demanding that he remove his sunglasses. During
the New Hampshire presidential primary, one of the officers in the police escort pointed to his partner and said the
latter had received word the previous night that his son had
been killed in Vietnam. Saddened by the news, Newman
offered the policeman his condolences and then said,
"What do you think about some creep, some Hollywood
peacenik coming in here and telling you about the war?"
The policeman assured Newman he didn't resent what the
actor was doing. "Even if a war takes your boy," he said,
"that doesn't make it right."

"I think he is the best of the liberal tradition," says
Marxist documentary filmmaker Emile de Antonio, who
was offered help by Newman on his film about the McCar-

thy hearings. "I would define him as the best of the liberal tradition who gives more than money, gives of himself, and isn't totally frightened. For the cassette version of my film *Point of Order,* he gave a day of shooting time in which he read intelligently and beautifully an introduction of the film for a new generation," de Antonio continues. "He's a decent man, and it's hard to be a decent man in his position."

Newman is a decent man, and he is also a man of singular determination, bent on succeeding in whatever challenge he may pose for himself. "Paul likes to test himself," Woodward confirms, "that's what makes Paul run. He's got a lot of courage, a highly underrated element in people's lives these days." But he chooses his challenges wisely. In each of his fields of endeavor—acting, directing, activism, business, and car racing, Newman understands how to wait for the right moment and how to discriminate between realistic and unrealistic goals. He knows himself and has come to terms with his limitations, but that doesn't preclude an irresistible urge to push against those limitations, to learn from his mistakes and try again, sticking to what can often be a tortured process until he has done what he has set out to do and, (this is also significant), the world recognizes his accomplishment. Paul Newman is concerned with his standing in the world, but not in a superficial or egotistical manner. His strict definition of success means gains through one's own efforts only, and these gains are not measured by material wealth but in acquired skill, knowledge, correct action, and the respect of one's peers. Success for Newman means doing the best with what you've got.

A line from *The Hustler* seems to echo his personal value system. "Whatever you do, if you do it good, then you gotta get a good feeling from it." Another line, from *Hud,* also symbolizes Newman's credo: "You don't look out for yourself, the only helping hand you'll ever get is when they lower the box." But the real Paul Newman is not a true loner. He just likes to be the boss. He may not be looking for the helping hand, but Paul Newman always acknowledges his debts of gratitude, particularly to those who have helped him develop his acting craft.

For a good part of his life, Newman's challenge was acting. He has often referred to himself as a terrier. If a role comes easily, Newman distrusts it. If he can say, "I did it with my brain and my hard work," he is as close as his perfectionism allows to satisfaction, but there's always something else to be achieved. This is why, for example, he has publicly given more credit to his work in the unpopular but morally ambitious movie *W.U.S.A.* than to that in *Hud* or *The Hustler.* The roles of Fast Eddie Felson and Hud were easier for him; they were characters into which he was able to slip more easily because his Paul Newman persona had already begun to jell and the parts were tailor-made to suit the image. *Hud* and *The Hustler* were less work than *W.U.S.A.* and, therefore, in the Newman moral hierarchy, less valuable.

Newman may have suffered insecurities concerning his acting abilities, fears of failure exacerbated by his relatively inauspicious screen debut in a four-million-dollar disaster called *The Silver Chalice,* but in retrospect that early embarrassment at age twenty-nine may have been the best beginning for his film career. Mediocrity and failure merely whet the Newman appetite for excellence, and he spent the next thirty-five years in intensive effort and study, particularly at New York's Actors Studio. He gives painstaking attention to technique and to preparation for each role. Over the years Newman has persistently mined his comparatively narrow range and focused his considerable intellect and energy on creating what has finally become an assured, highly suggestive, completely believable acting style, with no traces of the turning of mental wheels or the reliance on charming mannerisms that marred his earlier performances, even the most brilliant.

One motivation for taking so much control over all aspects of his films was to be able to rehearse for at least two weeks before shooting: "It gives me the chance not to just sit and intellectualize about a part but to get up on my feet and run through it. If you can rehearse a dozen key scenes with the other actors and get the style and progression of the character, you've got the part licked."

From his second film, *Somebody Up There Likes Me,* Newman developed the habit of spending time at the location, soaking up local culture and mannerisms long before the arrival of the rest of the company. Before a foot of film ran through the camera on *Somebody,* Newman had logged weeks of study with the real Rocky Graziano, observing all he could of the fighter—his walk, talk, every minute tic. For *The Long, Hot Summer,* Newman's first costarring role opposite Joanne Woodward, he journeyed to the small southern town where they were to film and hung around the local watering holes, convincing the inhabitants that he was just another good ol' boy from the next town or so over, until the rest of the company arrived and his cover was blown. He studied pool with a master before filming *The Hustler* and became so adept that all the shots in the film except one were executed by Newman himself. He learned to play the trombone for *Paris Blues,* lived in a bunkhouse and performed all the usual chores of a cowhand for weeks before filming *Hud,* went on a roundup before making *The Left-Handed Gun,* lived on an Indian reservation before shooting *Hombre,* and traveled to Mexico to soak up the nuances of holding up adobe walls in sleazy little cantinas before playing a bandido in *The Outrage.*

He has said, "If I feel that a character is close to me, my homework is minimal," but in explaining his elaborate working methods, he says, "I write voluminous notes to myself on the back of a script. It all breaks down to the way the character walks or uses his hands, his motions and his movements. I think that once you get the physical quality of a character, the inner person comes by itself." This attention to building a character from observed details of reality rather than by simply borrowing second-hand characterizations from stereotypical images projected by the mass media is known as The Method, a working style for which New York's Actors Studio has long been famous.

Ironically, the intent of any Studio actor is to avoid the cult of personality, to create individual, unique characterizations from role to role rather than going from one "Paul Newman role" to another. No actor likes to think he is simply playing endless variations on a single, identifiable character. When asked, "What is a Clint Eastwood movie?" Eastwood calmly replied, "To me, a Clint Eastwood picture is one I'm in." But, as the public knows, his persona looms large on the screen and its magic dwarfs every other element. The same is certainly true of Paul Newman. As uncomfortable as the realization may be for Newman, the truth is that for his entire acting career, the Newman screen persona has been so deeply ingrained in our imaginations that while he may not be playing his real self—the private Paul Newman known to family and friends—whenever he attempts to play anything but this romanticized image his acting seems strained, fake, utterly unacceptable. When Newman is working within the territory staked out by his movie persona, he is good—at times great—but when he ventures out of those bounds, his own self-awareness intrudes and renders his performance clumsy. It's almost as if he were in the middle of a speech and suddenly broke concentration. Hearing his own voice booming at him, or stepping outside to see himself attempting to mask his beauty under makeup and facial hair, or pretending to have feelings much too far from his own, he seems to go cold. He freezes in a spasm of self-consciousness.

Newman has often admitted that acting doesn't come naturally to him, that he has to work at it. He labels himself a "cerebral" actor, unlike Woodward who operates on instinct. "Some people are born intuitive actors and have . . . the talent to slip in and out of the characters they are creating," he told author Jonathan Kerbel. "Acting to me is like dredging a river. It's a painful experience. I simply do not have the intuitive talent. I worry about acting and constantly complain to myself about my own performance."

No one is more aware of his limitations than Newman himself. "I tried for classics and fell on my face," he acknowledges. "Let's face it—there a few actors who can avoid limitations. Only the great, great actors have an inexhaustible source of variety. Brando, when he is really on, when he is interested, when he is involved, can do it; so can Olivier, Gielgud, Richardson, Guinness. My wife, Joanne, can do it. But not me."

Though Paul Newman's career has certainly exceeded Joanne Woodward's in terms of box-office drawing power and magnitude of stardom, in the minds of most she is more the actor's actor. Intuitive and brilliant, unencumbered by the crippling effects of the self-consciousness that has sometimes hindered her husband, Woodward seems to throw herself fully into a role without looking back. She sheds her own skin, and, chameleonlike, becomes any of a variety of characters without imposing an identifiable persona of her own. In contrast, by virtue of rare photogenic looks that can hardly be subdued, a natural reserve, and a fear of pretension, Newman has rarely been able to submerge himself totally within a character. He is a prototypical star, a personality and an image that travel intact from one role to the next, one of those magical beings who realize the dreams of others. His withdrawn nature operates as a suggestion of dark, exciting secrets held back from what we see on the screen. This seduces us, draws us in. The magnetism of Paul Newman colors and dominates each character.

In his earlier years, Newman experimented with roles generally considered out of his range, taking parts for the sake of challenging his abilities rather than for what they could do at the box office—comedies such as *Rally 'Round the Flag, Boys!* and the ill-named *The Secret War of Harry Frigg;* romantic period pieces such as *Lady L;* and character parts like that of the Mexican villain in *The Outrage.* But Newman's omnipresent aura of intense seriousness weighed down the frothy concoctions, and the sheer glamour of his physical presence fought against the visual ordinariness he strove for in the character roles. Slowly, painstakingly, Newman stretched his range and learned, eventually coming to terms with and mastering that which fell within his scope. As this screen persona evolved, assembled from bits and pieces of his character portrayals, and as Newman sought out creative, compatible people who understood him and with whom he could work in partnership, the characters began to be created to fit the image that was building, and thus the persona was refined and solidified.

From the prize fighter in 1957's *Somebody Up There Likes Me* through the memorable protagonists of *The Left-Handed Gun, Cat on a Hot Tin Roof, The Hustler, Sweet Bird of Youth, Hud, Hombre, Cool Hand Luke, Butch Cassidy and the Sundance Kid, The Sting, Slapshot, Fort Apache, the Bronx, Absence of Malice,* and *The Verdict,* to 1986's *The Color of Money,* Newman's intelligence and sweat applied to his God-given magic have created a larger-than-life figure that has maintained its grip on the public imagination worldwide for over forty years. Ambitious, ruthless and cocky, the Newman hero is redeemed from comic-book style flatness by flashes of a hidden sensitivity and the suggestion of past hurts; yet the same vulnerability that makes us love him is more often than not his downfall, the stumbling block to the success he so single-mindedly craves. The Newman hero never gets the girl, but that's because he doesn't want her. He never aligns himself with the female principle. His physical bravery is breathtaking, but women are just too dangerous. In the early years the Newman hero loved them and left them because he was that much of a rascal. In more recent years, however, he leaves them not because he's fickle but because they threaten the fragility of his newly found moral stance. He's a man's man, and women love him for it.

What has made Newman's man's man so memorable, so different from the gallery of legendary personas that have gone before him, is that he humanized the cardboard macho image personified by the swashbucklers and the gun-toting heros. John Wayne and even Clark Gable now seem anachronistic to a thinking public, although the stereotype is played with by Clint Eastwood and in somewhat less of a tongue-in-cheek fashion by Arnold Schwarzenegger. But Sylvester Stallone's Rambo proves that a crude view of manhood still thrives.

Newman has always projected too much humanity, too much nobility to ever be all bad. The singular intensity blazing from those startling eyes seems to have a hidden source. The reckless charm of his grin suggests something masked, perhaps a secret hurt, a shadow side that desperately craves acceptance even as our hero fears exposure. The youthful version of the persona was a pure rebel, but Newman was able to capture the insecurity and anguish of being young at the same time as he presented masculinity in its pure form, unalloyed and unapologetic.

A whole new generation of actors has come into being, largely due to the element of vulnerability Newman brought to the icon of maleness. As much as he may have tried to play the irreclaimable rogue, the warmth of human sympathy always beat under the cool exterior of his characters. The audience loved them, often to his chagrin. In the case of Hud, an uncompromising portrait of an unregenerate scoundrel whom Newman and his co-filmmakers had fought to protect against the studio heads when they insisted on sugarcoating the villainy, the public responded to the character with gushing, unconditional love. "To think that after *Hud* and *Cool Hand Luke* and all the parts I've dug into, I come off as the guy women would most like to go to bed with," Newman has commented. "It's frightening."

Newman's movie persona has grown and expanded from the fifties to the eighties, in step with the maturation of Newman's public and private personalities. Unlike other heros of the screen that are linked to a certain period of time, Paul Newman has never become dated. The rebellion he symbolized in the conservative fifties became, in the social upheaval of the sixties, relatively conventional, but at the same time more directed, more focused. Dean and Brando, who with Newman portrayed the wild defiance of youth, were now out of the picture—Dean through his untimely death, and Brando through his own decision to withdraw. Newman reigned alone until the advent of Steve McQueen, for whom his own image had paved the way. The relative inactivity that characterized the social climate of the seventies was mirrored in Newman's work, where long absences from the screen were interrupted by appearances in unabashed potboilers such as *Towering Inferno,* and by the huge box-office successes of *Butch Cassidy and the Sundance Kid* and *The Sting.* In the eighties, Newman finally entered his full maturity in *Absence of Malice; The*

Verdict; and *The Color of Money,* a reprisal of his early brilliant success as Fast Eddie Felson that clearly shows how far thirty years have taken the actor.

By sheer force of personality, hard work, grit, and ambition, Newman has endured as one of the biggest stars of his time. Throughout his career he has won a number of awards, including Academy Award nominations and a premature honorary Oscar for "lifetime achievement." In 1987 he finally won a real Oscar for Best Actor of 1986, for *The Color of Money.* Though he has shrugged off his pretty-boy movie-star image, the undeniable fact is that he remains as handsome as ever. Even as recently as 1987, at the age of sixty-two, Paul Newman was voted by 46 percent of the women polled by *Europa* magazine as the man they most fantasized about having sex with.

Thus, while Paul Newman has epitomized a particular brand of antihero, a rebel with a cause who broke with the stagnant Hollywood notion of the classic leading man, he also took with him some of that old-fashioned glamour, the masculine ideal of physical beauty and a heroic sense of destiny. Though he remains lean and muscular, and those fabled orbs blaze with the same intense icy blue, Newman now sports a head of slightly thinning white hair. His classic Greek profile now pared down to a Hebraic sternness, the innocent upward-tilted line of his raised brows now drawn down close over hooded, wary eyes no longer open wide, his pouting upper lip now thinned out to a stern line of disapproval of what he sees around him (sometimes including himself), Newman has earned that face, a granite bust etched over time by the consistent exercise of character. The public and private Newman have never been closer, and he has never been more beautiful. After years of struggle against a myriad of forces trying to sell him as something other than what he really is, Newman has finally gained the esteem of his peers in the film world on his own terms.

It is ironic that Newman became a sports star long after he had been established as a movie star, because his particular brand of charisma is more typical of a Joe Namath or O.J. Simpson. The connection these men have with the public was initially due to their unusual prowess in preeminently masculine pursuits. For, ultimately, the Newman persona represents something more than just acting— hardly "man's work." Paul Newman symbolizes primitive masculine energy transmuted into something higher, something grand and romantic, and this quality is not just projected upon him. He has lived it. Because his private life has come to support and even ennoble his public image, the Newman hero has developed into the exemplary male with an uncanny ability to fulfill the requirements of traditional masculinity even as he mocks it and exposes its foibles. From mere Brando clone, Newman has become a public figure whose life and career have brought him nearer to the status of idol than to that of superstar. He has used his masculine energy—in all his pursuits—with passion and intensity. He has incorporated and carried his particular type of glamour without getting lost in it, and he has managed to portray it on-screen without threatening us. In his life and on-screen, Newman symbolizes a sense of purpose that takes on a collective, spiritual quality. He seems capable of making real some far-off, noble possibility. Newman represents the drive for adventure, a blend of all the wonderful characteristics of masculinity: courage, shrewdness, statesmanship. He is a real hero with a sense of destiny, the embodiment of that urge inside all mankind to live life to its fullest. No matter how unsympathetic and unregenerate a villain or how defeated the characters he plays may seem to be, the Paul Newman hero always has the energy and the will to make it all happen for us, so he will always be a true romantic leader, a modernist version of the gallant medieval knight. Newman is a complex man, with secrets that perhaps no one shares or even has a right to, but his integrity shines out clear and simple. That is why the 1987 Academy Awards audience rose to its feet for a man who represents the antithesis of everything Hollywood stands for. Who else but Paul Newman could be revered by the very powerbrokers to whom he has always turned his back?

The screen legend who might easily have passed an uneventful life selling footballs at the family store was born on January 26, 1925, in Cleveland Heights, Ohio. The second son of Arthur S. Newman (himself one of seven children of German Jews) weighed in at a robust eight pounds, distinguished from the other babies in the nursery by his brilliant light blue eyes. Paul's father had been an ambitious, hardworking child who had to help support the family from age eleven, when his father died. Arthur and his brother Joe founded Cleveland's first radio store in 1915, and by the time of Paul's birth Arthur was secretary-treasurer of the large and thriving business. The Newman-Stern company had switched to sporting goods when private radio broadcasts were banned during World War I. Paul's mother, Theresa (Feutzer) Newman, also a second-generation American, was a Hungarian Catholic who converted to Christian Science shortly after her marriage. Though Paul and his year-older brother, Arthur, Jr., attended the Christian Science church between the ages of six and eleven, Newman says the faith "didn't really take on me." Arthur Newman, Sr., was not particularly religious, and Paul says he calls himself a Jew only "because it's more of a challenge." While Paul was still an infant the family moved to a spacious eleven-room house at 2983 Brighton Road in Shaker Heights, an insular residential community composed of private homes, landscaped hedges, and gardens.

"Shaker Heights is one of the three most affluent communities in the United States," Newman later told reporter Bob Thomas. "It had the best educational system in the country, and my one regret is that I didn't take better advantage of it."

The young Newman may not have been an avid student, but he was a fairly dutiful child who showed few signs of the rebel persona for which he would become so celebrated. His future was secure. His life would be as easy and as uneventful as his father, the son of struggling immigrants, could wish for his child. Paul would take over the family business with his older brother, marry a nice local girl, raise two or three children, and spend pleasant Saturday nights at the local country club. That was his comfortable legacy, one Paul gradually came to know he could never accept, though for a long time he didn't know why.

Though neither parent seems to have exercised a striking influence in shaping the man the boy was to become, one can see in the child the seed of the paradoxical image projected by the future movie star: classical masculine virility shot through by a fault line of vulnerable sensitivity. Paul loved sports and dreamed of distinguishing himself as a jock. Today, at five feet ten and 145 pounds, he is an above-average-size man, but as a youth he was scrawny and got "the bejesus kicked out of me regularly in school." The humiliation taught Newman to withdraw and to numb himself from emotional pain, lessons he had to unlearn later in order to function fully both as a man and as an actor. "That isn't a very valuable quality for an actor," he admitted to *Time* magazine.

Newman has described his father as "bookish" and "gentle," with a stern sense of discipline that apparently was problematic for his son, though as a parent himself, he adhered to similar principles. Though his dad owned the biggest sporting-goods store in town, Paul didn't receive his first baseball mitt until he was ten. Humanistic but strict, Arthur Newman, Sr., was determined to instill a strong morality in his sons and to squelch any signs of entitlement that might easily appear in the sons of a relatively rich man who owned a business overflowing with the sort of stock little boys dream of. If one were searching through Newman's life for clues of the germination of his remarkable determination to succeed, his diminutive size as a youth and his relationship with his disciplinarian father would be the most likely sources.

Apparently Paul felt a powerful need to prove his worth to his father. Newman now speaks of him with sadness and longing: "I think he always thought of me as pretty much of a lightweight. He treated me like he was disappointed in me a lot of the time, and he had every right to be. It has been one of the great agonies of my life that he could never know. I wanted desperately to show him that somehow, somewhere along the line I could cut the mustard. And I never got a chance, never got a chance."

Though his mother attempted to instill the beliefs of Mary Baker Eddy in her sons, the teachings made little impression upon Paul, and his father saw to it that despite his mother's belief in faith healing the boys received conventional medical care, a particular consideration in Paul's case since the accident-prone youth seemed to have a facility for falling out of trees, scraping himself on pavements, and cutting himself with kitchen knives. A sensitive, refined woman—almost saintly—Theresa Newman harbored unfulfilled theatrical ambitions that she passed on to her younger son with whom she was connected in some deep, sympathetic manner. Both Newman and his mother were attracted to acting for the outlet it provided for their half-understood, inarticulate emotions. "She was a frustrated actress, I guess," he has said.

Mrs. Newman encouraged Paul to join a children's theater, The Curtain Raisers, and Newman has somewhat disturbing memories of his first role at age five as a court jester in *The Travails of Robin Hood,* yodeling a song composed by his uncle, Joe S. Newman. At twelve, probably just as painfully self-conscious as seven years earlier, he starred as St. George in his first thriller-adventure, *St. George and the Dragon.* "I played Saint George, the dragon was a bulldog, and I put salt on his tail," Newman recalled thirty-three years later. Reminiscing with Charles Hamblett, Theresa Newman described her son as "the neighborhood clown. He yodeled and sang and acted in all sorts of little stunts. Always into some mischief. He was such a beautiful little boy," she laughed. "In a way, it was a shame to waste such beauty on a boy."

The conventionality of the Newman household was occasionally disturbed by visits from Arthur's brother Joe, who fired the younger son's imagination with insights into literature and encouraged the boy's appetite for books. A well-known Ohio journalist and poet, Arthur Newman was, according to his nephew, "a brilliant, erudite man with a marvelous, whimsical sense of humor," who had a great influence on Paul. At seventeen, Joe had been the youngest reporter ever hired by the Cleveland *Press,* but he had quit this career to shoulder his share of responsibility for the family business. One could almost say Paul Newman had two fathers, both ambitious and responsible, but one clearly more eccentric—the one who represented for the young boy the endless possibilities offered by the creative life.

Newman's academic career was as uneventful as his family life. He attended local elementary schools and graduated from Shaker Heights Senior High School in January 1943. He seems to have been an ordinary kid, pulling fair grades and distinguishing himself at nothing except for an atypical interest in dramatics. Like any normal youth, he discovered girls and played football, baseball, and basketball. Like most young men, Paul yearned to be known as a letter man. Rather clumsy and slight in build, always appearing younger than he was—and very defensive about it—Paul barely managed to make his class's football team. But many years later, Newman would claim that he, alone among the Newman men, did not lose his hair because of the crew cut he adopted as the symbol of the athlete. "My father, my uncle, and my brother became bald," he told Bob Thomas. "I would have too, except that I kept the short haircut and, from the time I was eleven to my mid-twenties, I brushed my hair every day with a stiff brush." What little time was left after his unsuccessful attempts to excell as a jock was devoted to his class work, the debating club, and theatrical pursuits that included stage-managing and acting, though he didn't always get the parts he went out for.

Though the family was well off, Paul held a series of part-time jobs after school and during vacations, among them working as a sandwich boy at Danny Budin's corned beef palace in Shaker Heights. In an interesting episode that could be regarded as a rehearsal for his adult career as film producer and food company executive, Paul sold encyclopedias door to door and made a thousand dollars during one college vacation. The budding entrepreneur sold the business for five hundred dollars, but he showed less acumen when he invested the profits in a show that soon flopped.

Though Paul Newman's youth was the picture of mid-western wholesomeness, there were indications, for those who could see, of the shadow side of the all-American boy: an unusual seriousness would sometimes overtake his love of fun; a veil would drop over his eyes, suggesting secrets. All of this would later translate onto the screen as a particularly heady brand of charisma. One neighbor who remembered Newman from Cleveland related an impression to author Charles Hamblett that jibes a bit more with the image of the romantic loner that has held the public's fascination for forty years:

> "There was something dangerous about him, you felt he was not really tamed, that just beneath the surface there was a streak of violence. He was very popular, there were a lot of girls who wanted to date him. But he wasn't a chaser, he always seemed to be going someplace else. . . . His eyes already had that intense, direct look and were bright blue just as they come across on the screen. He was very sure of himself, you got the impression that here was a guy who really knew where he was going."

Unwilling to go into the family business straight from high school but still undirected as far as a career, Newman enlisted in the navy immediately after graduation and marked time for the four months before he was called up at Ohio University in Athens, where he "majored in beer drinking" and minored in his ostensible course of studies, economics and business. Newman remained sober enough to play one of the leads in the Speech Department's production of Lynn Root and Harry Clark's *The Milky Way,* and then Pearl Harbor provided a temporary respite from the guilt he suffered at not being able to fulfill his father's wishes. Newman was able to delay the fate awaiting him as co-owner of Newman-Stern Sports with the noble excuse of service to his country. He had his first serious relationship before the war started, but while Newman was in the middle of the Pacific he received a Dear John letter. His girl had met someone else. "My first love sent me a Dear John letter while I was in the navy. I often wonder what my life would have been like if she hadn't," he mused many years later. What would *her* life have been like is the more interesting question, one she might well ask herself daily.

When he was finally sent by the navy to Yale for training as an air corps pilot, it was discovered that those beautiful blue eyes were color blind. Still slight in build, with the small man's defensive tension about his size, the disappointed would-be war hero, who was once mistaken for a Sea Scout, grew six inches in the next three years, perhaps through an effort of will. But the childlike sailor failed to see combat. "I got through the whole war on two razor blades," he jokes now. Newman spent the war in Guam, Hawaii, and Saipan as an aviation radio-gunman, third class, on naval torpedo planes. Even this early, it was apparent that Lady Fortune smiled on Paul Newman. One day his was among six crews to be sent on a carrier landing, but when his pilot developed an earache another crew was sent in their place to what turned out to be its death on a ship that was destroyed by a kamikaze pilot.

After his discharge in April 1946, still reluctantly moving on automatic toward his preordained destiny as heir to Newman-Stern Sports, Newman enrolled on the GI bill as an economics major at Kenyon College in Gambier, Ohio, where he passed three happy-go-lucky years drinking beer and chasing girls, only occasionally burning the midnight oil. Drama was still a hobby rather than an aspiration, but after two years of college Newman switched his major to English and speech. One factor may have been his persistent failure to excell in his first love, sports. Though he had made the second-string football team, Newman was involved in a barroom brawl and was thrown off the team. The free time now diverted from football allowed him to exercise his inherited business sense and love of theatrics. After searching out a little store, Newman converted it into a student laundry depot. Two kegs of free beer flowing all day and night induced students to drop off their dirty clothes, so that with 25 percent of the gross from the laundry that was actually washing the clothes, Newman was able to net about sixty dollars a week. But what was lucky for him proved a disaster to the student who bought the bustling business. On the original owner's advice, the unfortunate young man bought a keg of beer and opened for business at 10:00 P.M. on a Saturday night. One student, apparently working harder on getting drunk than doing his laundry, staggered onto the street and attempted to perpetuate an obscene act on an innocent horse. The horse bolted and the police closed the laundry-depot-*cum*-beer room. Now that sports and laundry no longer occupied his time, when Newman happened to hear of auditions for *Front Page* he read for the lead and had his "first, heady taste of acting," which apparently struck him as a great way to get attention, second only to football.

Later in life, at the age of forty-three, sports would still attract Newman more than acting, he maintains that if he had been more successful at athletics he would have pursued that rather than acting.

"It was simply because I couldn't play football anymore and I didn't want to study that I went back to the theater," he said of his early participation. "About ten days later I got my first part in a play there—this was my junior year—and I was in ten subsequent plays as a result of that."

One of his drama professors, James Michael, recalls "having trouble not casting Paul as the lead in every play."

But even from the beginning, Paul found acting to be a painful experience. "You have to learn to take off your clothes emotionally onstage. I was lousy. I couldn't let go, yet I wanted to act." This need to express himself was clearly stronger than his inhibitions, and Newman participated in productions of *R.U.R.*, *The Alchemist*, and *Charley's Aunt*. Almost as self-conscious and self-critical now as he was then, Newman looks back on those performances as the worst examples of amateur college acting, inept and unformed. Those early embarrassments drove him to overcome his insecurity by approaching acting as a challenge, as a craft to be studiously learned and doggedly mastered rather than as an art, a God-given ability with which one is either blessed or not. Throughout his long career Newman would studiously and laboriously prepare for his roles, battling his inability to trust his instinct and follow a feeling, to let go of his emotions and intuitively allow his performance to create itself. He shored himself up against failure with minute preparations and thorough rehearsals.

But his aura of something held in reserve was not a total handicap by any means. A sense of something kept back can be powerfully attractive. All fine actors know this, but the key to fascination is not emotional constipation; it is the suggestion of a dangerous flood of emotional turbulence held in check, as implied in the screen images of actors such as Marlon Brando, James Dean, and Steve McQueen. At his best Newman has emitted that powerfully seductive quality of emotion barely contained; at his worst, however, he has projected a stiff self-consciousness.

Already learning whatever he could from what he regarded as his early college embarrassments, by 1948 Newman was hooked enough to sense that his personal opportunities for excellence lay in working in the theater, and he spent his summer vacations turning in respectable efforts in summer stock at Plymouth, Massachusetts.

In some vague manner, Newman assumed Newman-Stern Sports was fixed in his future, so he again delayed the inevitable by leaving immediately after graduation from Kenyon (with a second degree, a "Magnum cum Lager," awarded him in the yearbook) to claim a room-and-board scholarship at a small theater company in Williams Bay, Wisconsin. He debuted in Norman Krasna's *John Loves Mary,* played in *Suspect; The Candlestick Maker;* and performed the role of the gentleman caller in *The Glass Menagerie,* the beginning of a long and profitable association with the work of Tennessee Williams.

No conscious decision had been made, but instead of taking up his place in the family business, he joined the Woodstock Players in Woodstock, Illinois, in the fall after leaving the Williams Bay company. Newman says, "I didn't know what to do. So I drifted into a season of summer stock in a small theater in Wisconsin. Then instead of going into the family business, I joined the company of another theater in Woodstock, Illinois, where I appeared in sixteen plays." Woodstock Players and similar groups were the training grounds, scattered all over the country, where a young thespian might build a set one day, star in a production the next night, and handle props the following week. Newman estimates that he directed and acted in over sixteen productions, among them *Cyrano de Bergerac; Icebound;* and *Dark of the Moon,* in which he costarred with his future wife, Jackie Witte, a humorous and vivacious brown-eyed blonde, who saw the unfocused ambition seething beneath the "square" midwestern exterior. In December 1949, a few months after they had met, Jackie and Paul were married, and the industrious young husband supplemented their slight income by working as a laborer on a nearby farm. But that April, Paul's father became ill and he had to go home to help his uncle Joe, who was still writing on the side, run the business. "It was a marvelous shop," Newman recalled for Jane Wilson much later in life, "and sold all kinds of things—camping equipment, cameras, odd radio components. There's no question there can be great romance and exhilaration in retailing." But Newman wouldn't find the "romance in retailing" until many years later, when he and his buddy A. E. Hotchner started a business they would come to call a multimillion-dollar joke.

Arthur Newman, Sr., died in May 1950, the same year Paul's son, Scott, was born. Paul had gone as far as buying a house with the intention of fulfilling his notion of filial obligation, but after his father died he felt less obligated to take over and the business was sold. This brief unhappy period, during which Paul dutifully followed his family's wishes, had convinced him that even if acting was not going to be his true vocation, happiness did not lie in business. "I was stuck," he once recalled, "doing something a lot of other people could do just as well. I simply had to make up my mind. Who was I, and where was I going?" Newman knew he had to find a different life, and the emotional, colorful world of the theater was pulling him more and more. "When I decided to go into acting, I wasn't searching for my identity. I didn't have greasepaint in my blood," he explains. "I was just running away from the family retail business—and from merchandising. I just couldn't find any romance in it. Acting was a happy alternative to a way of life that meant nothing to me."

More is revealed about Newman in that statement that he undoubtedly intended. He may have denied that acting was a means to find himself, of "searching for his identity," but what else does an actor do but draw out bits and pieces of himself and expand upon them in order to reconstruct and express the motivation and behavior of another person? What better way to find oneself than to try on different characters and discard them like so many ill-fitting suits of clothes, retaining only those features that feel true to oneself? Ironically, Newman was later to discover that the "business suit" he had discarded as a young man would become one of many costumes that now seemed tailor-made.

Newman was twenty-seven years old, a husband and father, but he had been only marking time since his father's death and the sale of the family business, waiting, as it were, for a sign, bringing in the bacon in the meantime by managing a local golf range and making a few appearances on local radio. He was doing fairly well at what he didn't really like. "I was very successful at being something I was not," he told the *Daily News*. "And that's the worse thing that can happen to a person." Suddenly, in September 1951, he took the plunge and left, over his family's protests, for the Yale School of Drama, taking with him his wife, his baby, and four thousand dollars.

Even then, the "plunge" could more accurately be described as poking a cautious toe in the waters: Paul Newman's azure eyes were focused not on Broadway, but back toward Kenyon College, where he hoped to return as a professor of speech and drama.

"All this crap about greasepaint!" Newman later scoffed. "And after Yale I didn't have stars in my eyes. I knew what this rat race was. I wanted a master's degree because my dream was to return to Kenyon and teach. I just fell into acting."

In the fall of 1951, Newman moved his family into a tiny apartment on the top floor of one of the numerous wooden-frame houses in New Haven, and set out to support his family with his old sideline career as encyclopedia sales-man, supplemented by his wife's income from occasional modeling jobs in New York City. Still reluctant to entertain ambitions of acting professionally, Newman majored in directing, which interested him equally. Struggling against his emotional inhibitions, Newman had to sob in his first part at Yale, in Shaw's *Saint Joan.* "It was the hardest thing I ever tried to do," he recalls. "But I knew it was sob or give up acting. I had quit my job and sold my house in Ohio. I had a wife to support. So I made myself do it.

"People laughed at first. I felt like a fool, but after a few rehearsals, it was easier. Then I really began to feel my oats."

Newman took the script down to the boiler room of his boarding house and worked on that part until he felt comfortable enough to perform before people. This marked the beginning of his perfectionist habit of preparing and studying for a role in private well in advance of his work with his colleagues. Newman ended up appearing in six one-act plays and at least four full-length productions at Yale, one of which was a student-authored work about the life of Beethoven. Sitting in the audience of the little theater was the husband-and-wife agent team Liebling and Wood. They did not laugh at the young actor; in fact they invited him to look them up if he ever came to New York City. That may have been the encouragement Newman needed, or perhaps money for tuition was too much of a strain on the young family's budget. In any event, after nine months at Yale, Paul Newman made that long and fateful hour-and-a-half trip to the Great White Way, promising himself that if he couldn't make it on Broadway after a year he would return to Yale, finish his degree and take up his career in academia.

True to the course of his charmed life, Newman didn't have to peddle encyclopedias for very long. "I was very, very lucky," he now admits. After a few days in a cheap downtown hotel, he found an inexpensive apartment for his family on Long Island. Leaving his wife and child early every morning that first summer, Newman attacked the chore of getting work as an actor as methodically as any other young job-seeker commuting from the suburbs. He began his rounds of producers, agents, and casting calls promptly at 9:00 every morning, nattily dressed in his carefully pressed and only good suit. "It got so that receptionists would announce me with, 'Here's the guy in the seersucker suit,'" he later laughed to Sidney Skolsky.

The fifties were one of the most exciting times in the history of the New York theater. A miasma of artificiality and conservativism was being assaulted by young, innovative American playwrights such as Arthur Miller and Tennessee Williams, who espoused a bold new naturalism, and Europeans such as Jean-Paul Sartre and Jean Genet, who laid the tracks for American revolutionaries such as Andre Gregory, John Guare, and the Open and Living Theaters. The Actors Studio was preparing a new breed of actors, internal and shockingly natural in their approach, among whom Marlon Brando and James Dean were most emblematic. Into the midst of this fervor of creative upheaval strolled the young man from Ohio, and Newman began to get his breaks almost immediately.

After only a few weeks of pounding pavements, he won two walk-ons on live television, in those days just finding its territory, discovering all it could do before it became hamstrung by the rules and conventions burdening more established communication art forms. These were early days of the medium, just before the McCarthy hearings robbed the theater, motion pictures, and television of their best and brightest. A more daring, experimental approach was still viable, and the small screen abounded with live, dramatic shows such as "Playhouse 90," "Philco," and "US Steel." These programs provided great opportunities to train and work for young, talented writers creating material for the myriads of young actors and directors who had come to New York to make it on Broadway and had found equally interesting opportunities in this new medium. Newman made associations in those early days that have grown into present-day collaborations, for instance with Sidney Lumet, then a young television director who guided him through his sixth Academy award–nomination performance in *The Verdict.* Newman recalls those days of live TV as "exciting. Men like Tad Mosel and Paddy Chayefsky and Max Schulman were writing for television, and they made it an inventive era. Call it kitchen sink, inner search, what have you—it was great." His admiration for the style of that era can be seen in his own directorial efforts, characterized by a naturalistic, slice-of-life quality.

Newman's first role, as an old man applauding President McKinley in *The March of Time,* earned him seventy-five dollars, and his first speaking role was in a weak attempt at science fiction, *Tales of Tomorrow.* But by September he had already appeared on *The Web, You Are There, Danger,* and *The Mask,* and had won a running part on *The Aldrich Family* series that earned him regular payments of two hundred dollars per month. John Foreman, then a young agent at MCA, recalled for writer Bob Thomas the day Newman arrived at the agency. "He looked like a Greek god. I sent him over to read for a part in a television series, *The Web,* and he got the part. Paul was cast for nearly every part he tried out for."

That fall Newman helped out a fellow actress auditioning for the Actor's Studio by playing a scene with her from Tennessee Williams's *Battle of Angels* (later to be renamed *The Fugitive Kind* and made into a film starring Marlon Brando and Joanne Woodward). Acceptance by the Studio required passing an initial audition before a large group. Only then could the actor audition before Elia Kazan and Cheryl Crawford. Though Newman considered himself an "untuned piano," not yet ready to compete at these Olympian heights, he must have made an impression: The actress was not accepted but Newman, in a breach of procedure, was offered membership in the most prestigious acting club in America without having actually auditioned.

Many years later, Newman recalled the experience for *The*

Aquarian. "When I heard that Elia Kazan, Cheryl Crawford, Frank Cosaro, Karl Malden, Kim Stanley, and Geraldine Page were sitting out there, I was so terrified I was physically shaking and that's what the scene was supposed to do.

"So they mistook a case of nerves that I had for unlimited rage. I got in on one audition—one of the few who ever did that. An actor's discomfort sometimes works well for him. It is not out of the realm of possibility to have the audience mistake discomfort for rage. At which time the actor is way ahead of the game."

In awe of his extraordinary classmates—Marlon Brando, James Dean, Karl Malden, Geraldine Page, Kim Stanley, Eli Wallach, Rod Steiger, and Julie Harris—Newman has described his early days at the Studio as "monkey see, monkey do. Man, I just sat back there and watched how people did things and had enough sense not to open my big mouth." It was then that Newman realized he had "spent the first thirty years of my life looking for a way to explode. For me, apparently, acting is that way." For the first time in his life, Newman was where he belonged.

Over the years, Newman has consistently sung the praises of the Studio, helped to raise money for its continuance, and attributed much of his success to its training and support: "The Actors Studio, whether they like it or not, has either credit or blame for what I've become as an actor. I certainly came out of a very academic background, which was not very helpful, and I learned everything I've learned about acting at the Actors Studio."

Things continued to move forward for the novice with unheard-of rapidity. In November 1952, William Liebling, the agent who had first shown interest in Paul, sent him up for the leading role in William Inge's new play, *Picnic,* directed by Joshua Logan. Though Newman thought he did a poor audition, his judges were less harsh. Initially he was hired to play the leading role of Hal Carter, the charismatic drifter who upsets the lives of several women in the small quiet town, but when Ralph Meeker stepped into the picture, Newman was cast instead as the shy, staid college boy, Alan Seymour, who loses his girl to Hal.

Though this was certainly the first and the last time in his career Newman's special brand of charisma would be overlooked, he received good reviews. Just six months after taking his leave from Yale he had landed himself in his first Broadway play, a Pulitzer Prize–winning smash that ran fourteen months and helped him win *Theatre World*'s nomination as one of the "Promising Personalities" of 1953. He did get to play Hal for two weeks when Meeker was indisposed, but when Newman asked director Logan if, on the strength of his performance, he could take over Meeker's role in the road company, Logan again failed to discern leading-man material in the slight, blue-eyed young man. "I don't think so," he told a disappointed Newman, "because you don't carry any sexual threat." Newman recalled for *The New York Times* that "at that particular point, I probably didn't. That sort of thing has a lot to do with conviction." Logan advised the young actor to get in shape. "The way I translated that was six hours in the gym everyday," Newman said, and thus was created the famous tautly muscled physique, an integral part of Paul Newman's later "sexual threat." Logan's comment never stopped rankling the sensitive Newman. "I've been chewing on that one for almost thirty years," he has admitted.

The young understudy to *Picnic*'s two female leads was named Joanne Woodward, a twenty-year-old blonde with a corn-pone drawl that softened the edges of a razor-sharp intellect. She and Newman had met before, in agent John Foreman's office where Paul had stayed longer than scheduled for his appointment and kept the young actress waiting for hers. "So I was introduced to her by way of apology," Newman recalled many years later. "She was an actress and my part of New York was full of actresses. She wrote me off as a snobby college boy. . . . We exchanged polite hellos and I went my way, no sweat." But Newman clearly recalls first seeing his future wife onstage. "I remember seeing her in Noel Coward's *Hay Fever*. I thought, 'I don't know that woman. She must be a real scorcher.'" Working together for almost one and a half years led to a close friendship, which for five years Newman and Woodward were determined to keep as just that.

At the end of *Picnic*'s Broadway run in 1959, Paul was offered a five-year contract by Warner Brothers, and Susan, the Newmans' second child, was born. By now Paul was fully engaged in a promising career and spending a great deal of time at the Actors Studio. There was no question of returning to Yale to follow through with his plans to become a professor. Newman had allowed himself a short period in New York, almost as a means of getting any ideas about professional acting out of his system so his latter years would not be plagued with unfulfilled dreams, but work was coming even more smoothly than he had dared to hope.

But the relative ease with which Newman was winning recognition as an up-and-coming actor was offset by the intensifying struggle to keep his marriage intact despite his growing romantic attachment with Joanne Woodward. Five long years later, it would be Jackie who finally resolved the situation, freeing Joanne and Paul to openly acknowledge their relationship and marry.

An offer he couldn't refuse bought Paul Newman some thinking time as it took his young career in a new, exciting direction. Warner Brothers's offer of a thousand dollars a week was something no young actor, no matter how principled, could ignore, and it was a chance to put a continent between himself and his marital difficulties. Newman decided to forgo the national tour of *Picnic* in favor of making that archetypal trip West. He would take on the beast of Hollywood.

Despite the leap in salary and the contract, Newman approached Hollywood with the skeptical regard of someone viewing an oasis that suddenly appears in the midst of a vast stretch of desert. It could be a mirage. He checked into a cheap motel near the studio and paid Warner Brothers a visit, feelings of foreboding churning his gut.

His intuitions proved correct. From the beginning, signs did not augur well. He had a meeting with Sam Siegel, who had once changed his name to S. P. Eagle and tried to talk Newman into changing his name to something more American. "Why should I change my name?" Newman demanded. Spiegel muttered something about Newman not being phonetic. "All right," Newman replied, "I'll change it to S. P. Newman."

Things rapidly went from bad to worse. He had already lost the part of the year in *East of Eden* when he was cast in

The Silver Chalice, a movie Newman has since dubbed "the worse film made in the entirety of the 1950s—the worst American film in the entire decade." Elia Kazan had narrowed down the casting of Cal Trask to two finalists, both known to him and to each other from the Actors Studio: James Dean and Paul Newman. The part went to Dean, and Newman got the booby prize, *The Silver Chalice.* To make matters worse, the two films were shot at the same time on adjoining soundstages, with Pier Angeli, James Dean's real-life love, starring opposite Newman. So while Dean made screen history in a role that defined the tortures of misunderstood youth for all time, Paul Newman was condemned to a desperate search for something salvageable in a role that called for him to wear "a cocktail gown" and utter inanities such as "Oh, Helena, is it really you? What a joy!"

Newman never got over his embarrassment about his performance in that bizarre religious epic, a film so monumentally bad that over the years it has achieved a certain distinction as a camp classic of cheese. The notion must have particularly struck Newman with a sickening thud that, unlike a bad stage performance, his first movie role as Basil the slave would live on longer than he, preserved in larger-than-life technicolor. It took him two years to gather the nerve to make another motion picture. Many years later, when Paul Newman was an established star, long forgiven for Basil the slave by everyone but himself, the movie was scheduled to appear on Los Angeles TV. Newman took out a black-bordered advertisement in a Los Angeles newspaper saying, "Paul Newman apologizes every night this week—Channel 9." Though meant to be a joke, his action was a clear message of discomfort, and the attempt backfired. Attention was called to the film and ratings were far higher than the movie would otherwise have garnered; in fact, it pulled one of the highest ratings in the history of

Los Angeles. On another occasion he got a print of *The Silver Chalice* and showed it to friends in the screening room of his Westport home, fortifying everyone with a bowl of Newman's Own popcorn and arming them with metal pots and wooden spoons to drown out the worst spots. "It was fun for the first reel," he admits, "and then the awfulness of the thing took over."

Produced and directed by Victor Saville, the clumsy plot weaves biblical lore into the story of Basil, a slave and silver smith of early Christian days faced with the choice of his innocent Christian wife, Pier Angeli, and his pagan seductress, Virginia Mayo and opposed in his mission to create a receptacle for the chalice from which Christ drank at the Last Supper, by an evil anti-Christ magician, played with scenery-chomping relish by Jack Palance, the only actor who got out of this debacle alive. An article in *Silver Screen* described Newman at work on the set in true Method style, thinking through his character's motivation in a scene and debating aloud whether or not the dialogue written for the scene was appropriate. "If you had just seen a vision, what would you do?" he mused. "Wouldn't you want to be completely quiet and go off by yourself for a while?" But the musings of a serious young actor were hardly appropriate for this celluloid joke. One of the many hilarious anachronisms occurs in a scene picturing Caesar lolling on cushions in his palace dining hall before a procession of slaves bearing trays of what looks like papier-mâché food painted gold. A voice enthusiastically intones the list of delicacies: "Quail's eggs wrapped in the tongues of larks done to a golden brown, grasshoppers dipped in purest honey and roasted to a turn." All these items are described in language more suggestive of a Greek coffee shop than of ancient Greece.

Not surprisingly, *The Silver Chalice* opened to largely derisive notices, with critics falling over themselves to exercise their humor at the expense of everyone involved. One memorable review by the *New Yorker* critic joked, "Paul Newman delivers his lines with the emotional fervor of a conductor announcing local stops." Perhaps even more wounding to his film career were the many comments on his resemblance to the hottest young star of the time, Marlon Brando, whose *On the Waterfront* and *The Wild Ones* had been the sensations of 1954. The *New York World Telegram* made a typical comment in pointing out "an astonishing resemblance to Marlon Brando, an excessively sullen Brando." Newman would retort more than once, "Someday, dammit, they're going to say that Marlon Brando looks like *me*!"

There were certain similarities, physically and in their acting styles, but the physical resemblance was certainly negligible and the naturalistic acting style was the hallmark of an entire school that had studied at the Actors Studio. Brando and Newman both had elements of the rebel at the core of their screen images. The difference was that in Newman, one usually sensed a line he would not cross, but with Brando one never knew what would happen. He seemed that crazy. And that is why, of course, Brando was the genius, the hare who didn't finish the race, and Newman the tortoise, slow but steady, ultimately a winner.

Newman often expressed anger over the comparisons. "Why does everyone have to put labels on actors?" he demanded of a *Newark Evening News* reporter in 1958. "It never fails. Sooner or later every newcomer to Hollywood is told he is 'another somebody or other.'" According to Newman, Brando had "a rebellious attitude, which I don't believe I have." He and Brando were radically different actors, Newman insisted, describing Brando as the kind of actor most successful in roles close to his own personality, whereas Newman's technique was to draw as little as possible from his own character, fabricating his roles from his imagination. "It's the opposite with me," he explained. "I'm more effective playing parts which are farthest from my own self. I also enjoy doing them most."

Newman also objected to comparisons with James Dean, whose quality was "a lot like a little boy point of view." But Warner Brothers, true to Hollywood studio form, was more than eager to exploit the situation and chose to promote Newman as a "second Brando," playing it safe with a known crowd pleaser, rather than taking a chance in allowing him to develop his own image. Time would prove all these resemblances to be superficial and fleeting, a result of the need of facile minds to categorize and stereotype rather than deal with the unknown. In reality there were only a few generational similarities and some unfortunate coincidences in the three men's careers.

Newman had arrived in Hollywood just as the winds of change began to blow through the West Coast film community. The bad boys, T-shirted and blue-jeaned, announced their arrival roaring down the Sunset Strip on their motorcycles. Newman had a casual friendship with Brando, who treated his alleged look-alike with uncharacteristic respect, but Newman and Dean enjoyed a closer camaraderie. They had met through the Actors Studio, and stranded in California, they occasionally rode their motorcycles down to the beach and commiserated over beers about the Hollywood philistines.

But the old Hollywood would not be toppled by a gang of motorcycle-riding, black-leather-jacketed Method actors alone. More established actors, such as Kirk Douglas, Bette Davis, and Olivia de Havilland, were determined to wrest control of their projects away from the iron grip of the studio bosses, who told actors what to do and when to do it. They fought by attacking where it hurt most—by their valuable participation from projects they did not want to do, despite their own financial losses. Newman observed

and filed the lesson in his memory. Though his first Hollywood experience seemed a waste, the Newman charm had
occasionally glimmered through the muck. No matter what
the cost, Paul Newman would grab the first opportunity he
spotted to be his own man.

The Silver Chalice opened on December 25, 1954, a year
marking a happier premiere: Jackie and Paul's third child,
Stephanie. Newman had another reason to be thankful: the
clause in his Warner Brothers contract allowed him to do
two plays on Broadway. After viewing *The Silver Chalice*,
he knew what to expect from the critics. He had heard that
a new play, *The Desperate Hours,* was casting the perfect
role to antidote the insipid Basil—an escaped psychopath
who holds a family at gunpoint in their home—just the
kind of casting against type that could prove his worth as an
actor. Before shooting on *The Silver Chalice* had even
ended, Newman had wired his agent with the demand,
"Get me back on Broadway." He later recalled, "I called
my agents in New York, and told them, 'You'd better have
me on a stage when this thing is released or I'm dead!'"
But Warner Brothers exacted a stiff price for Newman's escape East, one he likened to having sold part of his body.
He was now tied to a new seven-year contract in which he
would give Warner Brothers two films a year with an option
on a third.

Once again the Newman combination of luck and savvy
saw him through. He walked onstage right into another
Broadway hit; on February 19, 1955, he began a six-month
run in *The Desperate Hours.* As Glen Griffin, the lead
hoodlum of a trio of escaped convicts who hold up a family
while awaiting their getaway money (a role later played by
Humphrey Bogart in the movie), Newman's performance
seethed with unresolved Oedipal hatred. The swarms of
backstage autograph hounds and the rave notices he received from the critics rebuilt his faltering self-confidence

and almost canceled out the critical pans drawn almost simultaneously by *The Silver Chalice.* Brooks Atkinson of *The New York Times* commented, "Paul Newman plays the boss thug with a wildness that one is inclined to respect. The play shatters the nerves." Walter Kerr wrote, "Paul Newman's grinning gunman with close-cropped skull and a firm assurance that there's something in it—may start off with the throttle too open, but it is finally an effective performance on a splashy level." Most enthusiastic was John Chapman of the *New York Daily News,* who described Newman's performance as "evil, neurotic, and vibrant—a first-class piece of work . . . there could be no more stir-crazy and animal-crafty desperado . . . a splendid, tensely maniacal performance." After one month, the producers took note of these reactions and the ever-growing clutch of eager young girls milling around the backstage door, and they raised his billing to costar status. There was nowhere for Newman to soar but up.

During the course of his Broadway run, Newman went home to his family on Long Island every night, visited the Actors Studio twice a week, and looked for other work during the day. He contrasted the psychopathic Glen Griffin with a very different role as George, the high-school boyfriend of Emily, in NBC's musical version of Thornton Wilder's *Our Town,* also featuring Frank Sinatra and Eva Marie Saint. Despite clear evidence of his talents, the mere fact that he costarred with Miss Saint, who had just won an Oscar for playing opposite Brando in *On the Waterfront,* coupled with his long run with Karl Malden in *The Desperate Hours,* burdened Newman with continued comparisons to Marlon Brando.

Though Newman was linked with Brando in the public and studio eyes, his professional path actually crossed more with that of co-rebel and buddy James Dean. Newman had continued to work extensively in live television drama and was scheduled to play Nick Adams, the narrator of Hemingway's *The Battler,* which Arthur Penn was directing from a teleplay written by A. E. Hotchner. Dean was scheduled to play the aging ex–boxing champion, but his death at the wheel of his Porsche left the part open just before telecasting time. "We were forced to fill the part by risking young Newman in the lead," lamented A. E. Hotchner in a letter to Ernest Hemingway. Hotchner was later to become Newman's close friend and business partner.

Newman, devastated by Dean's death, was barely able to perform his own role, but he was persuaded to take over Dean's part of the battler who is seen both as a punch-drunk wreck of fifty-five and a lean and hungry young champ. The part would have been a tour de force for any young actor, with its welcome challenge of proving himself under pounds of disfiguring makeup.

Meanwhile, Warner Brothers had been rather lack-adaisically looking to place their new contractee in a role to follow up Basil the slave. This was fine with Newman, who was perfectly content to remain on the East Coast, attending Actors Studio classes and appearing on live television. When *The Battler* was broadcast live in October 1955, director Robert Wise and producer Charles Schness, who had been planning a film version of Rocky Graziano's autobiographical *Somebody Up There Likes Me* (again starring James Dean), knew they had their replacement. Now Newman was not only being compared to Brando, but in the wake of Dean's death, he was inheriting the latter's parts as well.

Just before shooting on *Somebody* was to begin, Glenn Ford dropped out of a Warner Brothers film about a court-martial during the Korean war, leaving available the part of the young indicted marine, Captain Ed Hall, Jr. Two years after *The Silver Chalice,* the studio rushed its property into the part.

A potentially sensitive film marred by its static treatment, *The Rack* nevertheless proved Newman's worth as a
leading man and gave him his first chance to demonstrate a
gift for revealing the core of fragile emotion beneath the
crust of the macho male. From this role would grow
the complex mix of vulnerability and hard-boiled cynicism,
the signature quality of the Newman hero. Portraying a decent young man undone by the experience of psychological
torture at the hands of the enemy and accused by his peers
of delivering pro-Communist lectures to his prison camp
mates, Newman's hesitant, somewhat mannered performance struck some critics as mere Actors Studio mumbling
and others as powerfully affecting, particularly in the
scenes with the father (Walter Pidgeon) that reveal their
damaged relationship to be the cause of the young man's
fatal susceptibility. Though the film marked the birth of an
embryonic Paul Newman hero—alienated, vulnerable, always the loner—and though he turned in a solid, interesting characterization, the tag of Brando clone remained
fixed to Newman's public image. Newman judged that the
film "really aspired to something, and nobody went to see
it." Typically less kind toward himself, however, he went
on to call his portrayal "a fine example of me trying too
hard."

But Newman was again lucky. *The Rack* was pulled out
of release after only a few premieres and held back for
wide distribution until after the huge success expected for
him in *Somebody Up There Likes Me*. The film would show
the critics and the public once and for all that Paul Newman
was more than a decorative presence on the screen; Paul
Newman was an actor of scope and versatility.

Somebody Up There Likes Me still holds up as a stellar
example of the youthful-rebel-with-a-cause genre so popular in the bland, conformist fifties; it even included in its
supporting cast another embryonic screen rebel, a very
young Steve McQueen. The script, by Ernest Lehman, fol-

lows the general story of the Rocky Graziano autobiography, telling of his childhood in the ghetto, his juvenile delinquency, and the fixed fights of his early days. The youthful Graziano must choose between a career as a prizefighter and life as a criminal. He finally opts for a life of integrity built on a career in fighting that earns him self-respect and worldwide acclaim for his own honest efforts. Just as the character he played knew an opportunity when he saw it, Newman saw this role as a chance to prove himself and was determined to capitalize on it. Playing the fighter offered many opportunities for Newman, not the least of which was the chance to strip off his shirt and reveal the chest of a potential screen idol. The studio could hold on to their sex symbol, and Newman could show the world he could act.

He began by researching his character exhaustively so that his performance would have the proper ring of authenticity. He had the advantage of being able to study the real character on whom the role was based. Newman spent a good deal of time talking with Graziano, studying his physical and vocal mannerisms and his boxing technique, before he had to leave New York for Hollywood to film the movie. Once in Hollywood, Newman trained at the Hollywood YMCA for several hours a day and took coaching from boxing professionals.

The critical raves that greeted the film's release confirmed that his efforts had not been in vain. With the guidance of director Robert Wise, known for his ability to bring out the best in his actors, Newman was able to create a faithful screen interpretation of Graziano, complete with the cocky walk, the Italian New York mumbling accent, the shifty look, and the defensive, dancing mannerisms of the professional boxer; never lapsing into caricature, always suggestive of the complete personality. He captured realistically the crudity of the man, softened by a touch of the tender buffoon. Newman had become so accomplished a boxer that one of the most exciting moments of the movie is an authentically re-created fight scene between Newman as Graziano and Tony Zale, the former middleweight champion, playing himself.

But even this role was marred by the endless comparisons with Brando. Ironically, Brando had also modeled a role on Graziano, as the fighter relates in his autobiography:

This kid took to hanging around me in Stillman's gymnasium, training along beside of me, shooting the breeze. He looked like he might have been a fair fighter once, but he was in bad condition for the ring now and his punch looked slow. I felt sorry for the kid. He rode around town on a second-hand motorcycle, wearing patched-up blue jeans. Whenever we went downstairs for a cup of coffee or anything, I always paid for it.

One day, after he's been hanging around maybe a month, he says come and take a walk down Eighth Avenue with him. He takes me into Forty-sixth Street and points up at the marquee up over a legitimate theatre.

"Rocky," he says, "that's me. That's where I work. I want you and your wife to come see me."

Up on the sign it said "Marlon Brando" and the name of the play was *Streetcar Named Desire*.

When he gave me the tickets, he says, "Thanks for everything, Rocky. Thanks." What he's thanking me for, I don't know, unless it's for all them cups of coffee . . ."

A few months later I found out why Marlon Brando said thanks to me. I am watching television, and they introduce this show about fighting and his name is on the screen, and then he comes on and it's me! The son of a bitch is talking like me and walking like me and punching like me! How you like that! I got conned into learning this bum his part by a motorcycle and a pair of blue jeans!

Both Newman and Brando had built performances on a study of the same man, and though Newman's performance could not be faulted, the reviews were still full of comparisons and snide remarks about Brando and Newman, for example Bosley Crowther's review for *The New York Times:* "Let it be said of Mr. Newman that he plays the role of Graziano well, making the pug and Marlon Brando almost indistinguishable." The *Christian Science Monitor*'s grudging compliment was, "Although Paul Newman's shambling, impulsive performance as Rocky has inevitably recalled Marlon Brando's portrayals of Neanderthal types, Mr. Newman nevertheless adds his own insights and vivid portraiture." The truth, of course, was that Newman was accused of copying Brando only because Brando happened to get to the source first.

Despite the Brando label, *Somebody Up There Likes Me* made Newman a star of the fifties neorealistic school of "the rebel with a cause he cannot even articulate." William K. Zinsser was typical in his prediction that Paul "should jump to movie stardom with this role." The comparatively lackluster *The Rack* opened in the shadow of *Somebody Up There Likes Me,* so its rather bland impression hardly registered.

This should have been a happy period of his life, but "it was not a very good time," Newman later said. He had been busy commuting between Hollywood and the East Coast, where he was living with Jackie and the children. In New York he continued to do television, appearing in *The Rag Jungle,* the original television production of *Bang the Drum Slowly,* and *The Five Fathers of Pepi.* Despite their repeated resolutions to stop seeing each other, fate kept bringing Joanne Woodward and Paul Newman together.

Their feelings for each other had grown past the point where they could be contained. Woodward, herself the child of divorced parents, did not want to be responsible for taking Newman away from his three children, and Newman could not bring himself to leave.

In an attempt to deal with the stress, Paul found himself drinking to excess. This led to a minor confrontation with the Nassau County, Long Island, police on July 7, 1956; unfortunately the incident received major news coverage. After leaving his wife and friends in a restaurant and bar in Roslyn, Newman was picked up by the police at 2:00 A.M. for running a red light and leaving the scene of an accident in which he had demolished a fire hydrant and some shrubbery.

He allegedly boasted to one of the patrolmen, "I'm acting for Rocky Graziano. What do you want?" The patrolman's name happened also to be Rocky, so he snapped back, "I'm Rocky, too, and you're under arrest." After a slight struggle, Newman was brought in handcuffs to the Mineola police station, where a gaggle of reporters and photographers lay in wait for news of a kidnapping case. "This is a big deal!" Newman exclaimed, thinking the reporters had been alerted of his own arrival. "How did the newspapermen know I'd been pinched?" When the situation was explained, Newman reportedly said, "If they want a kidnapper, I'll make like one," stamping his foot and striking a threatening pose. "Rocky" Newman ended up spending the night in jail, despite his protests that he suffered from claustrophobia.

Finally Jackie ended an intolerable situation by asking her husband for a divorce. The separation appears to have been conducted with a minimum of recriminations, and, considering the potential of the story as grist for the overactive gossip mill feeding off Hollywood citizens, the breakup was carried out with a surprising lack of scandalized reportage. In fact, relations between Newman and his first wife have been so amicable that under the stage name Jacqueline de Wit, she has appeared in bit roles in many of her ex's films.

But Newman, the father of three children, hardly walked away from his first marriage unscathed. He later said, "I felt guilty as hell about it, and I will carry that guilt for the rest of my life." In his life thus far, Newman had made three agonizing decisions, all of which involved hurting those closest to him, all of which hindsight confirmed as necessary if he was to become his own man, but none of which seemed at the time "the right thing to do" to the traditional-minded, moral son of middle-class America living under the facade of a rebel image. Luckily, Newman's sense of honesty ran deeper than just doing the right thing. The same inner voice that led him to abandon the family legacy of a life in the suburbs tending the family store, to uproot his new family to pursue a dream of acting, to risk Hollywood just as his career onstage was taking off, also led him to leave his wife and three children to marry the woman he loved.

Born February 27, 1930, in Thomasville, Georgia, Joanne Cignilliat Woodward grew up, like Newman, in affluence, the daughter of Wade Woodward, a former state educator turned publishing executive who later became a vice-president of Charles Scribner and Sons. Her mother, Elinor Trimmer Woodward, a prototypical southern belle, raised her daughter alone after she and her husband divorced. Joanne rejected the southern-belle image early on, preferring to project her intelligence, independent spirit and outspoken manner, and to let the chips fall where they might. After two years at Louisiana State University she worked briefly as a secretary and then returned to her hometown of Greenville, where she studied acting with her high-school drama teacher, Robert Machare, and joined a theater group under the supervision of Albert MacLain. Like her future husband, Woodward played in little theater productions, notably as Laura in *The Glass Menagerie,* the film version of which the Newmans would collaborate on almost forty years later.

Unlike her future husband, Woodward had her heart set on acting from early childhood, and from Greenville she went first to Chatham, Massachusetts for a season of summer stock, and then to New York City, where she studied with Sandford Meisner, joined the Neighborhood Playhouse, and, later, the Actors Studio. Two days after graduating from the Neighborhood Playhouse, her agent at MCA got her a job in a *Robert Montgomery Presents* television show, "Penny." John Foreman was also Newman's agent and would become his partner years later in a number of Newman-Foreman film productions. Like Newman, Woodward regularly worked in television in such shows as *Omnibus, Kraft Theater,* and *Studio One.* She made her Broadway debut in 1956 in *The Lovers,* after she had acted in two films for Twentieth Century–Fox: *Count Three and Pray* and *A Kiss Before Dying.*

Joanne Woodward had begun her film career as inauspiciously as had Newman, with three undistinguished films in a row and a growing reputation among the studio bosses as trouble. Smart and independent, Woodward never shirked from offering her opinions on the pap the studio force fed the public. She wanted nothing to do with it.

The Wayward Bus was to have been her next film. She was scheduled to leave for California the next day, when she received a telephone call from her mother reporting that she had read in the newspaper columns about a wonderful new book, *Three Faces of Eve,* which was to be made into a film. Rumor had it Judy Garland was being considered for the role. Woodward told her daughter the role had to be hers. Recalled Woodward many years later,

"I said, 'Why mother, I haven't got a chance of getting a part like that. That's a star part. They want a star for that.'"

But the studio was having trouble casting the film with the difficult and challenging role of a woman with a multiple personality that was based on a real case, related by two psychiatrists. Almost by default, Joanne was cast by executives who half hoped the irksome young actress would fall on her face. The day after the conversation with her mother, Joanne received an urgent telephone call from the studio telling her to forget about *The Wayward Bus*. Another script was on its way by messenger, and this was to be her next film. It was, of course, *The Three Faces of Eve*.

Although the production values of the finished film indicate the studio had little faith in the commercial viability of the movie, during shooting word began to spread about the daily rushes. Everyone knew something special was happening. Woodward turned in a bravura performance as a woman afflicted with three totally distinct personalities: Eve White, a drab, repressed, mouse of a housewife; Eve Black, tramp, loud, and vulgar, an explosion of everything Eve White suppressed; and Jane, the integrated personality, the one who would eventually take over. While the film itself is largely an indifferent piece of work, it became a classic due to Woodward's landmark performance. If she had never made another film, she would still be remembered on the strength of this single characterization. Woodward easily captured the 1957 Oscar for Best Actress, the only period in their careers when Woodward's star threatened to outshine Newman's.

Though 1957 was not as successful a year for her lover as far as his career was concerned, it brought the peace of resolution to his personal life. The past few years had been difficult and tumultuous, and Newman had decided to take time for a bit of accelerated internal growth. He entered psychoanalysis for a period, and "found it a most enriching and rewarding experience," as he told writer Charles Hamblett. "What measure of serenity I have in my life today is the direct result of analysis," Newman acknowledged. "It brought me every possible benefit. My acting improved and I achieved a greater control over myself."

Newman's next film, a maudlin soap opera about four sisters called *Until They Sail,* was his third loan-out, this time to MGM, and it reunited him with his *Somebody Up There Likes Me* director, Robert Wise. Playing a loner, Jack Harding, in a role that offered few challenges, Newman distinguished himself as a star in the innocuous story of a shell-shocked alcoholic American soldier stationed in New Zealand during World War II, whose duty it is to investigate marriages between servicemen and New Zealand women and who falls in love himself. The mediocrity of the film merely served to reaffirm that the Newman charisma would prevail, even if the Newman acting ability could not quite completely conquer inferior material. The character of Jack Harding added an element of romance to the Newman persona that was rapidly taking form in the public imagination: the defeated yearning at the core of the cynic who seeks relief from his pain in the bottom of a bottle. In *Hollywood Stars,* Lawrence J. Quirk wrote, "In *Somebody Up There Likes Me,* Paul Newman revealed himself as a solid character actor. In *The Rack,* he showed he could handle heavy dramatics with the best of them. And now, in *Until They Sail,* he gives every evidence of becoming a matinee idol *par excellence.*"

Before returning to the Warner Brothers lot to film *The Helen Morgan Story,* Newman indulged himself in a display of his eccentric sense of humor. He had a picture snapped of himself exiting a deep freeze with the caption, "Paul Newman, who was kept in the deep freeze for two years because of *The Silver Chalice,* has at last been thawed out by Warner Brothers to play the cold-hearted gangster in *The Helen Morgan Story*" and sent it to studio boss Jack Warner.

But however lightly Paul tried to approach his second Warner Brothers project— a formulaic Hollywood star bio—difficulties with the director, Michael Curtiz, notoriously unsympathetic to actors, and a pastiche of a script that had suffered too many cooks since Warner Brothers had bought the rights to Morgan's story, resulted in another conventional and commercially successful effort. Newman lit enthusiastically into his role as an arrogant gangster of the love 'em and leave 'em type, but his attempt to galvanize a one-dimensional, stereotypical role failed to rescue the film from drowning in its bath of sudsy melodrama. *The Helen Morgan Story* didn't help to establish Newman as a gifted actor, but he projected such a powerful aura of masculine eroticism that it didn't hurt his career either. In fact, as Larry Maddux, a smooth-talking seducer who exploits anyone and everyone to achieve his ambitions, Newman was so attractive that the female members of the audience seemed more than willing to endure the harsh Maddux treatment. That inability to discourage female attention, no matter how nefarious the character he portrayed, would later annoy Newman, but it was an important contribution to the construction of the quintessential Paul Newman film hero that was coalescing swiftly, film by film. Newman's later self-criticism of his acting in this role: "Ugghh."

Despite his growing popularity, Newman was understandably unhappy with the work he'd been offered by his studio, and displeased with the fact that Warner Brothers was making $75,000 on loan-out for each picture he made outside the studio, while he continued to earn only a thousand a week. This lopsided financial arrangement held true in his next loan-out, in which he and Joanne Woodward costarred in *The Long Hot Summer* for Twentieth-Century Fox. This was the first of their acting collaborations, and perhaps the most successful.

The second picture Woodward had made with Actors Studio alumnus Martin Ritt, it was Newman's first with the director. Their collaboration would be repeated with fruitful results throughout both men's careers. Even this early on, Ritt was a true actor's director.

In preparation for his role, Newman spent several days alone before the shoot in Clinton, Missouri, where he passed the time hanging around the bars and pool halls, absorbing the local culture, fixing the drawl in his mind, and passing himself off as just another good ol' boy.

Newman's careful work paid off in more ways than he expected. When an ambitious newsman tried to insinuate himself among the locals in order to get the scoop on the Newman-Woodward romance, Paul's new friends took the reporter to the back of the bar and convinced him that leaving town would be a good idea.

As Ben Quick, the "stubborn, proud, wary hustler" who sharecrops when he isn't burning barns to settle grudges, Newman woos a reluctant Clara Varner with the encouragement of her father, a dominating patriarch played by Orson Welles. Quick finally wins Clara through her humanizing effects on him and he, in turn, releases the repressed virgin in Clara Varner.

Newman's meticulous preparation created a ruthlessly ambitious character that prefigured many of his great roles: the amoral man corrupted by greed who gets what he wants through seduction and charm, but who reveals at some point, usually near the picture's end, some saving grace of vulnerability and humanity. In the final analysis, the Newman protagonist comes off not as a complete villain but as an appealing kind of anti-hero, the kind of man every woman in the audience knows she could help "turn good," the kind of rascal every male wishes he was free to be.

Though Newman claims that when he views the film now he is "aware of how hard I was working," he did bring more complex dimensions to what could have been a flat, one-note role, and he received deservedly excellent reviews for his efforts as well as the Best Actor Award at the 1958 Cannes Film Festival.

Bosley Crowther, writing for *Time,* singled Newman out as "the best" of the distinguished ensemble of actors [including Orson Welles, Joanne Woodward, Anthony Franciosa, Angela Lansbury, and Lee Remick in her second film], and described his role as that of

> the roughneck who moves in with a thinly veiled sneer to knock down the younger generation and make himself the inheritor of the old man. He has within his plowhand figure and behind his hard blue eyes the deep and ugly deceptions of a neo–Huey Long. He could, if the script would let him, develop a classic character.

Though the American critics did not wholly appreciate the film adaptation of Faulkner's tale of family intrigue and greed in the deep South, *The Long Hot Summer* continued the process of building what would become a classic American character, the unforgettable Newman persona that would keep the actor within the boundaries of whatever makes one a star, a golden circle that Newman would view at times as a prison from which neither critics nor audience would let him stray.

By the time the picture wrapped, Paul's Mexican divorce from Jackie had come through. Newman and Woodward had been living openly together with writer Gore Vidal at a Malibu beach house the three rented together, but the lovers were now free to marry. Before they did, in January

1958 they costarred in a Playhouse 90 production, *The 80-Yard Run,* an adaptation of an Irwin Shaw short story. As a college football hero whose later life falls short of its early days of glory, Newman won rave reviews for what many still consider his best television work.

Two weeks later, on January 29, 1958, the couple was married in a Las Vegas gambling establishment, the Hotel El Rancho Vegas, with Sophie Tucker, Joe E. Lewis, Eydie Gorme, and other casino stars as the unlikely witnesses. The Newmans left immediately for New York, where they flew to London for a winter honeymoon. This was a happy time for Newman, who told the *Daily News* many years later, "Without her I'd be nowhere—nothing. She really opened me up." The honeymooners passed their first married days together exploring the countryside, taking long walks in the London parks, attending the theater, and sampling British brew in little pubs. "I have loved London ever since," Newman has said. In the years to follow, both Woodward and Newman have returned to England many times, both together and separately, to enjoy the relative anonymity allowed them by the less star-crazed British public.

After their honeymoon, the Newmans settled somewhat uncomfortably in Hollywood. It would be four years and ten different houses and apartments later before they determined to settle permanently in the East, a continent away from the insular film colony and the earthquakes that terrified Woodward. For many years they lived in a remodeled carriage house in Connecticut, and later, after their three daughters were grown, they bought a penthouse on Manhattan's East Side.

Despite initial circumstantial difficulties—the fact that their union was built on the wreckage of Newman's first marriage, and the initial resistance of his children to accept their new stepmother, neither partner was a novice at relationships. Paul, of course, was already a father of three;

Joanne had been engaged three times before, to writers Gore Vidal and James Costigan, and to an unknown man; and though they possessed very different personalities and interests, Woodward and Newman welcomed the differences as expansive of their union rather than as a source of divisiveness. On the matter of twin careers in one marriage, a rock upon which many a marital ship has floundered, Woodward's work clearly took a backseat to her husband's, particularly after their children began to arrive. Though at times she has stated this was a deliberate choice to maintain the balance of her marriage, at other times Woodward has said that she has not worked more because of a lack of good scripts. The truth is probably a bit of both. Three children have resulted from the Newman-Woodward union, and as their mother, Woodward felt she could hardly fulfill that role while she was off on locations playing others. "As I look back," she told *Time,* "I think what I really wanted was to have a life with no children, but I was raised in a generation that taught us otherwise. I felt very torn at times, lured away by the satisfaction of acting, which is a worthy thing, and by my own sense of ambition, which isn't. Acclaim is the false aspect of the job, which screws you up. You start to need it, like a drug, and in the final analysis, what does it all mean? I won my Academy Award when I was very young, and it was exciting for five or ten minutes. Sitting in bed afterward and drinking my Ovaltine, I said to Paul, 'Is that it?' Now I think being a full-time parent would be OK with me. With what I've learned, I'd enjoy it a lot more."

In the beginning of their marriage, the Newmans worked together as often as possible, and they made some unfortunate choices. In later years, particularly when their three daughters had grown older, they settled into a more comfortable arrangement in which they each pursued their own interests when they weren't working together.

By the time of his marriage, Newman had suffered the slings and arrows of nosy Hollywood gossip mavens as well as attacks by critics, some of whom clearly enjoyed exercising their wit at their subject's expense. Still tied to his studio contract, Newman was forced to pose for movie-magazine layouts depicting him doing "interesting" things like strolling through a zoo with a bird on his shoulder. He endured "visits with the newlyweds" showing the young wife standing on her head as her admiring new husband grins. As soon as he would become more independent in his career, the nonsense would end abruptly. Newman would consistently refuse to give interviews on personal matters, particularly on the subject guaranteed to titillate the imaginations of the public and therefore sell papers, his marriage. Despite the determined optimism of the press that their forty-year-long search would result in newsworthy scandal, they have failed consistently to come up with anything in the least bit shocking. It has taken that many years for the media to accept the normality of the Newman marriage, a solid and enduring union that is, by definition, eminently boring reading material.

The Left-Handed Gun, Newman's first film after his marriage, was an interesting though flawed western that has since become a cult classic. An adaption by Leslie Stevens of Gore Vidal's teleplay, it relates the Billy the Kid legend in a neorealistic style that merges classic Greek tragedy with twentieth-century neurosis. Billy the Kid's inability to adjust to society is shown to be attributable to unresolved early traumas and the lack of a father figure. The part, the type of role associated with James Dean— was psychologically arresting and off-beat enough to attract any young actor eager to show what he could do. But the originality that attracted Stevens, Newman, and director Arthur Penn, who had worked with Newman on *The Battler,* puzzled studio pundits, under whose dictums *The Left-Handed Gun* suffered innumerable changes. Though interesting in its exploration of the psychology of an outcast, a mixed-up kid with a potential for good, and refreshing in its naturalism, the film as it was finally made was marred by murkiness and occasional contrived attempts at an artful realism.

As the Kid, Newman's portrayal reflects the fascination of intellectuals of the time for on-screen Freudian analyses, in which the behavior of the character expresses the protective mechanism of the personality at the same time as it hints at early trauma blocking development of the true self. Newman tries to convey the Kid's adolescent frustrations and inability to tolerate human contact through inarticulate mumblings and long wordless stretches in which his body expresses what his speech cannot.

Almost totally unawares, Newman was further defining his screen image as the withdrawn iconoclast with a hurt mouth. Though now in his early thirties, Newman still suggested the malleability of youth, the salvageable bad boy whose hostile ways were balanced by a redeeming vulnerability.

Filmed in only twenty-three days on a shoestring budget, the film's unusual characterizations and unorthodox shooting style proved unpalatable to the majority of the public. But a few critics discerned the film's worth and, over the years, a cult audience developed that could appreciate its prefiguring of revisionist treatments of stale, outdated genres. Although its audience had to grow up to the picture, Newman himself later dismissed the work to a *Time* interviewer as "artificial," albeit "a little bit ahead of its time and a classic in Europe. To this day I still get eight hundred dollars at the end of the year. Go to Paris right now, and I bet you it is playing in some tiny theater."

Paul's next film, a neutered treatment of Tennessee Williams's successful play *Cat on a Hot Tin Roof,* again cast him as an ex–college athlete unable to put aside memories of youthful glory. Despite a role restricted by the mutilation of the original play, his performance won him his first Academy Award nomination.

The publicity surrounding the casting of Newman as Brick opposite Elizabeth Taylor as Maggie the Cat, focused more on the pairing of their eyes—glacial blue opposite warm violet—than on their acting abilities. But the hype did not negate the fact that both turned in more than effective performances, despite Taylor's tragic loss of her husband of only a few months, Mike Todd, halfway through the filming and the distortions censorship rules wreaked on the motivation of the characters and the general logic of the original plot. The film version of the story was forced to omit the central conflict generating almost all of Brick's behavior: an unacknowledged homosexual attachment to his best friend, Skipper, and repressed guilt over Skipper's suicide. Without this motivation, Brick's cold resentment to his wife seems overstated, petulant, and infantile.

The plot of *Cat on a Hot Tin Roof* revolves around a turbulent southern family, the Pollitts, whose patriarch discovers during the course of the play that he is dying of cancer. His children know the truth before he does, and Brick, his younger son, refuses to battle his brother and scheming sister-in-law (played beautifully by Jack Carson and Madeleine Sherwood), for the estate that Big Daddy will leave. Brick has broken his ankle during a drunken run on a football field, a vain attempt to conjure up happier days and to raise the ghost of his best friend. For reasons initially unclear to the audience, he blames his wife, Maggie, for his friend's death, and the film version so mutilates the original play, that his bitterness never does become entirely clear.

As Brick, Newman spends the first half of the film refusing to make eye contact with any of his family, and responds to the other characters, if at all, with a heavy dose of sarcasm. In the second half of the film, though, Newman pulls out the emotional stops for an explosive contrast. In the end Brick comes to admire Maggie for her bold, sad lie to the family that she is pregnant. The film's final life-affirming scene shows the couple mounting the stairs to their room, reconciled and intent on making good on her claim.

Though a considerable number of critics grumbled at the havoc wreaked on Williams's script, the public was oblivious, more than content to revel in the spectacle of a bare-chested Paul Newman hobbling around on a crutch, more attentive to the drink in his hand than to the lush charms of Elizabeth Taylor spilling out of a revealing slip. Newman turned in a well-modulated, minutely crafted performance, alternating between grim cynicism that suggests a deep un-assuagable hurt and guilt, and prepares for his wild, emotional outbursts. But as Newman comments now, one can still see how hard the actor is working, and those almost visible turning wheels cut into the character's believability. In fact, Newman so thoroughly projected the intensity of concentration associated with the Method style of acting on the set that a joke he played during rehearsal was mistaken for typical Actor's Studio zealousness. "I suddenly tore off my pajama top and started trying to climb into my wife's gown, crying 'Skipper, Skipper!' There were twenty people on that set," Newman recalled for the *Daily News*, "and do you know, not one of them laughed? To them, this was the Method in action and they stood in respectful silence."

Despite its many flaws, the acting was uniformly good to excellent, and *Cat on a Hot Tin Roof* was the top money grosser for 1958. *Variety*'s review was laudatory, dubbing Newman "one of the finest actors in films, playing cynical underacting against highly developed action. His command of the articulate, sensitive sequences is unmistakable and the way he mirrors his feelings is basic to every scene." Newman had finally arrived as a star based on merit, but even after winning an Academy Award nomination, he was still criticized by the *London Observer*'s Penelope Houston for having "the look of a sulkier Brando [which] seems, if anything, a little too strong for Brick." Over twenty years later, Newman was to shrug off the Academy Award nomination, "Nah," he insisted, "That was too early."

In his next film, Newman tried once again to extend his range as an actor—to stretch the limits of the Paul Newman persona before it solidified too firmly in the audience's mind—and to translate the closeness of his relationship with Joanne Woodward into a successful movie that would be a change of pace for them both. But, as was to be the case in several more motion pictures, this first attempt at bubbly screwball farce, in *Rally 'Round the Flag, Boys,* was flat and humorless.

Though directed and produced by veteran Leo McCarey, who had directed classic film comedies starring the Marx Brothers and W. C. Fields, and who had been responsible for the pairing of Oliver and Hardy, no one could overcome the formula screenplay involving a Connecticut housewife (Woodward) who neglects hearth and home in favor of community interests. She sends her husband (Newman) to Washington to argue against the choice of their town as a missile site, and a vampish neighbor, played by Joan Collins, pursues him. The ensuing misunderstanding places husband and wife on opposite sides of the missile debate.

In comedic roles, Newman's innate seriousness worked against him. One cannot work seriously at being funny, or at least let the strain of the work show, and his performance was damned by critics as arch, broad, and forced. "I was probably weak," he later acknowledged. Though Woodward had certainly displayed a wicked, often self-mocking sense of humor in previous roles, neither she nor Newman demonstrated a flair for light comedy in this wooden film that was relieved, ironically enough, by Dwayne Hickman's comical caricature of an American teen, à la Brando's black-jacketed motorcyclist in *The Wild Ones*.

During 1958, the year *The Left-Handed Gun* and *Cat on a Hot Tin Roof* were released, the Newmans had lived in a series of rented apartments and houses, mainly in California. The following year was to find them more settled. On the verge of the decade during which he would dominate the box office as the superstar of the sixties (almost by default, since James Dean had died and Brando had given up a career he had always disparaged), Newman and Woodward fled the mansions of Beverly Hills. They gave their landlord thirty days' notice, packed their bags and went East, moving into a cozy Greenwich Village duplex on East Eleventh Street, complete with small garden, fish pond, and trees. They filled their home with early American antiques, including the brass bed they had bought in New Orleans while on location for *The Long, Hot Summer*. The den featured a mantle, on which perched Woodward's Oscar for *Three Faces of Eve* and an "Oscar" bearing a close resemblance to Rocky Graziano given to Newman by the producer, cast, and crew of *Somebody Up There Likes Me*. The Newmans were awaiting the birth of their first child, whom they planned to name Joshua if it was a boy, for Josh Logan (who directed *Picnic*, where they officially met), or Quentin if it was a girl (after Woodward's character in *The Fugitive Kind*).

Neither prospective parent wanted any part of the Hollywood life. "Here's what happens," Newman outlined for the *Louisville Courier-Journal*, "You start making more money than you have ever thought existed. First you buy a mansion so big that even the rooms have rooms. Your children have to have individual governesses. . . . Comes April 15 and the income-tax people want $200,000. You call your agent but the only scripts available are real dogs. You have to take them anyhow. Either that or fire a couple of governesses."

In New York, the Newmans lived a decidedly unglamorous existence. "Three or four nights a week I cook up a batch of popcorn and open a couple of beers and read a book," Newman told columnist Earl Wilson. "That's what I call gracious living." Woodward spent much of her time perfecting her dressmaking and knitting skills. She had made the evening gown in which she accepted her Oscar, thereby incurring the wrath of the old guard who equated any drop in the sequin-and-lamé quotient as a dangerous moral slackening. "Joanne Woodward has set Hollywood glamour back twenty-five years," blared Joan Crawford, who was, ironically, the star after whom Joanne had been named. But Woodward was unperturbed. After only one year of marriage, she had knitted her husband thirty-seven sweaters, more than this man, who owned only four suits and whose daily uniform was a sweatshirt or T-shirt and jeans, could ever use. In fact, in *Rally 'Round the Flag,* part of Newman's wardrobe—bathrobe, sweater, socks, and sports shirt—is handmade Woodward originals.

Wary of the strains long separations and dual careers can exert on family life, Woodward had begun to allow her career to take a backseat to her husband's. Since *The Three Faces of Eve* she had made two films, generally unsuccessful despite highly respectable literary antecedents: *The Sound and the Fury,* from Faulkner's novel, and *The Fugitive Kind,* from Tennessee Williams's play, originally entitled *Battle of Angels.* Though basically hokey and preposterous, *The Fugitive Kind* is redeemed by its superlative cast—Marlon Brando as Valentine Xavier, the drifter with "superhuman powers" who seduces the wife of a small-town general-store owner; Anna Magnani as the improbable but fascinating wife; Victor Jory as the cancer-ridden husband; and Woodward, disguised in white pancake makeup and kohl-rimmed eyes, as the fey, alcoholic nymphomaniac, the last, dying twig of a many-branched aristocratic southern family. Woodward has rather cryptically commented, "Marlon was not happy at that time," but despite critical pans the film retains a cult following to this day.

Since her marriage, she had worked only on films with her husband. When he was working without her, Woodward would pack up her knitting and click away at the needles on the various locations of his films. "They refuse to be separated," a friend said. "Many an actress has got her big chance in a role that Joanne turned down because it would keep her away from Paul." While Woodward tended the nest, Newman brushed up on his technique at his beloved Actors Studio and planned to do more work in the New York theater. "Every so often an actor has to be kicked in the head to wake him up," he told the *World-Telegram and Sun*. "I go back to the studio to have . . . mannerisms pointed out, then to shake them. I'll continue to attend the Actors Studio as long as I can, or whenever possible. One must never stop learning," he vowed.

Newman negotiated the snarls of New York traffic and the overtures of female fans by traveling to his classes at the Studio and to his voice lessons, where he was working to correct his tendency toward hoarseness, on his motor scooter, an unlikely vehicle for a star and therefore the perfect disguise. With a cap and shades covering the famous eyes, his anonymity was assured. Newman would continue to use this method of transportation for several years, until an accident injured his hand and forced him to give it up. "It's the only way to get through midtown traffic," he explained to the *Daily News*. "It took me forty minutes by cab to get from my apartment to the studio. On the scooter, I could make it in ten." Though he protected himself from public recognition, in those earlier days Newman was less annoyed by the often rude approaches of his fans. One middle-aged couple are today the proud owners of a home movie in which Newman agreed to "perform," pretending with a straight face to pour the contents of a beer bottle into his ear.

Stung by what he felt was negative criticism directed unfairly at himself, and increasingly irritated by Warner Brothers' policy of offering him inferior scripts and then loaning him out to other studios at huge profits, Newman wanted to break his contract and retreat once more to Broadway. There, weak moments lasted only as long as the audience's memory, and he thrived on the infusion of energy only a live audience can give an actor. At a Hollywood press luncheon sponsored by Warner Brothers during the period he was shooting *Cat on a Hot Tin Roof* on loan-out to MGM, Newman had reportedly emptied the room with a bitingly humorous account of the exploitation he had suffered at the hands of his home studio. "It's wonderful to know that I can go to see the head of the studio any time," he announced to his lunch companions. "Like last year when I went to see him when he did me out of five thousand dollars. He couldn't have been nicer. Of course, I never got the money and I did get ushered out of the office but he smiled all the time."

Frank speech such as the above, and his reluctance to talk to a press anxious to squeeze all the juice from his private life, had drastically lowered the Newman popularity quotient with the gossip columnists. In an article he wrote for the *Newark News* in 1958, on the issue of movie stars as public property, Newman had protested, "I feel as if I have exposed enough of myself in front of the camera, if I'm successful, instead of prattling on and on about what I go to bed in and who my close friends are and what I do during daytimes when I'm not working."

To get out of the Hollywood game, Newman would have to buy his freedom. In this case, part of the price exacted by Warner Brothers was to play in *The Young Philadelphians,* an adaptation from Richard Powell's smoothly entertaining literary saga of intrigue among the wealthy and powerful of Philadelphia. Judson Lawrence (Newman) is the illegitimate son of a woman whose aristocratic husband proved impotent on their wedding night and killed himself. She ran back to the boyfriend she jilted to marry well, and became pregnant. Unaware of the true circumstances of his birth, the son grows up to be a ruthlessly ambitious young man, a lawyer who builds a lucrative practice by defending tax evaders but who finally finds his integrity, redeemed by the love of a good girl (Barbara Rush) and by defending his college buddy on murder charges. Lawrence is the second of Newman's larcenous charmers (the first being Ben Quick), another cynical young man on the make who gets away with it by a last-minute change of heart. It was a role seemingly cut to measure, but in the case of *The Young Philadelphians,* the charm outweighs the larceny and Newman seems to walk through the elaborate, glitzy sets on automatic pilot.

Going through the motions may well have been what he was doing, for more and more Newman chafed at the strings tying him to Warner Brothers. The situation was intolerable: not only were they making a huge profit on loan-outs, but they had the right to force Newman to perform in projects he considered unworthy. When the studio reneged on an agreement allowing him to do an outside picture, Newman confronted Jack Warner and demanded to be allowed to buy himself out of his contract. The matter was not settled right away, and Newman bought time by once again exercising his option to work on Broadway.

On March 10, 1959, Newman opened at Broadway's Martin Beck Theater in his third smash hit in a row, one that ran forty-two weeks. Another work by Tennessee Williams, this was the first play in which his performance would create the role, that of Chance Wayne in *Sweet Bird of Youth*. Directed by the preeminent actor's director, Actors Studio head Elia Kazan, and starring studio members Geraldine Page, Rip Torn, and Madeleine Sherwood, *Sweet Bird* was adapted for film in 1962 by Richard Brooks with almost the entire cast traveling intact from Broadway—an unusual occurrence.

The play's themes of lost youth and doomed innocence were brilliantly articulated by Williams's script, highlighted by the performances of Paul Newman and Geraldine Page playing their characters' last few years of youth for all they're worth. Chance Wayne was a perfect synthesis of all the elements that could now be called a Paul Newman role, and the actor received his best notices to date.

One month later, on April 7, Joanne Woodward gave birth to their first child, a daughter they finally decided to name Elinor Theresa, later to be nicknamed Nell Potts. In August 1959, three months after *The Young Philadelphians* opened, Newman bought out his contract to Warner Brothers. In the five years he had been with the studio, he had made only three films with which he had been satisfied, and all of these had been on loan-out to other studios. The contract, which had three years left to run, reputedly cost Newman $500,000, an enormous sum in those days. But in the long view it was a bargain, considering that he had been getting $17,500 per picture, and, after the release of his next film, *From the Terrace,* he would receive $200,000 per movie. The move would strap Newman financially for several years, but it was well worth the price. One can only speculate on what kind of career Newman would have had if he had remained under contract to Warner Brothers, certainly the most energetic, active studio of the time, but also the one that squeezed the most out of its directors and actors for the least price without giving serious thoughts to their artists' long-range career goals. If he had remained at Warner Brothers as a contract player, Newman might well have wound up as a distant memory, just another pretty face. The security of the contract was not worth the constraints on his talents and income and the constant battle against being packaged as an empty sex symbol. Newman's independent nature dictated that he make it on his own, succeeding or failing by his own efforts.

Toward the end of *Sweet Bird*'s run Newman began shooting *From the Terrace,* for which he would receive a much-needed $200,000. He was costarring for the third time with his wife by day and appearing in the play at night. In January 1960, he left *Sweet Bird of Youth* and went to Hollywood to finish the film, a "pretty good soap opera" demanding a minimum of effort, according to its star. Once again the Hollywood truism that the better the literary source, the poorer the cinematic translation, seemed to hold true. A diluted version of John O'Hara's best-selling novel, *From the Terrace* paralleled *The Young Philadelphians* in its setting and its plot, involving the rise of a charming young opportunist. Alfred Eaton steals and lies his way to success while neglecting his wife, played by Joanne Woodward, who jokingly remarked to a reporter on the set that playing hostile scenes with her new husband was "a relief. We get all our hostilities worked off on the set. Then when we get home—wow!"

The film was a commercial success, but it was an interminable bore according to some critics, despite Woodward having the time of her life playing an upper-crust bitch. Newman was again accused of just going through the motions, but, as usual, he fascinated the audience in spite of his struggle with the material and his awkwardness in tender scenes with Ina Balin. Love scenes were never his forte. John McCarten in the *New Yorker* even dragged out the old Newman-Brando comparisons: "Paul Newman (the lead) is a dead ringer for Marlon Brando, complete with built-in pout." But at this point it almost didn't matter what Newman did. He was hot at the box office, and the fans came out in droves to see their idol and his new wife. Newman could joke now about the alleged resemblance to Brando. "I may do a movie for him," he told *New York Post* columnist Sidney Skolsky. "Not long ago I told Brando I have signed more autographs with his name than he has," Newman quipped elsewhere.

Both Newmans had been anxious to finish filming so they could go to Israel for a few weeks before shooting *Exodus,* to be directed by Otto Preminger from former black-listed screenwriter Dalton Trumbo's script, which was adapted from Leon Uris's best-selling novel. Newman was to play Jewish resistance leader Ari Ben Canaan, and he looked forward to the film, not only because he enjoyed traveling to exotic places but as a kind of immersion into the ancient Hebraic heritage of his father.

Exodus features Newman in his most unequivocally heroic mode, the mastermind behind the escape of six hundred Jewish refugees from Cyprus to Palestine. But the experience was not to prove satisfying, in great part due to Newman's difficulties working with Otto Preminger. Notoriously dictatorial in his dealings with crew and actors, the director was hardly a compatible match for Newman, who was comfortable only with directors who would respect his careful attention to detail and who allowed him the time and space to prepare his character, even if they could not assist in the process. Unlike his wife, "able to create reality out of almost any situation, regardless of how bad the dialogue is, I'm a 'What does it mean?' kid," Newman told Skolsky. "Motivations, meanings, scene impact and quality of writing fascinate me. It sometimes results in disagreements with directors." As one friend explained it, "With

Joanne, you just give her the words and tell her where to stand. Paul, on the other hand, is careful, painstaking, studious, concerned with motivations."

Exodus was certainly one of his most painful experiences. Preminger was less concerned with helping actors birth their characters than with organizing enormous teams of technicians, and staging panoramic crowd scenes involving hordes of extras, in his attempt to create a three-and-a-half-hour technicolor, Super-Panavision spectacle, a grandiose celebration of the birth of Israel that involved monumental sets and heroic, milling action—all within the constraints of a fourteen-week shooting schedule. Preminger had neither the time nor the inclination to discuss with his actors such matters as character motivation and believability of action. When Newman talked with Preminger the day after he arrived, the director responded caustically to the several pages of suggestions the actor offered him. "Very interesting suggestions," Preminger commented. "If you were directing the picture, you would use them. As I am directing the picture, I shan't use them!"

Newman chafed under Preminger's militaristic control. Diminished in the midst of another vast cinematic spectacle, visions of Basil the slave must have danced through his head as he listlessly trudged through the interminable epic. According to Joanne Woodward, filming *Exodus* was such a painful experience, the $200,000 salary notwithstanding, that her husband cannot bear to talk or even think about it to this day. Many years later, his only comment about the film to *Time* was a terse "chilly."

Despite the great quantities of money and time lavished on the production the film was a critical flop, marred by an aimless script and by the wooden acting turned in by Newman and others who wandered through spectacular sets that barely rescued the picture from total failure. Typical of the critics' reactions was Bosley Crowther's in *The New*

York Times, describing the film as "massive, overlong, epi-
sodic, involved and generally inconclusive 'cinemarama' of
historical and pictorial events . . . an ambiguous piece of
work."

Luckily for those involved in the financing of the picture,
particularly for Preminger, who grossed over one million in
profits, the audiences didn't seem to read the reviews, or if
they did they didn't care what the critics had to say. They
turned out at the theaters in droves, making it Newman's
second-biggest grossing picture thus far—second only to a
film he would make eight years later, *Butch Cassidy and the
Sundance Kid.*

After three years of playing in mediocre productions,
Newman rebounded from the almost unbearable experience of *Exodus* to one of the most satisfying of his career,
certainly the first role to fully showcase his special talents:
that of Fast Eddie Felson, the young pool shark of *The
Hustler.* By the time *Exodus* premiered, Newman had
shelved its memory in a distant corner of his mind. He was
already back in New York, totally immersed in preparing
and filming a complex, dark, and uncompromising movie
about a young drifter who learns a hard and bitter lesson.
Co-adapted by Robert Rossen and Sidney Carroll from a
somewhat less rich novel by Walter Tevis, *The Hustler* was
produced and directed by Rossen in a grim and realistic
style of striking integrity. The dying man knew this would
be his last film. It was performed with passion and absolute
believability by Newman, George C. Scott, Jackie Gleason,
and Piper Laurie. Shot by brilliant cameraman Eugene
Shuftan in an exquisite chiaroscuro of blacks and whites
reeking of the film's grimy world, and shaped by an equally
legendary editor, Dede Allen, into a rhythm that propels
the viewer along with its protagonist on his inevitable fall
from grace, *The Hustler* relentlessly unwinds the brusquely
bitter fable of Fast Eddie Felson, an ambitious punk, who

makes his living pool hall by pool hall, suckering working
stiffs and rich men alike. He comes to New York with the
notion of taking the title from the champion of fifty states,
Minnesota Fats (Jackie Gleason), but through his innate
flaw of character—a hubris born of naivete rather than the
pride that comes of confidence—becomes the ultimate
sucker himself, robbed of his illusions and possibly his humanity by a professional gambler with the nerves of steel
he lacks. The character of Bert Gordon is played with
cool predatory shark eyes by George C. Scott. In the end,
Eddie does win the match against Minnesota Fats, but he
can win because he no longer cares, and the price of the
triumph is being banned from the game forever and losing
a chance to know love. Equally effective is Piper Laurie as
the alcoholic and disillusioned poetess whose love and Cas-
sandra-like vision Eddie cannot accept.

Newman has always maintained that he enjoys the preparation for a role more than the actual playing of it, and for
The Hustler the homework was even more pleasurable than
usual. Both he and Jackie Gleason were coached by the
greatest professional pool player of the time, Willie
Mosconi, and for the duration of the shooting period a pool
table dominated the Newman living room.

Critics scrambled for the words to translate the powerful
screen poetics of *The Hustler* into their reviews, and they
were virtually unanimous in their praise of the way Newman seemed to inhabit his character. Alton Cook, writing
in the *New York World-Telegram & Sun,* commented,
"Paul Newman is always a dominant figure in any scene,
but there is something extra this time in his intense ardor as
the man who treats a game with religious zeal that at times
mounts to mania. His standard is high but he has surpassed
it this time." Paul V. Beckley in the *New York Herald Tri-
bune* opined, "I'm not sure Paul Newman has ever looked
more firmly inside a role."

Despite the abundant praise from critics, Newman recently commented to *Time*, "Again, very conscious of working too hard, which comes partly from lack of faith in your own talent and lack of faith that just doing it in itself is all the audience requires." One critic writing for the *New Yorker* slyly concurred. "How he rejoices in the mastery of his craft! Luckily, it's a joy without a trace of self-satisfaction, and therefore harmless; the Academy may as well give him an Oscar right now and get it over with."

The Hustler did take nine Academy Award nominations, including Newman's for Best Actor, but only cinematographer Eugene Shuftan won, though Newman did win the British Academy Award. He had been well established as a star, but *The Hustler* confirmed that Paul Newman's position was secured by more than an attractive image of hero-outcast. Given the right role, Paul Newman could *act*. Unlike some of his less successful one-note portrayals, Newman's Eddie Felson was carefully nuanced, projecting all the contradictions and colors that compose not only a recognizable human being but a figure that in the right dramatic context becomes universalized, meaningful to us all.

Bert tells Eddie, "You're a born loser," a theme *The Color of Money* would pick up and explore twenty-five years later. These lines were the key to the peculiarly Newmanesque hero that took on a stark, tragic dimension with the release of *The Hustler*. The persona had developed into one with compulsive ambition and jaded, masculine charm, as indifferent to women (and the principles of intuitiveness and relatedness they represent) as they are obsessed with him. Callous and tough on the outside, always eager to test and prove his mettle, the Newman man is weakened by his inability to relate to his softer feelings and is therefore damned to failure: despite his bravado, he just doesn't have what it takes. Like the best of the Newman roles thus far,

Eddie is a rogue but not a pure one. Deep beneath the brittle exterior runs a thin vein of human sympathy. Despite the fact that he lacks the courage to draw upon his core of warmth and resiliency, and we rarely see evidence of its existence in his behavior, as far as the audience is concerned anything Eddie or any other Paul Newman character could do is understandable and forgiven. In fact, it is the tension of waiting for that humanity to finally show itself and complete the maturation process that makes Eddie an open-ended character, one that could be justified as the subject of another film twenty-five years later.

With *The Hustler* Newman was now more than famous. His screen image was fully assembled and given increasing believability by his growing reputation as an iconoclast and a remote, private man in real life. The persona of Paul Newman was now clearly identifiable and fixed in the public mind. Unlike Brando and Dean, Newman had not seared the world with his genius in a single identifying role, but had built up a fully faceted character over the course of several films. In three of his next pictures—all beginning with the letter *h,* a letter he had decided brought him luck—Newman further refined his image as the loner, the man who would say, as did Ari Ben Canaan in *Exodus,* "When the showdown comes, we will always stand alone. . . . We have no friends, except ourselves."

As *Time* magazine noted, his ability to find good parts— needles in the Hollywood haystake, as the writer put it— was too uncanny for him not to have been equipped with a magnet. The magnet, of course, was his own ambition and keen sense of purpose, but his unconquerable luminosity was a key factor in making the parts look good. The secret of Paul Newman's success resisted analysis, because the magnetism originated not in any single identifiable quality, such as the color of his eyes, but in his essence. Our eyes couldn't help but fix on him, partially because we knew we would never really know this man who embodied our own paradoxes, and partially because his special physical beauty defined the highest form of masculine appeal.

Soon after *The Hustler*'s release, there was much buzz to the effect that due to the burden of buying out his Warner Brothers contract, Newman was the only one not reaping tremendous profits from the film. But he had been cutting his recent deals in various ways, taking percentages that were often deferred—and though it looked like he was not making money, in later years, relieved of the burden of paying his way out of the contract and supported by solid producing partnerships, the profits found their way to his bank account.

Though Newman has demonstrated a gift for coming up with an inordinate number of apparently tailor-made vehicles, he has also shown an equally uncanny ability to take on roles for which he is obviously unsuited—notably in light comedy and what are probably erroneously labeled character parts. Mystifying to many, as well, is the failure of the Newman-Woodward acting team to come up with an unequivocal winner.

But the marriage was thriving. Though they still maintained a base in Los Angeles, the Newman family had moved from their downtown Manhattan duplex to an apartment in a venerable old building in the East Eighties with enough space to include a growing household. Soon to include a second daughter, Melissa, the Newman ménage already comprised their daughter Elinor; on occasion, Newman's first three children; a maid named Tressie; and two chihuahuas, El Toro and Little Brother. Newman still used a motor scooter to get through the congested streets, and if he was bothered by autograph hounds and could get away with it, he frequently signed Marlon Brando's name.

For his next film, Newman chose to follow his brilliant success with another attempt at a light-hearted romance

with his wife as costar. It was hoped that the subject matter
would be deepened by underlying themes concerning
racism, jazz, and expatriate Americans. The location was
wonderful, the perfect spot for a romantic working vacation—Paris in the springtime—and their coworkers were
ideal, notably close friend Martin Ritt, who was directing
them together for the second time. Going to the location
early was no hardship, and the Newmans took a little place
in Montmarte a few weeks before shooting where Newman's attempts to learn the trombone almost got them evicted.

Produced by Marlon Brando's Pennebaker Company,
Paris Blues was sweetened by a Duke Ellington score and a
cameo appearance by Louis Armstrong. Newman plays an
American trombonist, Ram Bowen, who with his black
friend (played by Sidney Poitier) is enjoying the bohemian
life of expatriates in the postwar Paris of the fifties. They
meet two American tourists (conveniently one white,
Woodward, the other black, Diahann Carroll). The plot
mainly concerns the vagaries of the dual couplings; one
would have hoped for more than a perfunctory and self-
conscious stab at exploring racism and passion, especially
given the fact that the two couples were actually in love off
screen. But trouble with the script was diagnosed early on,
and despite the best efforts of a script doctor who was
flown in, the basic plot structure was as substantial as tissue
paper and the film was little more than a romp through
"gay Paree," with little of the excitement promised in its
planning stages. *Paris Blues* remains a pleasant but ultimately superficial and bland vehicle, with lines like Newman's "Baby, I love music morning, noon, and night. D'ya
dig?" that drew howls at a 1988 New York City screening.

Cue rightly dismissed the movie as "frothy and self-con-
sciously 'socially significant': a loosely amoral, romantically
dreamy-eyed, casually interracial, pseudo-realistic tale of

music and music-makers, of love, conflict, boys-grab-at-girls, dope tragedy, and raucously wild music. And all so slickly fricasseed and illogical as to add up to a Frenchified tale that fobs off criticism." Newman himself admitted to *Time* that while he "had some fun with that," it was not a "great film."

Newman must have expected more of his next picture, the film version of *Sweet Bird of Youth,* for which he had won the best notices of his stage career and for which he was now being paid a whopping $350,000, plus a percentage. But Elia Kazan was not present to guide the actors and crew through a film version that, once again, was mutilated by director-writer Richard Brooks, under fire from the censors to forsake the harsh conclusion of the play and substitute the obligatory happy ending.

Cast as before opposite Geraldine Page, Newman reprised his role of Chance Wayne, a swaggering kept "boy" who takes a faded film star, Alexandra Del Lago, on a visit to his hometown, from which he had fled years earlier. In Williams's original play, the background of the story was that Chance had impregnated his girlfriend and infected her with syphilis. He had left town and she had been forced to undergo a hysterectomy. As the play opens he has just returned, ignorant of what has happened to his girl. Her tyrannical father finds out his daughter's spoiler is back and sends a gang of thugs, including his son (Rip Torn), to castrate him. Chance, knowing what awaits him, chooses not to fulfill his ambitions and run away to Hollywood with Alexandra, whose career has suddenly revived, but to stoically accept his fate. In the film version, however, the pregnancy, disease, and hysterectomy are reduced to a pregnancy and abortion. The castration becomes a beating, and Chance gets to run off with his love at the end, his happiness undiminished by a few bruises.

Though the acting was strong, the changes amounted to

distortions and the film lost a good deal of the play's impact. *Sweet Bird of Youth* was a mixed success largely because of this. Most of the New York critics had seen the play, but many of them failed to realize that Brooks had not been the only one to tamper with Williams's play. The playwright himself had rewritten the ending to omit the castration for a production on the West Coast. Newman defended the film version to journalist Al Morgan. "All right, so let's say the ending in the picture is different from the original Broadway play, but if you walk away from the movie with the same feeling and the same set of questions and the same self-examination that you did with the play, then the movie is a success."

Newman's next role was yet another attempt to not trade on his looks, to be "allowed simply to *act.*" For reasons best known to himself, but probably having something to do with his determination to break out of his increasingly restrictive glamorous image, Newman took a bit part as a middle-aged punch-drunk fighter in a cinematic treatment of Ernest Hemingway's *Adventures of Hemingway as a Young Man.* Hollywood was generally puzzled, even annoyed, at his unorthodox choice of a role.

"I really got them bugged out there," he told Al Morgan. "They screamed at me out there. I was cheapening myself by playing a bit, they said. I was a star, I couldn't play a bit. You know why I did it? It was the part of a forty-five-year-old, punch-drunk fighter. It was a good part and I wanted to play it for that reason alone." But Newman had another reason for playing the role. He had portrayed that character seven years earlier for television in *The Champ.* Playing it again was a marvelous opportunity "to see what I had learned about acting in seven or eight years." It wouldn't be until much later in his career that Newman would get another opportunity to return to a character and explore the possibilities of his development.

Newman's makeup for the cameo role was a total deface-
ment of his by-now legendary beauty, and though some
critics approved, Newman himself later told *Time* that "I
tried to do what I did in the TV show, and that wasn't the
way to go at it." But the assistance of director Martin Ritt
and a screenplay by Hemingway expert A. E. Hotchner
were insurance enough to make the actor willing to fly in
the face of convention for the chance to prove himself once
more. Another possible reason for the choice was that despite the hundreds of scripts he was receiving, few worthwhile projects had presented themselves.

Meanwhile, Newman had been reading more than
scripts. In 1962 he embarked on a six-week crash course on
the atomic threat, reading everything he could and collar-
ing experts willing to talk about atomic testing, fallout, and
the prospects of war and survival. Though he derided the
notion of being a movie star rather than an actor, Newman
understood the responsibility that came with his unwanted
title. "If I'm a member of that royalty," he told the *Daily
News,* "then it seems to me I have a responsibility to be
honest with people and to talk about the things I really
consider important."

Though generally contrasting in their interests, Newman
and Woodward shared political and social views, and had
become increasingly active. In the sixties their East Side
apartment became an unofficial salon for the new liberal
establishment of artists and intellectuals—who would later
be dubbed by writer Tom Wolfe the radical chic. When he
wasn't working on a film, visiting his gym or reading, Newman was acting on the responsibility he felt his position im-
posed on him to speak out on issues and to take an
increasingly active role.

His interests were broad and many: civil rights, environmental protection, freedom of speech. In September 1962,
he appeared at a public hearing of the State Joint Legis-

lative Committee on Obscenity to fight against governmental classification of movies. "Parents who are concerned with what their children will see will search out the information," he argued. "Those who don't care, will not. If we had classifications, those same parents who don't care would simply ignore them." He reported that the only one of his films his five children had seen was the relatively innocuous *Rally 'Round the Flag, Boys.*

Two years after his enormous success in *The Hustler,* Newman joined director Martin Ritt for their third collaboration, another archetypal Paul Newman loner/bad boy role, the most unregenerate of the lot and the second *h* in the trio of films that would compose the most enduring Paul Newman classics. Hud, a misanthropic, essentially weak man—"a pure bastard," as another character in the film describes him—was created on paper by writers Irving Ravetch and Harriet Frank, Jr. Despite pressure exerted by the studio, his character remained uncompromised by the censors' red pen. Ritt and the writers knew exactly what was original about Paul Newman and wrote specifically with this in mind for all three films they worked on with the actor: *The Long Hot Summer, Hud,* and *Hombre.*

Ultimately, the studio recognized the perfect fit of actor and role. "Paul Newman is Hud!" screamed the publicity machine, and, for once, they were not overstating the case. For several weeks before the shoot, Newman had worked on a Texas ranch, living in the bunkhouse, roping steer, mending fences, and performing all the duties of a cowboy, until he walked, thought, and talked like a lean and seasoned doggie. But despite his preparation for the physical aspects of the role, Newman was surprised at how easily he slipped into character without having to undergo his usual lengthy and painstaking process of research, analysis, and preparation, all the while battling his doubts and anxieties. "Very strangely, rightly or wrongly, or however the character turned out," he remarked with characteristic self-deprecating modesty to a *Films and Filming* reporter three years after the film's release, "that character came more easily to me than a lot of other ones. By the time we had reached four days of rehearsal before we started shooting, I knew pretty well what I wanted to do with him." The part was clearly customized for the Newman image, which refined several stops further with *Hud,* honing even sharper its outlines and details.

Adapted from a section of the Larry McMurty novel *Horseman, Pass By,* this American fable relates the coming of age of Lon, a young boy (Brandon de Wilde) caught between the rigid, old-fashioned morality represented by his grandfather (Melvyn Douglas), and the pragmatic amoralism symbolized by his corrupt but charming uncle, Hud, whom he idolizes. The two older men battle for control of the grandfather's ranch, and when one of their cows comes down with hoof-and-mouth disease, Hud tries unsuccessfully to persuade his father to sell off the herd before the government orders the required mass slaughter. Frustrated in his attempts to rescue what he regards as his rightful inheritance, Hud gets drunk and attempts to rape Alma, the housekeeper. Disillusioned by the behavior of the man he looked up to, Lon leaves the ranch to go his own way. The film ends with Hud watching his nephew go. He shrugs off any uncomfortable feelings and opens a can of beer. But the film's characters are less simplistically symbolic than that. The old man is not just moralistic, he is judgmental and unbending, and Hud's callousness toward his father implies a painful history that could justify his bitter contempt.

Though Newman tried hard not to let his natural charm dull the edge of Hud's sneering calumny, and though his portrayal reveals an unmitigatedly crude and arrogant cynic, a complete amoralist, Hud's vitality and humor coupled with Newman's innate attractiveness kept the character from being received as the total villain Newman, Ritt, and the writers had envisioned. Though Hud remains unredeemed to the end, the audience embraced the sexy bastard as their hero, much to Newman's chagrin. How could they help it? As Melvyn Douglas's character explains to the nephew, "Women just like to be around something dangerous part of the time."

After *Hud* and *The Hustler,* Newman's image was set irrevocably as that of the solitary rebel, ruthless in his quest to get what he wants yet ennobled by his relentless determination. Newman had left behind the more intellectual, sensitive, fragile roles he had played earlier in films such as *The Rack,* though that vulnerability was now incorporated into the fully evolved Newman hero who was, at bottom, a man's man.

Except for Newman's relatively minor disappointment in Hud's conquest of the female audience, the film was a triumph for its makers. They had made no compromises for popular notions of what an audience will or will not accept, and despite predictions of doom, *Hud* was a commercial and critical success, nominated for seven Oscars in 1963. Bosley Crowther spoke for many in his praise.

> While it looks like a modern western and is an outdoor drama indeed, *Hud* is as wide and profound a contemplation of the human condition as one of the New England plays of Eugene O'Neill. . . . The striking, important thing about it is the clarity with which it unreels. The sureness and integrity of it are as crystal clear as the plot is spare . . . with a fine cast of performers . . . people who behave and talk so truly that it is hard to shake them out of your mind. Paul Newman is tremendous—a potent, voracious man, restless with all his crude ambitions, arrogant with his con-

tempt and churned up inside with all the meanness and misgivings about himself.

But despite critical raves, Patricia Neal's Best Supporting
Actress award for a brilliant performance defining her
uniquely earthy appeal as Alma the housekeeper, Melvyn
Douglas's award for Best Supporting Actor, and James
Wong Howe's award for Best Black and White Cin-
ematography, Paul Newman lost the Oscar to his friend and
former costar Sidney Poitier, for a much less spectacular
but more socially redeeming performance in *Lilies of the
Field*. Newman had been quoted as saying, "I'd like to see
Sidney Poitier get it. I'd be proud to win it for a role I
really had to reach for." Once again, Newman was dismissing one of his finest performances. He felt that Hud was
too close to the Paul Newman image and that his performance traded too heavily on his powerful magnetism.
Many years later, he would comment on his work, "pretty
good, [but] again, working hard, working hard." Perhaps
the real reason Newman did not win the award that year
was what was interpreted as his anti-Hollywood stance and
his defiance of Jack Warner. Despite his widely acknowledged brilliance in this definitive role, the movie colony refused to honor one who was not willing to be wholly its
own.

In any event, 1963 found Newman even more concerned
and occupied with matters other than movie-making. He
publicly demonstrated his commitment to social causes by
participating in a fair-housing sit-in in Sacramento, by taking part in the civil rights march on Washington, and by
traveling with Anthony Franciosa and Marlon Brando to
Gadsen, Alabama, for a rally on racial problems led by Dr.
Martin Luther King, Jr. The mayor of this small town
was unimpressed, however, and refused to meet with them,

dismissing the distinguished thespians as mere "rabble-rousers."

With the birth of Claire Olivia, nicknamed Clea, Joanne Woodward was now the mother of three small girls. In addition to her family obligations, she had turned in an interesting performance in an otherwise forgettable movie, *The Stripper*. New York City seemed a less-than-ideal place to raise young daughters, so she convinced her hardly reluctant husband to move to Connecticut. Newman had recently commanded $350,000 for *Sweet Bird of Youth*. As number one at the box office, he could live where he wanted. They would come to him.

Thanks to actors and directors like Paul Newman, a new era was replacing the heyday of the giant studios when the bosses, backed by stables of stars, supporting players, writers, directors, and producers, commandeered every aspect of a production—from assigning a script to having the last snip of the scissors in the cutting room. Many of the new breed were forming their own production companies in order to insure the quality of the projects in which they became involved. Already independent of obligations to any one studio, Newman now turned his efforts to building financial stability through partnerships with producers and directors with whom he had worked, whose talent and judgment he trusted. With Martin Ritt, one of his favorite directors, he formed Jodell Productions (the name came from the first syllables in their wives' names, Joanne and Adele), but his partnership with John Foreman, who had served as agent for both Newmans in Newman-Foreman Productions, gave the actor real financial and creative gains. Unfortunately Newman's first choices for Jodell lent little credibility to his new career as producer. As determined as ever to have a success with his wife and to prove his range, Newman and company misguidedly chose an attempt at a genre he hadn't yet been able to master—romantic farce.

A New Kind of Love turned out to be a very old kind of flop. Woodward plays a gawky, naive duckling who comes to Paris, is transformed into a glamorous swan, and then mistaken by Newman's character for a prostitute. As Richard Coe in the *Washington Post* commented, "Even were the material witty, I have the sad feeling the Newmans wouldn't be at home in it."

In an interview with *Time* twenty years later, Newman recalled the circumstances of the film:

> Joanne read it and said, 'Hey, this would be fun to do together. Read it.' I read it and said, 'Joanne, it's just a bunch of one-liners.' And she said, 'You son of a bitch, I've been carting your children around, taking care of them at the expense of my career, taking care of you and your house.' And I said, 'That's what I said. It's a terrific script. I can't think of anything I'd rather do.' This is what is known as a reciprocal trade agreement.

The Prize, produced by MGM and directed by Mark Robson, was an equally leaden effort, this time in the mode of a Hitchcock thriller. The film seemed promising; it boasted a screenplay by Ernest Lehman, who had scripted *Somebody Up There Likes Me* and Hitchcock's *North by Northwest,* from which the plot of *The Prize* borrows the theme of the burdeoning dilemma of an ordinary citizen who finds himself enmeshed in the extraordinary events of international intrigue. Newman tried to hang on to the beard he had grown that year, saying that it would give him more of the air of the genius-novelist, but the producers had very specific theories concerning facial hair on their leading men. "Those poor idiots," Newman told *Life* magazine. "They kept saying things like, 'Gable's worst flop was *Parnell,* and that was the only movie he wore a beard in.'" But the beard couldn't have made things worse. Only the talents of Cary Grant, with his inimitable offhand touch of irony could have pulled it off. As usual, Newman's natural intensity did not serve him in the comedic scenes and simply called attention to the complicated plot's many improbabilities.

Newman claims he made 1964's *What a Way to Go!*—a film recently recalled by the *Village Voice* as "the all-time film excuse for a fashion vehicle, featuring Edith Head's mid-sixties high camp"—out of his fabled sense of "whimsy." This time he got to hide under a beard and mustache for yet another attempt at breezy romantic comedy, in a cameo role as one of the series of husbands—all played by big stars—who marry Shirley MacLaine, become rich, and then meet with unfortunate and improbable deaths, leaving her increasingly richer. Newman is husband number two, a Parisian artist who is devoured by his own invention, a painting machine, and though he is fairly witty in the role, the improvement of his comic abilities may have been due in part to the fact that since his participation in this inconsequential material was limited, he did not have to sustain his performance. As Stanley Kauffman wrote in the *New Republic,* "the film's only interest is that Paul Newman, so admirable in serious roles, gives one of his rare acceptable comic performances as an American painter in Paris."

Though his last three films had put his career into a kind of stasis, the lack of activity threatened to give way to a fast downward slide when Newman took on the part of a Mexican bandit in *The Outrage.* At first Newman felt (wisely) that the part was unsuitable for him and suggested it be sent to Marlon Brando. Brando was eager to play the role but couldn't commit himself; being occupied in Europe. The producer, also restricted by his commitments, had to begin shooting forthwith. Possibly on the strength of Brando's approval of the role, Newman decided to take it on. Always determined to show his versatility and broadness of range, he brought in his most compatible director, Martin Ritt, for their fifth project together.

The script, by Michael Kanin, adapted and transplanted to Mexico a play by Fay and Michael Kanin, which was based on Akira Kurosawa's film of medieval Japan, *Rashomon.* The theme is the notion that truth lies somewhere behind the eyes and that an absolute *truth,* therefore, is an impossibility. A murder and a rape have been committed. A number of people claim to have witnessed the crime, and each has a different account of the incident. Whose truth is *the* truth, this exercise in philosophy asks.

Ever the careful craftsman, Newman spent two weeks in Mexico, hanging out in derelict towns and sleazy cantinas, growing a scruffy beard and absorbing the singsong rhythms of Mexican Spanish in preparation for his role as Juan Carrasco, the villainous and unattractive bandit originally interpreted by Rod Steiger in the Broadway production. This time he succeeded in persuading the producers to obscure his beauty under Hollywood dirt, matted hair, and whiskers. He would succeed solely on the basis of his hard work and acting talents. Though Newman considered his portrayal of the uncouth Mexican his best thus far ("I liked that one," he said twenty years later), its broad mannerisms, with the technical seams of his preparation glaringly obvious, struck some critics as parody. Judith Crist ridiculed his characterization as a "sort of junior-grade Leo Carillo." *The Outrage* failed to successfully translate eighth-century Japan to twentieth-century Mexico; in modern-day western hands, the culturally bound themes of the original work degenerated into pointlessness.

But Newman cannot be faulted for breaking out of his star persona in order to challenge himself and grow in his craft rather than coasting on an image that guaranteed his stardom. Like Brando, who consistently ridiculed his line of work, Newman has at times disparaged acting as not being "man's work." However, his continual effort to stretch his boundaries into uncharted territories, and the concentrated intensity with which he tackles each role, show that he takes his work, and himself as a student of acting, seriously. Though he has a horror of making a fool of himself, Newman knows taking chances does not guarantee success. But without risk, one loses all opportunity to learn. It must have been no less painful to realize that virtually every time he veered from his strictly defined screen image, the result was disaster.

5

dhering to what was by now his pattern, Newman retreated to the theater to revivify spirits dampened by the vagaries of the movie business and to regain confidence in his ability to move an audience. Joanne Woodward, whose career was certainly at a low point as well, would join him on the New York stage. "The only thing I had to pass up was having a baby this year," she joked to the press. Both Newmans also wanted to repay the debt they felt they owed the Actors Studio, so they appeared in an off-Broadway production at the Little Theater, the profits of which were donated to the Studio.

Near the opening date, Newman joked to the *Newark News* about the history of bad reviews he and Woodward had received for their previous theatrical couplings. "We thought up a terrific advertising campaign. A poster reading 'Together again—You weren't fond of them in *The*

Long, Hot Summer, and you didn't care for them in *From the Terrace.* You thought they were quite awful in *A New Kind of Love.* Be driven to new heights of hatred in *Baby Want a Kiss.*"

Baby Want a Kiss opened April 14, 1964, directed by Frank Corsaro and written by Joanne's former fiancé, James Costigan, who also played the third character. The Newmans took home a little over a hundred dollars a week so that the Studio would retain maximum profits for the limited four-month run. The play was a success—of course. Everyone came to see Joanne Woodward and Paul Newman play a phony Hollywood couple who live inimically under their public mask of domestic bliss, and of course the audience enjoyed the thrilling subtextual implications concerning the real Hollywood golden couple playing the roles. But the comedy had merit on its own; it received good notices, as did the three actors. Much titillating (and undoubtedly wishful) speculation was also drawn from the observation that, for the second time in his career, Paul Newman played a homosexual hiding in the closet of his marriage.

Around the time of the play it was announced that Newman would costar with Sophia Loren in a film version of Arthur Miller's *After the Fall,* but when *Baby Want a Kiss* closed, Newman went off to Europe to join Loren in making *Lady L,* a romantic adventure about a female rogue. This project had clearly suffered from various changes in cast, writers, and directors, and from the red and green lights it had received since the late fifties, when Romaine Gary's novel had first been acquired by MGM as a vehicle for Tony Curtis and Gina Lollobrigida. The property was now in the very capable hands of screenwriter-director Peter Ustinov, but it was too late to rescue whatever merit it once had.

Playing a Robin Hood–style anarchist who is part of a

ménage à trois involving Loren, a laundress who somehow
becomes a wealthy noblewoman, and David Niven, a British nobleman, Newman the personification of the modern
alienist, was a confusing anachronism in a period piece already plagued with confusion of plot and style. The *New
Yorker* pointedly remarked that Newman "seems about as
far from Paris and anarchism as, say, Akron and the Young
Republicans are." Loren, at the peak of her earthy sex appeal, didn't fare much better, her passionate temperament
overpowering the lightweight material.

During the shooting, Newman celebrated his fortieth
birthday, but his mood was far from celebratory. "I woke
up every morning and knew I wasn't cutting the mustard,"
he later said. Newman's grim approach once again failed to
take him through the airy byways of romantic adventure,
which required a spontaneity and a dash of tongue-in-cheek
apparently antithetical to Newman's character and working
methods. Moreover, fans seemed unwilling to have their
hero step down from his rebel-hero pedestal to execute a
pratfall on a banana or to have a pie splattered all over his
beautiful face or even to see him *play* at love. Luckily the
studio decided to hold the film's release until after Newman's next film, *Harper,* the third *h,* had revived his box-
office appeal.

By 1966 Newman was in a major trough of his career, but
he would soon bound back to the top ten at the box-office
list on the wave of a pedestrian but stylish private-eye film,
Harper (a.k.a. *The Moving Target*), featuring him in the
customized role of an antihero private eye. Newman may
have failed at nineteenth-century swashbuckling or at being
Cary Grant, but with the release of *Harper* (two months
before *Lady L*), critics were calling him a worthy successor
to Bogey. According to Newman, there was no way he
could fail in the part, "an original character who would
simply accommodate any kind of actor's invention. There

was no way you could violate the character; he was so loose and funky and whimsical," he told *Time*.

Newman made the film for Warner Brothers, but any residual ill will directed at his old home studio must have been smoothed away by the $750,000 he received against 10 percent of the gross and a smooth-as-silk working relationship with director Jack Smight. As part of the publicity, Jack Warner visited the *Harper* set and posed for pictures with Newman. For that year's Christmas card, Newman sent his friends and associates, including Warner himself, one of the photos taken that day of him and Warner smiling together, with the caption, "Peace on Earth—Good Will Toward Men."

Eager to revive the hard-boiled detective–*film noir* genre, the makers of *Harper* blatantly aligned the movie with Raymond Chandler adaptations, specifically *The Big Sleep*. They even cast Lauren Bacall in a key role to evoke the spirit of Bogey, the essentially good man whose implacable wisecracking, tough-guy exterior doesn't quite obscure an incorruptible moral character. Under the stage name Jacqueline de Wit, Newman's ex played in one of the film's many clever scenes as a restaurant-bar owner in hair curlers, who flirts with Harper while he pries information out of her. The production was satisfyingly slick and hip, providing Newman with the vehicle he needed to firm up his star status. The formula plot, however, was stuffed with complicated maneuverings and assorted sub-plots—all of which dovetailed neatly into one another—and suffered from a ring of inauthenticity. For some critics, that false note sounded loud and clear.

Reviews of *Harper* were typical of the attitude film critics seemed to have toward Newman: He was damned if he did succeed and damned if he didn't, the credit for a success going to the suitability of the part rather than to his acting skill for making it *look* that effortless. Richard Schickel, writing in *Life,* was representative of most critics, who delivered their compliments with a heavy left hand:

> This is the kind of superficial role—plenty of action, jokes and manly sentiment—for which his superficial talent is ideally suited. *Harper* delivers us an unemotional memo on the way things too often are in our society, then shrugs and wisecracks. But in the prevailing conscienceless climate of American movie-making, it is good to see a film with at least that much awareness of its social context, that much critical objectivity.

For his next film, Newman leaped at the chance to work with master filmmaker Alfred Hitchcock in 1966's *Torn Curtain,* but his jump landed him in an abyss. Unfortunately Newman neglected to look first, particularly at the script, or to take the time to consider the fact that unlike the Actors Studio directors Newman preferred to work with, for Hitchcock the film was virtually created and finished on the storyboard. The presence of actors and camera were a bothersome, anticlimactic necessity to Hitchcock, somewhat akin to "painting in the numbers" after the design had been created. *Torn Curtain* was one of his rare failures, plagued by a boring, hackneyed script based on an improbable plot filled with contrived and confusing situations involving spies, a missile formula, and a leaden love match between Newman and Julie Andrews, who was identified in the public mind with the saccharine and sexless Mary Poppins.

Though Newman was unhappy with his experience on the set and with the results on the screen, which seemed like Hitchcock copying himself, *Torn Curtain* was an even greater commercial success than *Harper.* Despite his one-dimensional impersonation of a ruthless spy, the role posed no threat to the Newman box-office viability.

Following his disappointment with Hitchcock, Newman reunited with some tried and true collaborators, director Martin Ritt and screenwriters Ravetch and Frank. The winning team that had come up with *The Long Hot Summer* and *Hud* took on the challenge of Elmore Leonard's novel *Hombre,* an offbeat revisionist western exploring racism. This screen adaptation would be the final *h* following *The Hustler, Hud,* and *Harper.* Newman played the title role, his most uncommunicative and alienated "hero" thus far. An ensemble of fine actors completed the cast, including Richard Boone, Fredric March, Cameron Mitchell, Barbara Rush, and Diane Cilento.

Confronted with the challenge of playing a white man raised by Apaches who now feels he belongs to neither race, Newman approached the project with his usual thoroughness. He traveled to the location weeks ahead of the shooting schedule to immerse himself in the local culture; he concentrated on one man "who stood for an hour without moving, his foot tucked up behind him, and simply watched what was happening in the street. I stole that stance for *Hombre,*" he admitted.

As the silent, stoical John Russell, the outcast figure who has suffered the prejudice of the white man and disengaged from the rest of humanity in order to survive, Newman was daringly minimal in his acting technique. Thrown together with a group of whites whose stagecoach is attacked by bandits, Russell becomes their only possibility of survival. The most extreme of Newman's antiheros—unrelieved this time by any vestige of charm or humor, Newman strove in his characterization for an evocative silence, attempting to suggest more in those empty spaces than the other characters communicate through speech. Like a vacuum he draws attention to his stillness, an uneasy quiet suggesting an emotional implosion that could redirect itself outward at any moment. He is the center of the screen, pulling all eyes to him. Yet this extreme underplaying—barely more than a series of grunts emanating from a face expressionless except for a hint of sullenness—failed to render the stark character acceptable to many fans and critics. Joseph Gelmis spoke for many when he commented in *Newsday:* "In *Hombre* the *h* is silent, and so is Paul Newman. He's strong and silent and mean. If he has more than a page of dialogue in the film, it would be a surprise. *Hombre* has less impact than his previous gallery of *h* films . . . I liked *Hombre.* It is rough, funny, exciting. But I couldn't take it very seriously. Newman's blue-eyed Indian, a Caucasian raised by the Apaches, is somehow implausible, even when he is being his most nasty, inscrutable or violent." No one seemed to like it when Newman stepped "out of character" and left the glib, wisecracking cynic behind. But Newman stands by his performance, and rightly so. "By then I was doing it less and enjoying it more," he told *Time.*

At forty-two, Newman was at the top of his physical form, enjoying the benefits of "maturity without age." His blue eyes attractively framed by a few lines suggested the humor and wisdom of a man of experience rather than the toll exacted by Father Time. Though he was reportedly capable of downing six-packs of beer daily, a strict regime of light eating, regular push-ups, daily saunas, and, as the apocryphal and highly suspect story goes, donning a snorkel and dunking his head in a bucket of ice water for twenty minutes every day, kept him as lean and youthfully attractive as ever.

And Newman's next film, "the best script I've read in years," *Cool Hand Luke,* would prove unequivocally that Newman was at the peak of his talent and of his physical prowess. He turned in a compelling, complex, and multifaceted interpretation of the archetypal Alienated Loner in a role as physically demanding as that in *Somebody Up There Likes Me*—a role that finally allowed him to fully display his unique talents. "I had great fun with that part. I liked that man," he told *Time* years later.

Excited by the script, Newman prepared for the role, in which he would have to simulate a convict's many escape attempts, by working out even more strenuously than usual, often walking about in chains, and he spent some time before the shoot in the Appalachian location. Don Pearce, the real-life ex-convict on whom the character and story was based, was on the set as technical adviser and co-writer with Frank Pierson.

One could say, similarly to what the studio exclaimed in the case of *Hud,* that "Paul Newman is Cool Hand Luke!" Combining the rebelliousness of Hud, the cynicism of Harper, the fatalism of Chance Wayne, the relentlessness of John Russell, and the pure grit of Paul Newman himself, Luke Jackson, a convict imprisoned in the South who repeatedly attempts to escape no matter what the cost, may be Newman's most definitive estranged rebel hero thus far, redeemed and ennobled by his refusal to bend to a dehumanized, heartless society as represented by the South's penal system. Newman described Luke to the *Daily News* as "detached, indifferent to the world, having only his own strange kind of participation. The only rule he is exposed to is that you must be boss or eat dirt. Luke can't buck the system. He's caught up in a dilemma of rules and regulations. The characters I played in *Hud* and *The Hustler* faced the same kind of problem. To Luke there is no difference between regulations in the chain gang and regulations outside. You bust wrong and you get broken." In his indifference to the laws of men, Luke becomes a kind of Christ figure, a theme that runs throughout the film and of which few critics and audience members seemed aware. The convicts feed off the strength the prison officials cannot defeat. "You're going to have to kill me," he says more than once, and in the end, that's exactly what they have to do.

Luke is fighting an undeclared, half-conscious war against the system. With each almost breathtakingly reckless act of defiance, Luke's peers and the audience grow to increasingly respect and understand him; he becomes an emblem of integrity and indomitable courage. Luke knows he has nothing—not without his freedom. What appears to be rebelliousness taken to a suicidal extreme is, in Luke's mind, pure logic. He has nothing to lose, and he acts from that realization. The film ends with Luke's death after yet another futile escape attempt, and his fellow convicts, for whom he has been transformed from outcast to hero, are told that he died with "that Luke smile" on his face. At this point in his career, Newman had so captured the public imagination that every mind's eye in the movie theater could see that special grin.

With Luke, the "convict Christ," the Newman persona refined itself to the point of myth. Critics were nearly unanimous in their praise. The performance won Newman his fourth nomination for Best Actor, but once again he lost, this time to Rod Steiger for *In the Heat of the Night*—although Newman did capture the Golden Globe Award as the World's Favorite Actor.

Once more buoyed up on a great success, Newman followed *Cool Hand Luke* with yet another disappointing stab at light comedy in 1968, this time as a clumsy thug in the trite, overworked, unfortunately titled and just plain awful *The Secret War of Harry Frigg*. The plot concerns five Allied generals imprisoned in an Italian villa during World War II. Harry Frigg, infamous for engineering daring escapes from army prisons, is promoted to general and smuggled into the villa to spring the brass. Of course he falls in lust with the resident countessa and delays the escape plans as long as possible. He manages to pull off the escape anyway, and the lucky rascal gets to keep his countessa after all. His next posting is on a radio station in her villa.

Newman defended his baffling choice of vehicle to *The*

New York Times by saying he was a working actor, great roles didn't come around that frequently, and he had initially thought he could have fun playing his rebel persona in the context of a lighthearted farce. "Sure, I've made plenty of mistakes," he later admitted to the *New York Sunday News* magazine. "Every actor has, but if I worked in movies that appealed to me, I'd only make one picture every three years. But I'm the type of guy who can't lay off for a long time. It's physically and mentally important that I work steadily." Newman later analyzed this "mistake" for *Time,* calling it "a lurch at comedy. I didn't accomplish it very well." In fact, the movie ranks as one of Newman's most detested screen vehicles.

It was clearly the time for the ever-restless Newman to assess his position and make some changes. "When I was thirty-two, I had the emotional maturity of a child of thirteen," he had once admitted. "This comes from my middle-class upbringing." But he had certainly reached the maturity of mid-life by 1968, and, as he told the *Saturday Evening Post* that year, "When you get to be around forty, it's very necessary to make a break, or to effect some kind of wrench in your life . . . I find that I've been repeating myself in performances, and in judgments, because I'm burned out creatively. I can't invent anymore. I've done it."

Disappointed with the quality of the scripts offered him, he complained to *Film and Filming,* "I read a script now and say, 'Well, that isn't quite the same scene as *The Young Philadelphians* but it's the same intention, same background, same breed; that is a little bit of *Hustler* and *Hud* is in there . . . that's what he would do.' And it's very discouraging." Newman was also unhappy with some of his own choices that didn't prove as promising as they might have on paper, such as *Lady L* and *The Torn Curtain,* and he was speaking more and more of himself as something other than just an actor. "I am not an intuitive actor," he said, not for the first time. "I direct myself, which I suppose in the long run makes me more of a director than an actor."

Newman had made twenty-seven films, many artistically successful, others not, and whether he liked it or not, either his talents seemed unable to encompass as broad a range as he would have liked, or the audiences refused to accept anything but the "Paul Newman is Hud" type of role. Despite the elusiveness of the Oscar he had won many awards, particularly those relating to audience popularity. Newman was considered more of a superstar than an actor's actor, despite the fact that he had proved his worth as an actor many times over. What he really craved was official recognition by his peers. For the time being Newman had gone as far as he could as a film actor. His restless nature goaded him on to search out other ways to test his mettle.

Joanne Woodward, on the other hand, was not an image stamped in the public psyche, though she had received the official sanction of her peers with the Oscar she had won for *The Three Faces of Eve*. At this point, Joanne Woodward was considered by some female fans as little more than an obstacle, the irksome Mrs. Newman who stood between themselves and Paul. By the time she was seen on the screen in 1966, she had not made a film since the forgettable *Signpost to Murder* two years earlier. Though she had willingly forgone an all-out career effort for the sake of her family, the lack of suitable vehicles had not encouraged her to exercise her considerable gifts. It was time to remind people of who Joanne Woodward was and what she could do. For Newman, it was time to find new challenges.

Directing had been Newman's initial goal. He had majored in directing at the Yale School of Drama intending to become a professor of drama and spend his life directing student productions. Even as he addressed a group of

UCLA film students following a screening of *The Hustler,*
Newman admitted his ultimate aim was to do nothing but
direct. He told the group about his only effort thus far, *On
the Harmfulness of Tobacco,* a twenty-eight-minute black-
and-white film version of Chekhov's monologue performed
by Michael Strong; it had enjoyed a brief run in the art
houses.

Newman has always claimed to be a cerebral actor who
carefully analyzes and works out his characterizations, unlike Joanne Woodward, an "intuitive" artist able to somehow sense the essence of a character and assume her
behavior with the natural ease of someone putting on a suit
of clothes. "Joanne enjoys acting," he explained to columnist Sheila Graham. "I don't. I enjoy the rehearsing, the
intellectual exercise." The preparation phase of researching
and making choices in building a character has always interested Newman more than the actual playing, which, at moments, has revealed a discomfort resulting in heavy-handed
or mannered attempts to overcome that intrusive self-
awareness. "I guess I've never been that much of an exhibi-
tionist," he once said.

Around 1967, Woodward's agent came upon the galleys
of *A Jest of God,* a Canadian novel by Margret Laurance
about the last fling of a small-town schoolteacher hovering
on the verge of spinsterhood. The book had won the Gov-
ernor-General's Award, which is comparable to America's
Pulitzer Prize. It seemed to be a dream vehicle for Woodward, a part that would allow her to run through the gamut
of emotions. Stewart Stern, the writer of *The Rack* and a
close family friend, was asked to write the screenplay,
eventually retitled *Rachel, Rachel.* Although Newman was
not initially enthusiastic about directing his wife, perhaps
out of fear that since their working methods were so different it would cause undue strain on their relationship, he
did agree to act as producer. Then, when Stern and Wood-

ward experienced difficulty in raising the money and interesting a bankable director, Paul agreed to step in. His
name drew sufficient backing from Warner Brothers for the
film's modest budget of a little over seven hundred thousand dollars.

For Newman, directing a feature film was the logical next
step. Taking a position on the other side of the camera
proved he had more going for him than a pair of beautiful
blue eyes. "If blue eyes are what it's about, and not the
accumulation of my work as a professional actor, I may as
well turn in my union card right now and go into garden-
ing," he told writer Jane Wilson on the *Rachel, Rachel* set.
"I guess most people, particularly women, suffer from a
lack of being looked at. But half of my enjoyment in life is
watching other people, and I can't watch them if they're
watching me." Newman insisted that "the only reason I got
into it, directing Joanne in *Rachel, Rachel,* is that it's just
so hard to find parts." But directing also offered Newman a
cleaner means of expression, one untainted by either his
own self-consciousness in performing or his movie-star image as a glamour boy.

If the truth be told, Newman was plainly terrified, but as
Stewart Stern observed to *The New York Times,* Newman
is "the only man I ever met who decides what makes him
nervous—like directing a movie—and then, with his hands
sweating and his feet sweating, goes right into it." Determined to serve the property as best he could, Newman surrounded himself with the finest talent available to make up
for his lack of technical expertise. He called upon their
knowledge more extensively than an experienced director
might have, particularly since he had to mount the entire
production within a five-week period.

"He's sometimes stymied simply because he doesn't
know how to express himself mechanically," commented
one crew member to Jane Wilson. But Dede Allen, who

had cut *The Hustler* and is one of the greatest editors in the film business, was on the set daily, advising Newman on how to film the screenplay so that the shots would cut together effectively in the final editing stages. Of course Newman also had the advantage of the leading lady he admired and knew best, his wife, Joanne Woodward.

The making of the film, in a studio built inside a gymnasium in nearby Danbury, Connecticut, became almost a family affair, certainly a labor of love for all involved, with Woodward playing the repressed schoolteacher Rachel; the eldest Newman daughter, Elinor (using her nickname, Nell Potts), playing the infant Rachel; Newman's brother, Arthur, functioning as an associate producer; and friends such as Frank Corsaro, who had written and costarred with the Newmans in *Baby Want a Kiss,* filling out the cast and crew. Though the film was shot in the summer of 1967, it was not released until a year later, under the production company name of Kayos, a pun on Newman's wry self-comment.

According to its director, *Rachel, Rachel* "singles out the unspectacular heroism of the sort of person you wouldn't even notice if you passed him on the street. The steps the characters take are really the steps that humanity takes—not the Churchills, not the Roosevelts, not the Napoleons, but the little people who cast no shadow and leave no footprints. Maybe it can encourage the people who see it to take those little steps in life that can lead to something bigger. Maybe they *won't,* but the point of the movie is that you've got to take the steps, regardless of the consequences."

The story takes place over a summer in the life of Rachel Cameron, who, at age thirty-five, remains dominated by her mother, with whom she lives above a funeral parlor. Rachel senses life passing her by, and when a former high-school friend, Nick, comes back for a visit, she eagerly allows him to seduce her. Rachel assumes their sexual relationship means love and marriage, but the wary Nick invents a wife to thwart her plans. Rachel thinks she is pregnant and plans to move to Oregon. When she discovers her pregnancy is really a cyst, she leaves town anyway, determined to break out of her restricted existence and take hold of her life.

As one would expect from Newman's preferred style of working as an actor, the performances in *Rachel, Rachel* attested to his sensitive handling of the actors. "I think it's easier to direct if you're an actor because you understand an actor's problems, and you understand that certain transitions are difficult. Actors want to direct because they get fed up with the restriction of acting inside their own selves." *Rachel, Rachel* could easily have degenerated into a sudsy froth of sentimentality, but Newman's subtle and rich exploration of the characters' inner lives, through what they reveal in their actions and through Rachel's fantasies, transformed their ordinary world into something infinitely meaningful.

"He's marvelous," his wife exclaimed to Jane Wilson. "It comes as a great surprise to me because I had never thought of him in those terms. I wasn't really quite sure how it was going to turn out. Now I think he is the best director I have ever worked with—and not just because he's my husband."

At one point the prevailing sentiments of the time concerning personal liberation led some studio personnel to put pressure on Newman to have Rachel break completely from her mother. But Newman, a self-proclaimed "terrier type," had the tenacity to follow his own instincts. "There was insistence on that when I directed the picture," Newman recalled, "but I said, 'That's not the way things go, fellas.'"

The film's thoughtful honesty and gentle ironies drew

rave notices from the critics, both for Newman's direction and for Woodward's exquisitely modulated portrayal, which never romanticizes or mocks her character, and upon which the entire film hinges. Critic William Wolf commented: "Paul Newman is off to an auspicious start in a new career. If he hasn't set the industry on fire, he shows a truth-seeking directness that stamps his film with conviction and honesty. He also possesses a key quality; he knows how to be lean and judicious instead of cinematically verbose. . . . Admirers of Paul Newman will now have an additional reason for their esteem."

The film itself, Woodward, Stern, and Estelle Parsons were all nominated for Academy Awards, and lost. Woodward and Newman, though, won Golden Globes, as well as the prestigious New York Critic's Award for Best Actress and Best Director of 1969. An unforgiving Hollywood chose to pass over Newman even for a nomination, despite the fact that it is rare for a director to win the New York Critic's Award and not even garner an Academy Award nomination. But if Newman remained unpopular in Hollywood circles, the decidedly anti-sensational, minusculely budgeted film was a huge success with the public, grossing over eight million dollars. Newman recalled the experience for *Time* with "great fondness, great fondness. That is a really good film."

As he moved into the third decade of his career, Newman seemed more creative and diverse in his interests than ever, and this may have been adding insult to injury for the powers in Hollywood. He had taken time out from editing *Rachel, Rachel* to campaign actively for Eugene McCarthy's presidential campaign. A fellow campaigner commented, "What drove us all was the issue of the war. But Newman was active before, in civil rights, et cetera. He was really good in speaking for McCarthy. He had to be fed all the facts—the stats on McCarthy's position. He was not as good with off-the-cuff questions and answers; he was less comfortable with that. But he was sensitive about people saying, 'Where do you get off telling us how to vote? Who are you?' His stock answer was, 'I'm a citizen, I'm a father, and I'm a voter. I have the same concerns as all of you, and I'm speaking as a citizen, not as a movie star.'

"He gave a lot of time to the campaign. He went just about everywhere for the entire nine months. He would always show up when we needed him—Indianapolis, Milwaukee, Lincoln, Nebraska—everywhere."

Newman later recalled, "I was campaigning for presidential candidate Eugene McCarthy on the weekends. A Jaguar dealer kindly loaned me a car to use every Friday, Saturday, and Sunday. I learned that Nixon was using the same car on Tuesdays and Wednesdays, so I left a note in it. It read, 'Dear Mr. Nixon, You should have no trouble driving this car. It has a tricky clutch. Paul Newman.'" Perhaps Newman's little jest had something to do with his placement at number nineteen on Nixon's notorious enemies list, which finally became public in 1973.

Another act Nixon possibly viewed as antagonistic was Newman's service as a delegate to the infamous Chicago Democratic National Convention in 1968. "I feel I'm the better man—win, lose or draw—for having been a part of this campaign," he told *The New York Times*. "I wear this button with considerable pride and, for the first time, with a great deal of hope." He and Frank Perry coproduced a twenty-five-minute film on the New Hampshire campaign, entitled *All the Way to Jerusalem,* and donated the profits to McCarthy. Newman also campaigned actively for Joseph Duffy for the U.S. Senate. In the fall of 1968 he made a rare television appearance as host and narrator for a two and a half-hour NBC news special exploring the state of the nation, *From Here to the Seventies*. With Peter Fonda, Alan Arkin, Dennis Hopper, Arlo Guthrie, and Jon

Voight—all of whom at the time had successful films p!ay-
ing in theaters, and they owned a percentage of the profits—he asked the public to boycott those very films as an
"act of conscience" against the war in Vietnam. He and
Joanne Woodward were awarded the William J. German
Human Relations Award of the American Jewish Committee in recognition of their good works.

Newman felt it was his responsibility to speak out publicly for issues and candidates that he could believe in, but
he continued to maintain that catering to the public's penchant for intruding into the lives of movie stars was not part
of his duties. As he explained to the *New York Sunday
News* magazine,

> People think I'm a snob, but that isn't true. I'm just in-
> credibly uneasy when people make a commotion over me.
> When they go see my pictures, I'm grateful and hope I of-
> fered them something in return for their two and half dol-
> lars. But they don't own stock in me! I'm not a public
> corporation.
>
> When a Mrs. Jones marches up to me for an autograph,
> I'm supposed to immediately stop what I'm doing, whether
> it's eating dinner, playing with kids or making love to my
> wife. I'm supposed to say: 'Oh, sure, Mrs. Jones, I'll smile
> for you. I'll take off my sunglasses, then I'll put them back
> on.' The whole thing is ridiculous!

Public service did not mean Newman was slackening in
his work as director or as actor. While waiting for the right
script among the many he was asked to direct after *Rachel,
Rachel,* Newman further insured his control with more active productorial duties. He had formed the Newman-Foreman Production Company with agent John Foreman, and
with Barbra Streisand and Sidney Poitier, he created First
Artists Production Company, whose goal was to handle the

financing and distribution of films in which the stars would appear. They were later joined by another screen rebel, Steve McQueen, and occasionally by Joanne Woodward. Newman also entered into agreements with Jennings Lang, Stuart Rosenberg, and George Roy Hill, and though much time was diverted with political and social issues, Newman helped to produce the resulting films, in which he also starred: *Winning, Butch Cassidy and the Sundance Kid, W.U.S.A., Sometimes a Great Notion, Pocket Money, The Sting*, and *Slapshot*.

Winning, a 1968 Newman-Foreman production, costarred Newman and Woodward. After all that hard work on *Rachel, Rachel*, Newman wanted to have some fun while he made enough money to ensure the independence of his new productorial ventures. In fact, the film seemed to have been packaged to be as entertaining for its stars, particularly Newman, as it aspired to be for its audience. Originally planned in 1967 as a low-budget made-for-TV docudrama that would use some of the 1968 Indianapolis 500 race footage Universal already owned, with Newman's participation, the project ballooned into $7-million feature for which Newman received $1.1 million plus a percentage. Thrilling racing scenes—particularly those of the spectacular seventeen-car pileup during the 1968 Memorial Day crash at the Indianapolis 500—were well integrated with a suspenseful, albeit formula, plot. In their seventh on-screen collaboration and one of their most successful, Newman and Woodward are convincing as a couple who love each other but are torn apart by Newman's obsession with his career as a racing driver. It is no secret that Joanne Woodward was as unimpressed as the character she played with her husband's new and dangerous sport, as well as with his refusal to use a double for many of the race sequences. Part of this real-life couple's formula for marital success, though, has always been a respectful tolerance for each other's individuality, and Woodward has come to appreciate and enjoy her husband's passion for racing. The on-screen couple, however, do not enjoy the mutual understanding of the Newmans. They drift in separate directions, and the obsessed race driver loses his new wife to the affections of a rival driver, played by the Newmans' good friend Robert Wagner. Newman's character wins the big race that had so preoccupied him, but soon realizes life is empty without his woman, and the film ends with him trying to convince her to come back.

Paul prepared for *Winning* with even more relish than usual. He attended the Bob Bondurant School of High Performance Driving in Santa Ana, along with Robert Wagner. The 1965 World's Manufacturers' Champion, Bondurant, who had previously coached Yves Montand and James Garner for *Grand Prix,* found Paul to be such a willing and apt pupil that it took only a few weeks to bring him to the point where he could lap 143 mph at Indianapolis, and was prepared for even more professional training. For several years Paul had been arranging his work schedule to give him time off to attend important car races. He had formed close friendships with many of the drivers, so he reveled in the race-circuit atmosphere of the *Winning* set, tossing down beers and talking cars with the mechanics and drivers whenever he had a chance.

Perhaps more significant than the film itself is that it marks the point at which Newman's passion for car racing began to grow. Eventually, it would overtake the time and attention he devoted to acting. When the film ended, Newman pursued the sport with more intensity than ever. After three years of study he competed professionally, and later won all four of the Sports Car Club of America races in which he competed with the Datsun-factory team. He has even set a record at Watkins Glen, New York, one of the more difficult courses on the circuit, and in 1979 he tackled one of racing's most difficult challenges, the twenty-four hours at Le Mans, a grueling test of endurance and speed that has claimed more than eighteen lives over the years. Newman and his teammates rode to second place in a red Porsche 935 twin turbo, at speeds up to 220 mph.

Winning was widely acknowledged as exciting viewing—according to Newman, "a pretty good story about racing"—and the Newmans were lauded universally. As William Wolff noted, "Paul Newman and Joanne Woodward are zooming in stature as a film-world couple. They are doing it without leading private lives that catapult them into headlines. Their own special ingredient is *talent.*"

Though their pairing in *Winning* was lightweight compared with what they had accomplished in *Rachel, Rachel,* the team had come through smelling like roses, as much for their solid marriage as for their recent successful film partnerships. Their domestic tranquillity was a personal affront to professional scandalmongers, who began to hunt all the more feverishly for any suggestion of trouble. Though they came up empty-handed, this did not deter some columnists from exercising their imaginations and publishing hints and innuendos in lieu of available facts. Finally, in July 1969, the Newmans took out a two-thousand-dollar advertisement in the *Los Angeles Times,* half-seriously proclaiming, "We are not breaking up!" They then took off for a second honeymoon in London.

While Newman had been creating his public persona—an amalgam of his screen roles and the aura of nobility and mystique surrounding his personal life—in a sense he had been helping the next generation of superstars by providing them with a model they could adapt to their own personalities. The rebel-loner image was no longer Newman's alone. Steve McQueen had toppled his position at the box office, but this posed no threat to Newman. One could even say he welcomed the company; it had been lonely up there.

Newman had always been careful not to confuse his screen image with his real identity, and his ego remained unshaken. As a humanist and political activist, he had sailed smoothly on the winds of change that swept the nation. On the screen, he not only personified an antiauthoritarian, a rebel armed with a better idea of how the world should be run, but he had also helped to bring about these changes in real life, through his social and political work in the fifties, sixties, and early seventies. But with the mid-seventies, the real end of the decade of change called "the sixties," even the neo-hero defined by Newman in roles like *The Hustler* was somewhat out of fashion. More acted upon than author of his own destiny, this neo-hero—along with the anti-hero—the willful embodiment of everything society despises who is nonetheless often morally superior, was out of favor with a public enervated by the spiritual malaise that hung heavily over the nation like a gray fog. Activist heros like *Cool Hand Luke* seemed almost anachronistic. Disillusioned by the death of real-life heros such as the Kennedys and King (and with them their dreams), even neo- and anti-heros seemed naive, their rebellion pointless. They would soon be replaced, by perversions of the heroic mode, nightmare visions—like the insane assassin Travis Bickle, the protagonist of Martin Scorsese's *Taxi Driver*—and later by a regression to escapist fantasies of absolute power, as represented by the Rambo figure.

Disgusted with the scripts sent his way, and captivated by the challenges of car racing, Newman had diverted his considerable energies away from acting and toward competing on the circuit for the full season, as well as directing, producing, and continuing his political activism. But despite the neglect of his acting career, Newman rose again to number one at the box office with the 1969 release of his and Robert Redford's thirty-million-dollar *Butch Cassidy and the Sundance Kid* (a.k.a., by some irreverent wits, "Two Pairs of Blue Eyes").

Loosely based on the adventures of two legendary out-
laws around the turn of the century—"an adult fairy tale,"
as Newman dubbed it—the William Goldman script had
been making the rounds of producers' offices for some time
before Newman-Foreman got hold of it, first as a vehicle
for Newman and Brando (an intriguing prospect). When
Brando, more concerned at the time with social issues, indicated he was uninterested in working on any film, the
movie was planned for Newman and Warren Beatty, then
Newman and Steve McQueen. When neither Beatty nor
McQueen materialized, the role went to a relative newcomer, Robert Redford.

"If Marlon Brando had been in the picture as was suggested at first, I would have played the Sundance Kid. If
Warren Beatty had consented to do the picture, I would
have played Butch. It didn't make any difference because
they were both marvelous parts," Newman later told the
New York Sunday News magazine.

Though undistinguished as motion-picture art, the film,
directed by veteran George Roy Hill, cleverly exploited
both stars' immense reserves of charm, as did their later
hit, *The Sting*. The audience didn't stand a chance. Bedroom walls across America were graced by a poster of Newman and Redford, in black and white except for two pairs
of bright blue eyes. A true case of serendipitous casting,
the film made Redford a star on the mythic proportions of
Paul Newman, and it won Redford the British Film Academy Award for Best Actor.

As Newman told many reporters, "I don't think people
realize what that picture was all about. It's a love affair
between two men. The girl is incidental." He was later to
say to *Time*, "too bad they got killed in the end, 'cause
those two guys could have gone on in films forever." The
film did spawn a whole school of buddy pictures, including
a "prequel," *Butch and Sundance—The Early Years*, starring Newman and Redford would-be's Tom Berenger and

William Katt. Despite Berenger's pouting upper lip, vaguely reminiscent of Newman's, this pallid reprisal did little more than underscore the extraordinary charisma projected by the original duo.

Beneath the fun lay a message of solemn social import. "The legends of the West have left us with great hangovers, like the inaccurate representation of the American Indian," Newman told *Seventeen* magazine. *Butch Cassidy and the Sundance Kid* spoofed those legends, even as it celebrated the love of two friends. Unlike the serious and self-important *Hombre* and *The Left-Handed Gun,* also deconstructionist westerns, *Butch Cassidy and the Sundance Kid* treats the myth of the romanticized outlaw gently and with great humor. Butch and the Kid are seen as funny, amiable, not very bright, but above all human figures, deepened by the hint of sadness in their unacknowledged awareness that they are vestiges of a past that cannot survive.

Butch, leader of a gang, has hooked up with the Kid in a series of holdups. The president of the victimized train company decides to put an end to this and sends a crack team of agents after the robbers. Along with the Kid's schoolteacher girlfriend, Etta, Butch and Sundance decide to head down to Bolivia. But pickings are sparse, and when Etta realizes that the two are hell-bent on playing out their roles even to death, she leaves. The final scenes show Butch and the Kid trapped in a cul-de-sac. Death is certain, but the film spares us that grim sight and ends with a freeze-frame of the two men facing hundreds of troops, guns blazing.

Newman is at his best here. Mellowed and self-assured, less reliant on the habitual self-conscious mannerisms that had annoyed his critics in the past, his Butch Cassidy skillfully underplays to Redford's more bravura Sundance Kid, but as Lawrence Quirk notes, "Redford outplays but does *not* outshine his costar, who was never in better form."

While the film received mixed reviews, it was welcomed unequivocably by a huge public, to the tune of over thirty million dollars' gross. Newman continued to rise in critical esteem. As Lawrence Quirk noted, "A onetime intense-but-narrow-ranged talent seems unmistakably to be broadening, and the Paul Newman of the seventies should have rich characterizations to offer his admirers."

Eager to fulfill that prophesy, and to seize the film opportunities his reenergized superstar status could finance, Newman-Foreman bought Arthur Kopit's Broadway play *Indians*. Newman was to take the Stacy Keach role of Buffalo Bill, and George Roy Hill would direct, but the project failed to materialize. Later on it would be revived with a different title and director.

Newman's next project was just as close to his true interests. *W.U.S.A.*, a five-million-dollar honorable failure, had seemed in the planning stages to portray an America torn by civil rights, the war in Vietnam, and the political corruption apparently running rife through the nation. "Politically, movies have been back in the Stone Age, but I think *W.U.S.A.* brings film into the seventies," Newman optimistically told *Seventeen*. "It says something about the people who are cooled out and also about the nature of alienation."

Antifacist and proliberal in its bias, *W.U.S.A.* is based on *A Hall of Mirrors,* a Faulkner Prize–winning novel by Robert Stone (who also wrote the screenplay) about a newscaster (Newman) working in a right-wing radio station. The story structure incorporates a confused tangle of subplots, including one involving Joanne Woodward as a prostitute who kills herself, and another concerning Tony Perkins as a politically fanatic social worker naively organizing a bogus social-welfare survey on the orders of the station owner. Signs abound of the social chaos characterizing those times: rallies, an assassination attempt, and a riot. The film was clearly meant to galvanize the public into political awareness and action, but it failed to shock an audience in which most had already turned on, tuned in, and dropped out, or at least given the prospect serious consideration. The nation was living through a disenchantment brought on mainly by an unheroic war, the assassinations of three heroic political figures, and the 1968 Chicago Democratic National Convention. Those who were not already convinced that something was very wrong were clearly refusing to be moved, and they were certainly not persuaded by the overwrought drama of *W.U.S.A.*—despite Newman's unusual decision to make extensive personal appearances to promote the film and signal his ardent support. In a TV interview with David Frost, Newman asserted the film's importance, maintaining that it "should be in a time capsule to be seen a hundred years from now," for what it revealed about the corporate greed and public apathy afflicting the nation. Later, though, he would reassess his opinion, telling *Time* magazine it was "a film of incredible potential, which the producer, the director and I loused up. We tried to make it political, and it wasn't."

W.U.S.A. cost $4.8 million to produce, and was hardly seen in the United States. Liberal-leaning American critics were particularly vexed with the film, wishing it had more successfully accomplished its mission, and ridiculing it for its pretensions. Kathleen Carroll of the *New York Daily News* was typical in her reaction:

> *W.U.S.A.* was a complete turnoff for this reviewer. They, I suppose Newman and his coproducers, are trying to bury us with the message that this country's current trend toward neofascism is a dangerous thing. Their message is only loud, not clear; and the movie itself amounts to nothing more than a lot of sounding off.

But Newman's social message, this time concerning racial equality, had the ring of eloquence born of clarity in his narration of the award-winning documentary codirected by Joseph L. Mankiewicz and Sidney Lumet, *King: A Filmed Record . . . Montgomery to Memphis,* a less ambitious but more successful effort made during the same period.

Newman's next film, *Sometimes a Great Notion,* the story of a lumberjacking family stubbornly struggling to preserve old-fashioned principles in a changing world, was adapted from a novel by Ken Kesey, who had distinguished himself among the counterculture literati for his powerful *One Flew Over the Cuckoo's Nest.* The project seemed promising, with a cast including Henry Fonda and gifted newcomers Lee Remick and Michael Sarrazin, but it soon ran into trouble during the 1970 shoot in Newport, Oregon. Midway through, Newman was in a motorcycle accident resulting in a broken ankle. This delayed the film and pushed it over budget. Mounting costs and other problems forced Newman, already one of the producers, to take over directorial duties from newcomer Richard Colla so that the film could be rushed to completion within a few weeks. Though the finished project was certainly respectable, it wasn't ready until late 1971. By then it had lost momentum, and the distributor, Universal, botched the marketing.

Newman's efforts to rescue the film were characteristically heroic—though a movie about right-wing types was certainly a strange choice to follow up *W.U.S.A.* His ability to handle action scenes proved that his directorial talents were not limited to coaching his wife in slice-of-life intimate dramas. To this day Newman feels the film is a much better piece of work than its lukewarm reception indicated, and he was more amused than disturbed by its supposedly "reactionary" politics. "I'm afraid," he joked to *Show* magazine, "that Agnew is gonna wanna shake my hand and congratulate me for 'tellin' 'em what's what.'" Ironically,

Newman had just learned of his dubious honor of being in the top twenty on Nixon's infamous enemies list, probably as much for his avid support of Nixon's sole opponent in 1972, Paul McCloskey, whose campaign was an embarrassment to the incumbent's administration, as for the other offenses suggested earlier!

As Newman was struggling with *Sometimes a Great Notion,* Woodward starred with George C. Scott in another Newman-Foreman production, the eccentric fantasy *They Might Be Giants,* which she later described as "an absolute horror." This was the third 1970 failure for the Newman-Foreman company, who also produced the unsuccessful *Puzzle of a Downfall Child,* starring Faye Dunaway.

Disgusted by a moviemaking scene in which budgetary considerations ruled unequivocally over artistic concerns, Woodward took a deserved trip to England, indulged in her passion for theater and ballet, and spoke relatively freely to the British press about her career and her marriage, which, she affirmed, thrived on the couple's diversity of interests and on their ability to give each other the space to pursue them. She spoke also of her three daughters. Elinor, the oldest at twelve, had just finished a role in a television documentary and enthusiastically pursued the unusual sport of falconry. Melissa, known as Lissy, nine, enjoyed painting, composing music, and cooking. The youngest, Clea, five, was an avid trampoline artist.

In April 1971, Newman made another rare television appearance, narrating an ABC TV special, *Once Upon a Wheel,* that depicted the thrills and dangers of car racing, on tracks from California to Germany. Several racing champions appeared in the program along with celebrity aficionados such as James Garner, Kirk Douglas, and Glenn Ford, all of whom participated in a Pro-Am event at the Ontario Motor Speedway in California.

Despite his productorial control, Newman's films during

the seventies were generally indifferent efforts. Though his popularity seemed to be on the wane, he still commanded one to three million dollars per film straight into the eighties. First Artists had been formed in 1969, but projects planned for 1971 did not materialize—in *Hillman,* Newman was to play a man evicted from a hill he had constructed from garbage, and in *Where the Dark Streets Go* he was to play a priest. It wasn't until 1972 that the company released its first effort, *Pocket Money* (first announced as *Jim Kane*), with Martin Ritt directing.

Looking for a magical combination like the Newman-Redford team, this mediocre film paired Newman with Lee Marvin. It was a promising idea with colorful characters, but the project that was announced with fanfare never came together under Stuart Rosenberg's direction, and despite a fine script by the gifted Terence Malick and brilliant photography by legendary cinematographer Laszlo Kovaks, it became Newman's third failure in a row. Trying once again to submerge his natural heroic image, Newman portrayed a goofy itinerant cowhand in a meandering fable that wanted to be laid-back but just rambled pointlessly and ultimately went nowhere. As Joseph Gelmis wrote in *Newsday,*

> Stuart Rosenberg, who stylishly guided Newman through *Cool Hand Luke,* gets lost in this one. It bogs down in flabby, uninspired performances. Nothing works. It's supposed to be a funny contemporary western about a naive cowboy and his inept con man pal. There's not a laugh in the film.

Disgusted with the film business and falling more and more in love with car racing, more than once during this period Newman would say, as he did to *Women's Wear Daily,* "If I were fifteen years younger, I'd drop the motion picture industry in a minute . . . like a bullet . . . if I could drive in competition. But you don't start at forty-three."

6

Newman may have become increasingly disinterested in screen acting, but he distinguished himself once again as a director in the 1972 film adaptation of Paul Zindel's Pulitzer Prize–winning play, *The Effects of Gamma Rays on Man-in-the-Moon Marigolds*. In *The Films of Paul Newman*, author Lawrence Quirk makes an interesting, though a bit overstated, contrast between Newman the director and Newman the actor.

Marigolds demonstrates an odd and arresting fact about Paul Newman. When he chooses a film to *act* in, he seems to seek out pretentious directors. . . . The surface, negatively experimental, unsure Newman comes across in those films. But for the most part, when he picks a subject to *direct*, like *Rachel, Rachel* or *Marigolds*, he gets off his beer-swilling, existential, macho donkey and reveals himself for the intelligent, sensitive artist he in actuality is.

Though Quirk stretches the facts to prove his point (Newman is not *always* on a "macho donkey" when he acts in a film directed by someone else, and his directors are not generally "pretentious"), it does seem, at least thus far in his directing career, that Newman's instinct was to guide his actors into a style distinguished by an understated, almost reverent regard for the truths of ordinary reality. This is certainly the case in *Marigolds*. The choice of project did reveal a gap between the supermasculine, unfeeling image projected by the Newman persona, and the reality of a man sensitive enough to direct an almost entirely female cast—a man who, in real life, has admitted that women fascinate him. As he told *Family Weekly,*

> I find them all mysterious. I suppose it's purely sexual, because there's always *that* going on in addition to all the other things that involve communication. Your relationship with a woman is infinitely more interesting than with a guy, because it's on several levels.

Once again filming was a family effort. Newman directed his wife as Beatrice Hunsdorfer, the slovenly yet sympathetic middle-aged widow who lives in a run-down house with two daughters she is incapable of caring for properly, and who wastes her days in idle fantasies about fancy tearooms she will one day own. "Beatrice is a monster," Woodward said of her character some dozen years later, "and since I tend to take my characters home with me, I took Beatrice home. *I* was a *monster* for about three months. My kids hated me. Paul hated me. Everybody wished I would leave home. *I* wished I would leave home."

Newman concurred about the "alienating" effect the part had on his wife. "That was a pain," he said.

Woodward's screen daughters, both of whom have inherited at least some of Beatrice's defeatism, were played by Roberta Wallach, the daughter of Actors Studio alumni Eli Wallach and Anne Jackson; and thirteen-year-old Nell Potts, Paul and Joanne's daughter Elinor in her second screen appearance. As the shy, intellectual Matilda whose school science experiment gives the play its title, Nell almost walks away with the picture.

Woodward and Newman typically proved to be more effective in the roles of actress and director than in any of their on-screen pairings. "We're a kind of artificial couple," Woodward explained to *The New York Times*. "Paul is a great star. I'm a character actress."

Critics were warm in their praise of the entire company, particularly of Nell Potts, and of Woodward for her characteristically intelligent, finely shaded interpretation as the sarcastic and outrageous Beatrice. Newman was cited for what was now his signature, a sensitive and restrained directorial style. Typical was Joseph Gelmis's rave review in *Newsday:* "I can't remember when I've been more depressed and more moved on a nearly documentary level than I was with [*Marigolds*]." But though the film reaffirmed the talents of all involved, the applause was scattered. Perhaps because of its downbeat ending, it was not a commercial success. Newman himself doubted whether or not he succeeded in making the transition from stage to film in the production. He later assessed it for *Time* as "too much theater and not enough cinema. I screwed up there."

Woodward wanted to follow her success, for which the next year's Cannes Film Festival awarded her with the Best Actress prize, with the lead role in *40 Carats*. The role went to Liv Ullman, but Woodward went on to win the New York Critic's Award and an Academy Award nomination for her next role, Rita in *Summer Wishes, Winter Dreams,* scripted for her by Stewart Stern, who had adapted *Rachel, Rachel.*

Newman again failed to come up with a winner at the box office in *The Life and Times of Judge Roy Bean,* directed by John Huston, shot in Arizona, and released the same year. As Newman had often told interviewers, "I don't want to die and have written on my tombstone: 'He was a helluva actor until one day his eyes turned brown.'" So once again he attempted to mask his natural glamour behind a beard and aging makeup. This time his efforts were successful. "Marvelous," he said of the film to *Time.* "The first three-quarters of the film are classic. We never came to grips with the ending though. I loved that character." The film humorously spoofs another romantic myth of the Old West—this time the legend of Judge Roy Bean, whose life was transformed into a fairy tale by John Milius's screenplay. According to the film, Bean is a mix of the heroic and the absurd, a character who hangs people according to his caprice but is capable of a lifelong passion for the archetypal western belle, Lily Langtry, for whom he names the town he created and controls under a tight reign. Defeated in his attempt to meet the Jersey Lily and by the death of his common-law Mexican wife during childbirth, Bean leaves town. He returns to Langtry twenty years later, an old and beaten man. In a final heroic gesture he tries to destroy his creation, now congested with traffic and filled with oil derricks, but he is killed in a fire instead.

While Newman and John Huston had a great time romping through the desert and working with the mountain lion and the bear who almost stole the show, neither Huston's considerable talents nor Newman's generally successful efforts to interpret the character of the judge (played in earlier films by Walter Brennan in *The Westerner* and by Victor Jory in *A Time for Dying*) managed to make the movie a commercial success. Erroneous rumors flew through the press, claiming that the film's failure could be attributed to tension between the director and Newman, but their eloquent refutation took the form of teaming up once again in 1973, for *The Mackintosh Man*. The rumors were quelled. *The Mackintosh Man* was, however, Newman's sixth commercial failure in a row. The two men may have gotten along, but apparently they were unable to share the fun with the mass audience.

After this string of financial flops, it may have seemed that his long reign as a box-office king had ended, but superstardom never really deserted Newman. Even at forty-seven, he remained the personification of the youthful, charming rogue. All he needed was the right setting and he would shine as brightly as ever. He paired up once more with Robert Redford, now a huge star with a clearly defined screen persona of his own, in an appropriate vehicle for their charisma—the monstrously successful hit *The Sting*.

Slick and densely packed with two hours of solid harmless entertainment, *The Sting* features two easygoing grifters, as confidence men were known in Chicago in the thirties, who are quite a bit more crafty than Butch and Sundance. The movie brilliantly exploits the all-too-human fascination charming larcenists have for an audience. The film is so much fun, no one questions the obvious loopholes in the plot, and what it lacks in substance it more than makes up for in style. Newman prepared for his role of the suave con man by viewing about fifteen of William Powell's movies. And to great effect. Director George Roy Hill rightly calls the poker scene "one of the best pieces of comedic acting I've ever seen. I defy any actor to play that scene better." Though Newman had often been accused in his earlier comedic attempts of lacking the light, sophisticated touch of a Cary Grant, screenwriter Goldman told

Time that Newman "could be called a victim of the Cary Grant syndrome. He makes it look so easy, and he looks so wonderful, that everybody assumes he isn't acting."

"George and I have quite a marvelous relationship," Newman told journalist Leonard Probst. "He is, I think, an extraordinarily gifted man, he really has a concept of what a movie should be like. He has a great musical sense. He is loyal, affectionate, gifted, and the cheapest son of a bitch that I've ever met in my life." Neither Newman's admiration for Hill's abilities nor their great friendship prevented Newman from sawing Hill's desk in half in retaliation for not paying his bill "for liquor which he had borrowed from my office." Even more grandiose was Newman's next stunt, performed while Hill was enjoying *The Sting* wrap party. When the director left the festivities, thinking to drive home in his brand new sports car, it was parked where he had left it but was now in two pieces, courtesy of Newman, a stuntman, and a blow torch. Economically minded in other matters, Newman was fully prepared to pay for a new car just for the pleasure of seeing Hill's dismayed face.

He had been trading a series of elaborate practical jokes with Robert Redford as well, although on a slightly less spectacular scale. Redford had presented Newman with a Porsche that had met a telephone pole at 90 mph. Newman awoke one morning to find the vehicle sitting in his driveway, *sans* transmission, engine, and seats, so he had the car compacted, crated, and shipped straight back to Redford. "To the best of my knowledge it's in his vestibule right now," Newman told Probst. "I don't see how he could move it."

The two actors had apparently established an off-screen camaraderie not very different from their on-screen relationship. "I'd welcome another opportunity to do a picture with Redford," Newman told the *New York Sunday News* magazine, "but it would have to be something special, something as good or better than *The Sting*. I wish it would happen because we have such a marvelous time on the set. I'm getting to that age now where it's extremely important for me to have fun while making films. Yes, Redford and I are good friends, but the motion picture business is peculiar—you build very strong friendships for three or four months on a picture, then you don't see the guy for three years." In recent years, however, Redford has separated from his wife and has moved to Weston, a town neighboring Westport, so the two have been able to continue their real-life friendship.

The huge success of the *The Sting* reasserted Paul Newman's Olympic status among the Hollywood pantheon. Grover Lewis, writing for *Rolling Stone,* visited the set and observed that though Redford drew his share of fans, it was Newman who magnetized the crowds that had gathered.

> Newman picks up a Pied Piper–like entourage of followers, numbering at times around 300 people. Everybody wants to touch him, as if to reassure themselves that he really exists. Nobody attempts to separate him from his clothes, but the men scramble to shake his hand, and the women jockey for position to pat him on the arm, the shoulder, the back. To those who ask him for his autograph, Newman politely but firmly declines, muttering some variant of 'I'm waging a one-man war against autographs.' The same scene, the same dialogue could be taking place anywhere in the world except maybe the farther reaches of Outer Mongolia. Newman is global, a symbol as instantly recognizable and as potently magical as the sun rising over Malibu. Star value, box office.

With profits from *The Sting* pouring into his bank account, Newman, together with friends Marlon Brando and George C. Scott, brainstormed for a project that would communicate some of the more serious issues affecting the quality of life. The three men and others invested their money and donated their services for a documentary called *The Wild Places,* a beautiful and eloquently made case for the importance of preserving America's few remaining unspoiled areas.

Newman was also indulging more and more in his enthusiasm for car racing, and he had begun to race professionally at a time when most drivers consider retirement. In 1974 alone, he competed in at least a dozen races and won two national championship races driving a Datsun. Newman also served as commentator for a TV documentary on British racer Graham Hill. In the spring, he had a minor racing accident that was made much of in the press, but he refused to accede to the fears of his friends and his wife by slowing down.

Newman's next role, in 1974, was in the unabashed potboiler *Towering Inferno,* one of what threatened to be an interminable series of disaster films, a new genre that soon reached its nadir with the unattractively titled *Condominium.* Produced by Irwin Allen, who had provided a much-needed injection of green energy to the Hollywood machine with *The Poseidon Adventure, Inferno* followed a strict and proven formula of challenging a huge, star-studded cast of characters with a man-made or God-decreed disaster of biblical porportions. But *Inferno* was a bit more than just a bag of tricks; it distinguished itself with a script that retained some crumbs of intelligence. Allen was able to attract high-caliber actors such as Robert Wagner, Steve McQueen, Jennifer Jones, Fred Astaire, and Paul Newman, to go with the spectacular special effects portraying the conflagration of a 138-story glass office building. Newman later praised the film to *Time* as "of its kind, rather good. Get the actors off and the stuntmen on as quick as you can." The film was a huge success: those effects and stars burned at the box office. One interesting sidelight of the film was an anxious young fireman played by a handsome Scott Newman, who, his stepmother asserted, looked like a "French movie star."

Though critics grumbled at the "current addiction to Great Disaster cinema," they apparently had a good time writing about it. Vincent Canby in *The New York Times* called it "a nearly three-hour suspense film for arsonists, firemen, movie-technology buffs, building inspectors, worry warts—a gigantic cautionary tale for people who want the worst to happen." Dilys Powell in *The London Times,* looking out for the animal lovers, closed his review with the following quip: "I should add that despite the paucity of human survivors, somebody saves the cat."

After completing his duties on *Towering Inferno* for his usual fee of a million dollars plus a percentage, which in this case had to have been considerable, Newman returned to political concerns, traveling to New York to introduce ex–attorney general Ramsey Clark at a fund-raising event, making a television documentary with his wife on ecology, and working on a campaign to stop off-shore drilling in California. He also found time to race a Ferrari and begin rehearsals for his next film, *The Drowning Pool.*

Though Newman enjoyed the Harper character, the film was a disappointingly predictable sequel to *Harper.* Costarring Joanne Woodward as his ex-mistress, *The Drowning Pool* attempted to capitalize on the earlier film's success. Employing a glamorously gritty mise-en-scène and a convoluted but superficial plot that got in the way of creating meaningful characters, the film was overall a mildly entertaining but forgettable attempt. As William Wolf commented in *Cue,* "Even the presence of [Newman and Woodward] can't overcome the listlessness of this private-eye yarn based on the Ross Macdonald novel."

Amid rumors of the breakup of his marriage, rumors that

seemed to have their own natural cycle, reactivating peri- odically without any discernable reason, Newman busied himself in the mid-seventies by searching for projects. He announced several that never materialized, such as the mind-boggling proposition of his lead opposite Mick Jagger in a film adaptation of E. L. Doctorow's *Ragtime;* a part in *A Bridge Too Far,* which Redford eventually accepted; and a film version of Patricia Nell Warren's *The Front Runner,* a touching homosexual love story between a coach and a run- ner. Newman wanted to go ahead with the last project, but finally decided that his audience would not be able to accept him as a homosexual.

In 1975 New York's Film Society at Lincoln Center hon- ored both Newmans with a gala evening featuring their ap- pearance, celebrity hosts, and a specially assembled collage of clips from their movies. "I don't think they were too enthusiastic about it," commented a Film Society worker many years later. But their feelings were understandable in light of the fact that the previous recipients—Charles Chaplin, Fred Astaire, and Alfred Hitchcock—had all been in their wane, while the Newmans hoped to have many more active career years. Newman obligingly posed for photographs, but refused to sign his name on proffered scraps of paper. The evening was otherwise uneventful, ex- cept for the somewhat sad slip of tongue by one of the in- troducers, Tennessee Williams, who said he was here to honor "Paul Goodman." Included among the clips were a few minutes from *The Silver Chalice.* "A lot of laughs," was Newman's comment on his early embarrassment. "I never realized how skinny my legs were—and that terrible cocktail dress. At least Nero had his to the floor."

For his next project Newman exercised his option, bought for $500,000 a few years earlier, on Arthur Kopit's play *Indians.* He chose as his director maverick Robert Alt- man, who was known for turning genre filmmaking upside down to show how things really were. In this film Newman seemed to be celebrating America's two-hundredth birthday with yet another revisionist treatment of western myth, *Buffalo Bill and the Indians, or Sitting Bull's History Lesson*. Implicit in the film is the message that just as the heroics of Buffalo Bill's Wild West show are a staged fraud, so is the official story about how the American West was won, replete with tales of pilgrims risking life and limb for the right to practice their faith, hardy pioneers persevering through all odds, and bloodthirsty Indians. According to the filmmakers, America is built, at least in part, on the bloodstained land belonging by right to the aboriginal Americans.

Masking his glamour once more, this time behind a long pointed beard and flowing wig, Newman portrayed Bill Cody, the proprietor of a seedy Wild West show, in which not even Sitting Bull is authentic. Despite some interesting and valid reinterpretations wreaked on America's most cherished myths, the film's eccentricity did not sit well with many, and it was attacked as a self-indulgent bore by some, as an affront to the national dignity by others. *Films and Filming*, though, was won over. "To be sardonic while maintaining an impression of lightheartedness is no mean feat—and Robert Altman performs it with *Buffalo Bill and the Indians*, which personally I'd count among his better films." Vincent Canby in *The New York Times* half-jokingly spoke of the difficulties Altman created for those used to a diet of clearly defined and easy-to-locate genre films.

What are we going to do about Robert Altman? He simply won't stand still so that the movie industry, movie critics and the movie-going public can get a comfortable hold on him. He is praised for doing one thing right and he takes another direction to try something completely different.

Just about the time we think we've caught up with him, we turn a corner and he's vanished.

But these were lonely voices among the pack of critics who tore the film apart. "This presentation emerges as a puerile satire on the legends of the Buffalo Bill era," sniffed *Variety*. Newman was singled out for a particularly withering assessment by Penelope Gilliatt in the *New Yorker:* "Buffalo Bill is played by Paul Newman, with age lines of makeup on his forehead, and a wig of long fair hair that makes the character look peculiarly like the result of a sex change." Newman himself admitted to *Time* that he didn't "know what happened to that one. Made a mistake somewhere along the line. Great potential."

Newman followed this critical and commercial failure with a peripheral silent cameo part in Mel Brooks's *Silent Movie,* a gesture that, intentionally or not, seemed to speak for itself.

His next film of 1977, also a Newman-Foreman production, *Slapshot,* is a genuinely funny, offbeat and raunchy sleeper about a shoddy small-time ice hockey team managed rather lackadaisically by Newman until he hits on the notion of psyching out the competition with verbal and physical abuse. Well-paced and with hilarious performances by unknowns, the film offended many with its rough language, but supporters argued that the language was a realistic re-creation of a certain milieu. Richard Schickel in *Time* attacked the film, saying "There is nothing in the history of movies to compare with [this movie] for consistent, low-level obscenity of expression." John L. Wasserman in *The San Francisco Chronicle* disagreed: "The undeniably foul-mouthed language [helped] the major characters develop depth of personalities and relationships. . . . A marvelous and funny film." Newman himself holds it as one of his favorites, acknowledging, "Unfortunately that character is a lot closer to me than I would care to admit—vulgar, on the skids." While it did not receive the praise it merits, *Slapshot* has attracted a growing audience over the past ten years and is a favorite on network and cable television reruns.

In 1977 Newman was well into middle age—fifty-two years old—yet he drove a Porsche 911S in the twelve-hour endurance race at Sebring, Florida. He also participated in numerous races around the country, most notably in April 1977, when he finished fifth driving Clint Eastwood's Ferrari in the Daytona twenty-four hour Endurance Race. In the summer of 1977, he was driving a Datsun in a Sports Car of America race at Garrettsville, Ohio, when another car flipped and landed on top of his. But that and another accident at Lime Rock, Connecticut, failed to deter him despite Woodward's fears—though he did make clearly insincere promises that he would soon give up the sport.

The couple was more in accord on their work for the Native Americans on the Bellingham Reservation and the Washington Energy Action Committee, whose purpose is to pressure the government into a saner energy policy. "I'm what you would call an operational cynic," he told *Foundation* magazine in response to questions about his activist role. Would he run for political office was the question on most interviewers' lips, particularly since fellow thespian Ronald Reagan was now governor of California. "There would be no way I could survive," he said with a grin. "I mean, they'd never elect me anyway because my platform would be too outrageous to begin with." Newman admitted he'd been asked to run for office, and his friend Gore Vidal had always encouraged him in that direction. Newman consistently "declined on the basis that I think I can make my presence felt as well as an actor and can have as large a platform as I could if I were actively working as a politician." For a man who refuses to give autographs, maintaining "there is no reason why I should have to be stopped every twenty or thirty feet every day of my life," the goldfish bowl of political office would fast become intolerable. Besides, he had often commented, if his wife suddenly found herself in the position of holding formal dinners and functioning as first lady, "that'd be the end of the relationship."

In the spring of 1977 the Newmans went to London, where Joanne was to costar with Laurence Olivier in a British television production of *Come Back, Little Sheba.* Though the Newmans still spent part of the year in California and enjoyed frequent trips to London, for nearly twenty years they had made their home in a sprawling colonial house on three acres of wooded land. "This is home," Joanne Woodward told the *New York Post* in 1980. Life is pleasant. in California, where we often have to work. But it's just not me—or us."

Living in a quiet community such as Westport allowed the couple to pursue interests outside of moviemaking. Woodward could run three miles a day on the country back roads without inhaling Los Angeles smog, and she could do her exercises five days a week in the estate's ballet studio. Newman had his sauna and his office, and he was only an hour away from the racetrack where he drove most weekends.

"I can be much more private in Connecticut," Newman told the *Saturday Evening Post.* "People can't catch up with you as easily and I've never liked the California scene. No, I can't say that. What I really like is mobility. I love California for about a year. I like Connecticut for about two and a half years. The fact that I can move back and forth is a great luxury."

Despite their serene, low-key family life, the late seventies were not good years for the Newmans. Following *Slapshot* Newman took an eighteen-month self-imposed sabbatical from film acting. "I decided to take that year and a half off because it was time," he said. "I'd been working since I was thirteen, and I figured I was due to put a bunch of time together. It's really funny, though, because I found out that I didn't do anything of consequence. Either sweeping out the old head or the kind of travel that I would have liked to have done. Very peculiar."

For Newman the major problem was a lack of material depicting genuine human emotion. "It's manufactured. My fantasy of making the perfect movie is very simple. You have an idea for a film, you work with a screenwriter or a playwright. It can be either a film or a play. You get a marvelously inventive director and you cast it the way it ought to be cast, not because you have to cast it a certain way. You get together and you have four incredible weeks of rehearsal and then you shut it down. And no one ever sees it. That would be a marvelous movie. You never crank a foot of film and you never have an audience to come in and see it."

Although he was increasingly disillusioned, Newman was reluctant to abandon his career altogether. "I have a recurring nightmare in which I always dream that the whole bottom is going to fall out of my career; that I will have paid several million dollars in taxes and will have no annuity to live on in my later years." Newman attributed the nightmare to feelings of guilt. Because I've been fortunate enough to have made pictures that turned out okay, it is very difficult for me to comprehend why the reward should be so extraordinary. That's why I feel it might all come to an abrupt end. And if it did I would have to adjust to the circumstances. It isn't just the money, but the fact that I've become accustomed to a certain kind of living and recognition that may be totally destroyed. I worry so much that I'm lucky if I get five hours sleep at night, even between films."

Newman finally found what he considered to be a worthy project, an offbeat film with a message that would reunite him with friend and collaborator Robert Altman.

Released in 1979, *Quintet* tried to make significant social commentary through an improbable futuristic story about the scattered survivors of an apocalyptic ice age created by the misalignment of the earth's axis caused, in turn, by one nuclear war too many. The plot hinges on the conceit of a game played by the disaffected human remnants of the technological age that self-destructed. To bring home the message that these people live in utter boredom and without hope; the stakes are life and death.

The film's publicity was steeped in mystery and intrigue. Under orders from Robert Altman, none of the international cast members—including Vittorio Gassman, Bibi Andersson, Fernando Rey, Brigitte Fossey, Nina van Pallandt, and David Langton—or the crew could discuss what it was about. Newman, who played the hero, the last man who cares and, incidentally, the last man who can impregnate a woman, did comment later that the project had changed radically from the original script (written by Altman, Patricia Resnick, and Frank Barhydt). Newman described his character, Essex, as a "detective—a deducer. He's pretty well anesthetized except in this survival-detective kind of way. A lot of human functions, like making love, are simply vague memories in the back of his consciousness. Sometimes he remembers the taste of food other than fish or recalls something warm in all of the cold. Beyond that there really isn't much."

None of the cast members had to rely on acting techniques such as sense memory to create the feeling of a frigid world. *Quintet* was filmed on location in the environs of Montreal, Canada, and in Frobisher Bay during its arctic winter. Even the interior scenes were filmed outdoors, in sets constructed to withstand a below-zero temperature.

When Newman and company did the river scenes, it was forty below. According to the production executive, no feature film had ever been made under similar circumstances.

Despite the aura of mystery surrounding the project, the extreme attention to realistic detail, and the noble intentions of all involved, the film mired in heavy-handed, portentous symbolism constructed around ice, barrenness, and the waste of life on earth. Few members of the audience got to see what the secret was all about. *Quintet* barely got its message out through the confused plot concerning Newman's search for the killer of his pregnant woman. Though the film appears improvised, as if the actors had come to the set with only a rough idea of the action from which they would create their own dialogue, Newman defended Altman's methods, asserting that "there's very little improvisation in this picture. Scenes are rewritten. Sometimes you get them as you go on the set to shoot, but they are written. Its pretty hard to get away with improvisation. This picture is too out of our time, it's out of our vernacular. It has to be mysterious without being bewildering. It has to have a lot of double meaning, which is very difficult to add to with any accuracy. I think all this talk about Bob's ad-libbing is a lot of things that the actors bring in. This is what he wants. But these things are all incorporated and rehearsed before they're shot. You don't just get up on a set and start improvising and shooting."

Though critics were generally respectful of Altman's willingness to take risks—he had called *Quintet* a "whole new departure" in his work—they generally found the movie to be a self-indulgent, boring exercise, filmed through an "artsy" camera apparently generously smeared with Vaseline. "Altman—a Daring Filmmaker Falters" was the headline over Vincent Canby's review. He found the film "depressing not because it's about the end of the world, but because it's artistic vision is feeble." Even Altman fans couldn't resist the opportunities to be clever. Writing in the *New Yorker,* Pauline Kael likened the film to "a Monty Python show played at the wrong speed." Frank Rich in *Time* dubbed the game "a shotgun marriage between backgammon and Russian roulette." Only the *Christian Science Monitor,* with its eye cocked on Revelations, got the message. "*Quintet* emerges as an unexpectedly bold and powerful experience. Shortcomings notwithstanding, it is nothing less than a full-scale cinematic myth, using an audaciously far-flung tale to point a moral about the strength and heroism that can flame up in mankind under even the most dismal conditions." So few saw this film that on the occasion of Newman's next screen appearance in *Fort Apache, the Bronx,* many of his fans thought of it as a comeback.

As usual, however, Newman had been hardly idle. In 1978, at the age of fifty-three, Newman was appointed by President Carter to be one of three citizen delegates, paid $217.32 per day, to participate in the U.N. General Assembly's Tenth special session, the first devoted to disarmament. In an interview with the *Daily News,* Newman said,

> You know, I agree with the guy in *Network* who said, "I'm mad as hell and I'm not going to take this any longer." I think the American people should feel outraged as well. Somewhere, somehow, this madness has got to stop.
>
> At first I declined. Then I figured that most people in the United States knew little about the arms race. I gave the offer some very serious thought and agreed.

Newman cited his children as the major reason for his public service. "I don't want my children to write on my tombstone that there lies a lazy old man who was never part of his time. It's a part of our time to work for disarmament."

His peers at the conference rated his work highly. A Russian diplomat called him "talented and intelligent," and a spokesman for the U.N. mission noted that "he was here almost all the time. He worked long hours and he was really effective at the nuts and bolts stuff."

As Newman noted in his speech to the special session, "this conference can only prepare an agenda and provide the machinery for future negotiations. It can call attention to the necessities for arms reduction and put a spotlight around the world on it." The session fulfilled its objective: to draft a document that outlined an agenda for world disarmament. "Who would have thought we'd get this far?" Newman exulted. "We had a general debate. We reviewed and appraised the situation in light of the pressing need to make some headway in arms reduction."

Newman vowed to continue working with the U.N. in any manner deemed appropriate, stating, "Hell, I might even make a movie about it." Though he was disappointed in the lack of sufficient news coverage of the conference, enough reporters were in attendance to catch some of Newman's comments during the discussion, delivered in a characteristically direct and undiplomatic style. "Unless we have some way of regulating arms control or arms reduction, some nut somewhere might accidentally push a button and that will end that . . ."

"Do you know the story of the airline pilot who told his passengers, 'I've got some good news and some bad news. First, the bad news. We are hopelessly lost. Now the good news. We're making wonderful time.' That's the message."

"There are some military nuts in Washington playing king of the mountain. It makes me feel twitchy. They are playing it tit for tat—with our lives. There's paranoia in the Pentagon."

The Newmans had planned to host a celebration of the seventy-fifth anniversary of the Ford Motor Car Company, calling it Imagination in America. Involving technology, politics, and life-styles, the plans failed to materialize. Another dream of Newman's, more humble but undoubtably closer to his heart, did come true. In the fall of 1978, he returned to his old alma mater, Kenyon College, without his wife but with his portable sauna, to direct *C. C. Pyle and the Bunion Derby,* a play by prize-winning dramatist Michael Cristofer. Five years earlier Newman had been approached to contribute to Kenyon's proposed new two-million-dollar theater. He decided to direct the inaugural production for free. "I took so much out of this place," Newman explained, "I wanted to give something back." Whether or not the college offered to name the building after its most famous alumnus is unknown, but Newman says, "I wouldn't have allowed that. I do not suffer from the 'edifice complex.'"

But what should have been a happy experience of completion was marred by a tragedy Newman had fearfully anticipated for several years. Paul's first child, his son Scott, accidentally overdosed on alcohol and drugs. For years Newman had been telling friends, "I live in fear of that telephone call that will come in the night telling me something has happened to Scott."

On the afternoon of November 19, 1978, Scott complained of pains in his chest and side, which he attributed to a motorcycle accident of a few weeks earlier. Scott was a six-foot, muscular twenty-eight-year-old who seemed to outdo even his daredevil father in risk taking. He had made almost five hundred jumps from airplanes, opening his parachute at the last minute, and had done stunt work involving countless tumbles from horses and down flights of stairs. But he had also turned to alcohol and drugs for relief from his physical aches and pains, and, gradually, from emotional stress as well. On the afternoon of his death, Scott had driven to a friend's house. The two watched Sun-

day football as they slugged down rum. But the liquor
failed to dull Scott's pain. "God, it hurts right here under
my ribs and behind my shoulder," he complained. His
friend responded, "Maybe some Valium will help," offering five tablets. An hour later he gulped down five more.
That evening Scott consulted clinical psychologist Dr. Mark
Weinstein—Paul Newman had arranged for him to be
available whenever his son needed professional help. Scott
spoke that night of his feelings of inadequacy about not
having made a name for himself, and of his conflicts with
his father and stepmother. Dr. Weinstein gave Scott a small
sample of a painkiller, Darvon, to take home with him.
Scott returned to his friend's apartment, where they continued to drink. They were joined by an associate of Dr.
Weinstein's, Scott Steinberg, who was assigned to stay with
young Newman through his difficult moments.

Later that evening, Steinberg escorted Scott back to his
Ramada Hotel room in Beverly Hills, where they talked for
a short while before Scott went into the bathroom and took
some Quaaludes and cocaine. Feeling sleepy, Scott went to
bed around 10:00 P.M. He snored loudly until approximately 11:30, when the sound suddenly stopped. So did his
breathing. He was rushed by paramedics to the New Hospital, where he was pronounced dead on arrival.

Paul Newman finally received the dreaded phone call in
Ohio, at the college from which he had graduated over
thirty years earlier with a "magnum cum lager" and where
he had planned to build a career as a professor of theater.
Newman assembled his cast of students, telling them, "It
would help me if you'd all be as rowdy as possible,"
Newsweek reported. Later that night a group of students
appeared at his door, dressed in silly costumes, bearing a
bottle of whiskey and a case of beer. "It's the first time I've
touched hard stuff in eight years," Newman quietly re-

marked, taking the gifts gratefully and bidding the young people good night.

Paul Newman made the sad journey to California for the funeral, which was attended by immediate family only: Scott's mother, Jacqueline Witte Newman Robinson; his sisters, Susan and Stephanie; his stepmother, Joanne Woodward; and his half-sisters, Elinor, Melissa, and Clea.

Though Paul told Barbara Walters he felt he had been remiss as a father, close friends deny this, citing his deep sense of family and the guilt he had always carried for the breakup of his first family when Scott was seven years old. Friends also remember that Scott was always a difficult child, and that when they visited Newman and his first wife in their tiny New Haven apartment, they could barely converse for the racket the screaming, uncontrollable child created. The problem was worsened by Scott's confusion about the growing problems between his mother and father, and about his father's long absences as his career took off and he had to be on the West Coast to make movies. When his parents split up, Scott and his sisters stayed with their mother, who remarried; they spent part of their summer vacations with their father and Woodward, in either California or Connecticut.

Apparently the situation was never resolved between Scott and his father; during the teenage years—difficult for any child—the conflict worsened. Scott felt he had been deserted and that his father should therefore give him anything he wanted. But Newman lived by a credo of gain through one's own efforts only, and moderation in material things. He was determined not to raise a family of movie-star brats. For a long time, Scott also resented Joanne Woodward as the interloper, and the two would go for a year at a time without speaking. Scott was sent to private schools, where he consistently proved to be a disruptive influence, getting into fights and receiving poor grades. He was expelled several times. He attended college but dropped out after two years.

At nineteen, however, Scott did a complete about-face and declared his total independence. Living on his own and refusing any help from his father, he took up parachuting, a pursuit in which he must have felt he didn't have to compete with his father. He qualified as an instructor and taught parachuting to cadets of the United States Naval Academy.

Like his father, Scott began drinking heavily at age eighteen, but his problem was more serious than Paul Newman's ever was. Often violent when drunk, he got into many scrapes, one of which made the newspapers. In 1974, when he was twenty-three years old, Scott got into a drunken brawl at a ski-resort town, Mammoth Lake, in California. On the way to the station, Scott kicked one of the officers in the head and the car ran out of control into a snowdrift. Scott was charged with felonious assault with a deadly weapon, though as he sarcastically remarked, "the weapon was my boot," and he was jailed.

Though Scott had declared his independence, and had dug ditches for three dollars an hour rather than accept his father's money, the incident served to convince him that his dad was truly behind him. The elder Newman persuaded the officers to reduce the charges to a misdemeanor with a thousand-dollar fine and two years' probation.

Scott wanted to succeed on his father's turf, the world of entertainment. Though he felt conflicts about being known as the son of a superstar, he accepted a small role as a nervous young fireman in *The Towering Inferno,* and promoted the film on a six-city tour. When he heard that George Roy Hill, a close friend of his father's and director of *Butch Cassidy and the Sundance Kid* and *The Sting,* was making a movie about barnstorming aviators, Scott knew he could do the job based on his own experience. He felt

comfortable enough to capitalize on the personal relationship—he called Hill and got a job as a parachute
jumper. He had also performed in a guest spot on the TV
show "Marcus Welby, M.D."

"It's a brand new world," he told the *Daily News* as he
toured for *Towering Inferno*. "I love it, and I'm good at it.
I know what I want to do now. And it has given me the
opportunity to dispel some of the myths people have about
me." Scott denied that he was spoiled, citing the past four
years in which "I've made and paid my own way, except for
the help he gave me when I got in that scrape with the
law." He refuted the notion that he did not get along with
his stepmother.

Though Scott took his new career seriously, taking
lessons with acting coach Peggy Feury four times a week,
he never knew if he was getting the work only because he
was the son of Paul Newman. He used William Scott as a
professional name, and he branched out into an area of
entertainment never ventured into by his father—singing in
small nightclubs in the Los Angeles area. Scott shared
many of his father's traits: he was a proud young man, un-
afraid, eager to challenge his capabilities. He shared with
his father a certain charm: an insouciant, knowing grin
combined with a gentle sweetness that allowed him to
smooth over some of his more exasperating shenanigans.
Like his father he was ambivalent about acting, but his
streak of self-doubt ran deeper and wider. According to his
classmates, he seemed insecure about his abilities and had a
reputation for sabotaging rehearsals by being late or by not
showing up at all. Like his father, he had a somewhat eccentric but ruthless health regime, alternating his days of
drugs, junk food, and drinking with long hours of running
and sweating at the gym, fortified only by a green liquid
recommended by his nutritionist. Unlike his father, he was
also driven to self-destruction. His recklessness was ex-

treme, taking him into suicidal excesses of drugs and alcohol. Repeatedly he would declare to his father that he didn't need him, that he wanted no help from him, and that "I'm going to make it despite you." Yet he was clearly bound and hobbled by his unresolved emotions regarding his father, and he sought escape more and more, through alcohol and drugs.

Drawing on their common love of physical risk, Paul tried to interest his son in car racing, but by then Newman was so well established that Scott felt even here he would fail in attempting to compete with his illustrious father. At a loss, Newman turned to professionals for help in salvaging his son's life. He hired Dr. Robert Scott of the Advanced Health Center of Newport Beach, California, to counsel Scott on his alcoholism. Paul Newman was well acquainted with the problem of alcohol abuse and had received help himself from Alcoholics Anonymous and his own course of analysis. The counselor said that Scott was "terrorized by the idea of trying to be a professional actor. The risk of failure scared the hell out of him, so he relied on drugs and alcohol." But the treatment didn't help, despite Paul's attendance of joint therapy sessions in which Scott released his venom toward his father, whom he irrationally blamed for all his problems.

In desperation, Paul hired Dr. Mark Weinstein and Scott Steinberg as caretakers for his son, on call at any time. But nothing, it seems, could have diverted the course of Scott's self-destruction, which ended in death, labeled by the Los Angeles coroner as accidental. No funeral was held for Scott, but at the informal commemoration, emotions broke when someone spoke about Scott's reaching out to his father.

Paul Newman has been literally unable to speak of the tragedy. But Joanne Woodward has been more open, if only for the sake of other parents and children with similar problems. She has stated that "Scott was a bright kid, and maybe if he had known early on about the dangers of drugs, he wouldn't have started. You have to do a positive thing for kids. Negative things like throwing them in jail or sending them somewhere to be dried out won't work. What finally happened to Scott could have happened a lot of other times much earlier. We knew it and we had to live with it."

Woodward also revealed that Scott was not the only one of the Newman children to have experienced drug problems. Nell, Paul and Joanne's oldest daughter, the young actress so praised in *Marigolds,* also underwent a period of experimentation with drugs. "She never got to the addict stage, but what she did was to screw up school and everything else in her life so that at twenty-one she finds herself way behind her peers," Woodward said.

In an attempt to salvage some positive effect from the tragedy, the Newmans formed the Scott Newman Foundation, an organization dedicated to spreading information about drug abuse by awarding grants to writers, producers, and directors of prime-time TV programs dealing with drug-abuse prevention. In 1979 Newman worked with producer David Begelman on *Angel Death,* a film about angel dust, and he backed a movie project that did not see the light of day, called *Just Say No.* "This may sound corny," Joanne Woodward has said, "but we just didn't want Scott to have lived in vain."

In 1981 Kathy Cronkite, herself the daughter of a famous man, news commentator Walter Cronkite, wrote an article for *US* magazine—she talked about Scott, with whom she had attended acting classes, and interviewed Susan, the oldest Newman daughter at age twenty-five.

Susan Newman grew up with her mother, Jackie Witte. She began her real relationship with her father when she was older, partly because, she says, her father relates better to older children. Her early memories were of "glorious, divorced weekends, fairy-tale weekends, really. We'd have lunch at the Plaza and then maybe go to F.A.O. Schwartz and pick out one toy, of which mine were mostly dolls; then we'd take a carriage ride around Central Park or go to the zoo or something like that. They were very magical. And it had nothing to do with reality." But even these outings were marred by the constant harassment of rude stares and of fans who surrounded her father, sticking pens and papers in his face.

"Maybe that's where some of the anger comes from: You haven't seen your old man in four months, and you're trying to tell him how you flunked out of school and your boyfriend is a junkie—or whatever the major catastrophe is—and people are coming up. . . . Time elements are very disproportionate, and I think that affects the relationship." According to Susan, her father is still just "a nice, blue-eyed kid from Shaker Heights. Who was to know that old Skinnylegs Newman was going to become such a big thing?"

Newman's next film, immediately after this difficult period of 1980, was a blatant potboiler that afforded the Newmans a well-paid working vacation, a chance to heal a bit from their tragedy in the tropical paradise of Kalaleu, Hawaii.

Producer Irwin Allen attempted to inject seriousness into his tried-and-true disaster formula in *When Time Ran Out*. This time a volcanic eruption destroys a luxury resort and allows Newman to flex his heroic capabilities by leading the survivors to safety, but few of the audience members received the benefit of the film's weak attempt at moral instruction. Though the movie spins out a predictable but pleasant plot, and the timing of the release date—just as Mount Saint Helen threatened to bury half the state of Washington—was certainly fortuitous, *When Time Ran*

Out's time seemed to run out as rapidly as the lives of its characters. The movie closed almost immediately after it opened. Critics were not kindly disposed to Allen's pale imitation of a genre he invented practically single-handedly. Richard Corliss in *SoHo News* likened his viewing experience to "being trapped in a stalled IRT train during rush hour. The feeling is a mixture of annoyance and ennui." He did express astonishment, however, about Newman's youthful handsomeness, wondering "just what pact Paul Newman has made with the Devil to keep him so youthful and handsome. (I've got the answer to that last question: Newman swore to Satan that he'd appear only in movies like this.)" But those are unlikely terms, for *When Time Ran Out* was the last of Newman's few potboilers, and on the occasion of Newman's fiftieth birthday, the media had been flooded with articles detailing both real and apocryphal secrets to Newman's perennial youth and sex appeal. "It doesn't matter what you do to your body," *The Star* reported Newman explaining in a skewered version of Zen's yin and yang, "as long as you do something else to balance it." Among Newman's alleged recommendations were his 7:00 A.M. routine of sit-ups, regular jogging or swimming, a half-hour of sweat in the steam room, an icy shower, and cooling off with feet propped up and eye packs.

When Time Ran Out is probably memorable in the Newmans' minds only for events external to the film, such as the romantic surprise anniversary dinner à deux Newman arranged, on the deserted golf course by the sea, during which the earth really shook—the quake registered over five points on the Richter scale, and its epicenter was very close to the film's location. On the day filming started by the caverns of Kileauea Iki, geysers of steam spouted up from previously dormant underground wells. Producer Allen was delighted. "The special effects men were supposed to give us geysers just like that," he said, beaming.

But even this natural excitement was not nearly enough for Newman. Disappointed that no major auto racing was scheduled during the time he and Joanne were on location, between filming and looping the picture Newman managed to jack up the producer's cast-insurance rates by entering and finishing second with his teammates in the twenty-four-hour Le Mans race in France. During the same year, he devoted time to campaign for John Anderson in the 1980 presidential election.

Throughout the seventies and into the eighties, Newman was to show more sound judgment in his directing than in his acting. When asked by Vincent Canby why so much time had elapsed between directorial projects, Newman responded that he was much more selective about what he directs. "I'm whimsical about what I act in," he acknowledged.

One of his directorial successes was a television drama that incisively treated a daring topic—terminal illness. Based on a Tony Award and Pulitzer Prize–winning play by Michael Cristofer, the young writer whose play Newman had directed at Kenyon College, *The Shadow Box* starred Joanne Woodward, Valerie Harper, James Broderick, Sylvia Sidney, Melinda Dillon, and Christopher Plummer and was coproduced by Newman's eldest daughter, Susan. It aired on December 28, 1980.

Though the play was enormously successful, the television adaptation faced the obstacle of its difficult subject; dying is not a topic guaranteed to draw a mass audience. The play entwines the stories of three patients—a working-class family man whose wife refuses to accept the truth, a homosexual with a bitter ex-wife and a male lover, and an elderly woman—all of whom have come to a West Coast hospital complex for the terminally ill to await the inevitable. Through conversations among themselves and with the hospital staff, they share their views about their situation and philosophize about mortality.

In an interview with *The New York Times,* Newman said he chose the material "because it says we should use our time today, not wait until tomorrow or until we are facing death." The confrontation of emotions usually suppressed was one factor that attracted Newman to the property. Another reason, perhaps unconscious, could have been the play's connection to his own loss and its ultimately humorous, life-affirming attitude. The film also implicitly made a strong case for the hospice movement, the so-called "alternative way to die."

"You sense that society is anesthetizing itself," Newman observed. "It's very important to get to people's emotions, to remind them that they've got emotions lying around. If you just look at the bare plot line, you think that doesn't sound like much fun. But it's funny, bitchy, poignant, and, in the final analysis, very uplifting."

Despite the teleplay's obvious merit, even when Paul Newman agreed to take on directing chores, the networks needed convincing. Susan Newman, who had appeared in *I Wanna Hold Your Hand,* became involved with the project at the suggestion of her stepmother, and through her efforts and those of the coproducer, Jill Marti, the play finally aired. "Susan and Jill hustled their fannies off," Newman asserted proudly. "We were very thorough," acknowledged Susan. The project was mounted because she and her coproducer anticipated all the network's misgivings: "We got together all the reviews of the play. If they said, 'But it deals with death,' we said, 'But look at this review, which talks about how funny it is.' So, when we walked in with this package, which included Joanne and Paul, it was pretty impressive. It was hard to say no."

In the end the network was so persuaded that it not only said yes, it also gave them a $1.9 million budget, a longer-than-usual shooting schedule, and a two-week rehearsal period (unheard of in commercial television, but a point on which Susan Newman says her father was "very insistent").

The Shadow Box, Newman's first directorial project since 1972, received a 1981 Golden Globe citation and universal praise. Newman is justified when he says, "I take some pride in that one." John O'Connor, writing in *The New York Times,* called the program a "splendidly controlled realization of Mr. Cristofer's play," with performances that were

> uniformly excellent. Miss Woodward reveals still new layers of expertise as the nasty wife. Mr. Plummer turns the impossible writer into a terribly moving character. Miss Dillon is incredibly on target as the neglected daughter. I could go on, but the message is: watch *The Shadow Box* Sunday.

Just as Newman seemed to be moving into directing, the next several films in which he acted revealed he had entered a new phase. He had finally outgrown his golden youth, but his masculine charm had deepened, and his persona as Outsider had grown more complex and socially important. Director Sydney Pollack told *On Cable* magazine,

> You're seeing a greater degree of maturity in Paul. Maybe he's catching up with things that happened in his life. He's always been a hard-working actor, he's always been a sane actor with an enormous amount of intelligence and decency. You're seeing him now at the top of his form.

In *Fort Apache, Absence of Malice,* and *The Verdict,* Newman played a tough yet sensitive middle-aged man (always at least ten years younger than his actual age), who must call upon his most profound reserves of moral and intellectual determination to overcome seemingly insurmountable problems. From an emblem of misunderstood youth lost in a corrupt world, Newman had grown into an Everyman, an ordinary citizen of integrity who must take a stand to make a difference. The blindly rebellious vulnerable kid of his early roles had given way to a rebel with a cause, a man of conscience who knows what his difficulties are and takes on the responsibility to resolve them. In one of the films he would make in the eighties, *Harry and Son,* Newman came full circle, playing the opposite of the character he had defined in the fifties and sixties. As a widower whose son's wishes differ from his own, Newman portrayed the parental figure, the object of the young rebel's love and hate.

As Billy the Kid in *The Left-Handed Gun*, four years after Josh Logan, director of Broadway's *Picnic*, told Newman he wouldn't cast him in the lead because he lacked the requisite "sexual threat." Here Newman proves how wrong Logan was.

Two pairs of blue eyes. Newman and Redford in their 1968 partnering, *Butch Cassidy and the Sundance Kid*. Newman's straight man was beautifully executed, if anything underacted, allowing Redford's talent to shine through.

As alcoholic, ambulance-chasing attorney in 1983's *The Verdict*, one of Newman's favorite performances and probably his best.

Paul Newman and Joanne Woodward as friendly neighbors in *Harry and Son*. Newman cowrote, coproduced, directed and starred in the 1984 film. Wife Joanne was to direct while he was busy acting, but she liked her minor role so much, it was built into a major supporting character. When the film was finally finished, Newman swore "Never again."

Fast Eddie Felson of 1961's *The Hustler* wants to beat the best pool player in the country, but he lacks what Minnesota Fats has in abundance – character. When the film ends, he still has a lesson to learn.

Paul Newman as Fast Eddie twenty-five years later in *The Color of Money*. Director Martin Scorsese and Paul Newman felt the character of Fast Eddie was left unfinished. This film would depict his final lesson and give the actor a rare chance to reprise one of his most memorable portraits.

In a more relaxed moment, Newman is captured off-scre

Age has diminished none of Paul Newman's charm or good looks. Friends swear he never looked better.

Sidney Lumet, director of *The Verdict*, and Paul Newman, its star, are two mavericks who eschewed the West Coast film colony for the more intellectual East Coast. They go back a long way – to the beginning of both men's careers in the New York of the fifties.

Paul Newman, director, checks a camera angle for his award-winning television drama about four dying people, *The Shadow Box*. As usual in any Paul Newman-directed production, this was a family affair, produced by eldest daughter Susan and featuring wife Joanne Woodward.

On the set of Newman's film adaptation of Tennessee Williams's greatest drama, *The Glass Menagerie*, with John Malkovich (Tom Winger) and Joanne Woodward (Amanda Winger).

In 1957, Paul Newman and Joanne Woodward were "just good friends." Here, in their pre-nonsmoking days, they light up at a Hollywood dinner at which Paul Newman received an award.

Paul Newman visits his new wife
on location for 1960's *The Fugitive
Kind*, in which Woodward
appeared as an alcoholic
nymphomaniac wearing white
pancake makeup and kohl-rimmed eyes.

Both Joanne Woodward and Paul Newman are
honored by a retrospective of their careers in film
put on by the New York Film Society at Lincoln
Center in 1977. As former honorees were men and
women whose careers were definitely on the wane,
the Newmans were initially less than enthusiastic
about the occasion.

A man whose tastes have remained constant
throughout his life, this fifties publicity shot
proves Newman's predeliction for peering under
the hoods of fast automobiles – his souped-up
Volkswagen and his Nissan 300ZX racing car –
is not a recent fancy.

Paul Newman gets ready to leave the pits for his first
shot at the Indy 500. With 1968's *Winning*, Newman
caught the racing bug for good. Since that date, his
racing career has rivaled and at times overtaken his
acting and directing.

T though the general consensus was that Newman
had indeed entered a new, mature phase in his
career as film actor, 1981's *Fort Apache, the
Bronx,* an exciting police drama written by
Heywood Gould, met with mixed critical and
commercial success. Newman received three million to play
a role turned down seven years earlier by Steve McQueen
and then by Nick Nolte, who would have been paid two
million. The story, which underwent seven rewrites before
filming began, tells of a group of cops beseiged from within
and without by the hierarchy, corruption, and the turmoil
of drug deals, prostitution, robbery, murder, and general
mayhem seething within the devastated forty-block Bronx
ghetto that is their precinct, the Forty-first, nicknamed Fort
Apache, after the classic John Wayne film. "At one time,"
said Newman, "the Forty-first Precinct was considered the
most dangerous in the country and the cops assigned to it

were under constant seige." The murder of a pair of rookie cops has roused the newly appointed precinct commander to straighten out his underlings, solve the crime, and generally bring the community under control. Newman is Murphy, a veteran cop who plays by his own rules and faces a crisis of conscience that ultimately positions him against the precinct status quo.

In preparation for his role as the cop confronted not only by a difficult community and corruption among his peers, but by a new boss (Ed Asner), a by-the-rules autocrat who doesn't play by the Fort's rules, Newman rode around the South Bronx in a squad car with the former officers upon whose exploits the story was based, Tom "Red" Mulhearn and Pete Tessitor, known in the precinct as the Katzenjammer Kids. "Mulhearn and Tessitore used humor to solve many of the problems they encountered," said Newman. "So we've incorporated that into the film. Murphy isn't just another weary cop, he has humor and humanity in him. Like Harper, Butch Cassidy, and Luke, their hard-edged humor is what the public responds to and remembers." Mulhearn and Tessitore's humor, not unlike Newman's own brand of practical joking, found outlets in improvisational street punishments, some of which found their way into the script, such as gluing the hair of a glue sniffer to his head, taking a junkie's shoes so he couldn't go outside to score dope, throwing the keys of a drunk driver down the sewer, or chewing up and swallowing his driver's license.

"I think what I learned about the police is what a difficult thing it is for them not to become anesthetized by the suffering, the blood, everything. My own involvement with the police usually has been on an unfriendly basis," Newman acknowledged. "In fact, I became an actor because I was thrown in jail," he added, referring to an early college escapade that also got him thrown off the football team.

For their part, Tessitore and Mulhearn were impressed

with Newman. "He's a true professional," Tessitore commented. "We described a lot of our experiences, and I'm sure that was helpful to him. But what really impressed us was his power of observation, the way he was able to pick up the mannerisms and jargon of cops on the beat."

"Newman really captures the spontaneous humor of the men in the precinct," added Mulhearn. "You can't tell the story of Fort Apache without showing that side of the officers; the film conveys the humor quite well. In the midst of very difficult circumstances, the men would joke and kid around to relieve the tension of the work."

Despite the impeccable liberal credentials of all involved—producer David Susskind, director Daniel (*Raisin in the Sun*) Petri, and, of course, the star—the film was attacked, unfairly, Newman believes, by local black and Puerto Rican groups who charged the filmmakers with racism and denigration of their image in the interest of sensationalizing the film's themes. Their rallies in protest of the film did cause the owners of the Gemini Theater at Second Avenue and East Sixty-fourth Street in Manhattan to cancel the scheduled opening. Robert Mega, manager of the Gemini, said he had second thoughts about the movie after a meeting with the committee that was protesting the film, and after a boycott held outside his theater. But it was Mayor Koch's description of the film as "racist" that finally decided management against opening it, he said. "We didn't do it out of fear," the owner claimed. "Our theater is in the silk-stocking district, and we thought it best not to have demonstrations of this kind around. We did it to be a good neighbor." The controversy over *Fort Apache* became so heated that it reached the floor of the New York City Council, which debated on whether or not to call for a boycott of it, but the resolution proposed by the Committee on General Welfare was defeated by a vote of twenty-six to fifteen.

There were also unpleasant incidents on the set during the course of the fourteen-week filming. Some local teens jumped on top of a car, pounding on the roof and screaming epithets at Newman and Rachel Ticotin (the female lead), who were trapped inside. Another time, director Daniel Petrie accidentally set up for a shot right outside the headquarters of the Coalition Against Fort Apache. "We didn't know it was their headquarters," Petrie told *The New York Times*. "It was just a storefront. Naturally, the coalition emerged, got a lot of local residents involved, and every time I would shout, 'Action!' they would yell, 'Help stop Fort Apache!'" Petrie, who said he was just trying to "tell a good story about an unlikely hero," was driven to write an article on the issue of racism and *Fort Apache* for the blue-collar New York newspaper the *Daily News*. He gave detailed accounts of the distortions reported by the press, and stated that the intentions of the film and everyone involved were completely honorable, even antiracist. In the many interviews and press conferences he gave, Petrie recalled that during the second week of shooting, Newman, whose commitment to civil rights is well known, put his arm around him and said, "I haven't felt this good about a picture since *The Hustler*."

To a man known for backing up his long-standing opposition to racism with committed action, the posters of Newman's face smeared with the caption "racist" must have been particularly vexing. In a myriad of interviews responding to the furor and to a suit claiming libel (filed by attorney William Kunstler on behalf of the Committee Against Fort Apache), Newman dismissed the controversy as exaggerated. "Too much has been made of the controversy. I'm tired of it. I'm mad. The press has done this. Four guys handing out leaflets. The *New York Post* indicated there were riots when there were *no riots*. I can understand misinterpretation. But the invention of things that didn't even occur . . . amazing."

"I'd rather make films in the Bronx than on Park Avenue. The film is a tough film," Newman commented on another occasion. "It's tough on Puerto Ricans, Blacks, cops. If you're doing a movie about cops, you can't have Easter egg hunts and wedding parties. But does anybody out there think this is a racist film?

"There was an absolutely malicious invention of things that didn't occur. To the best of my knowledge, 90 percent of the South Bronx groups were favorable to the film," he said.

"It is not a racist picture," Newman maintained. "The two villains are Irish cops who throw a Puerto Rican off of a roof. . . . I've lived here, I've talked to these people. I was in Alabama long before Bill Kunstler was in Chicago. I've lived in New York since 1951. I've lived on the doorstep of the Bronx. It was a revelation, a shock to me. The acreage, the size of the blight. It's wishful thinking that people will look at this film and try to do something. Most of the people living there try to make decent lives for themselves, but it's not easy under those conditions."

In an interview with the *Daily News,* Newman's anger at the unjust assaults on his integrity, made by self-appointed Bronx community leaders, heightened. "I don't like being called a racist pig and being told I give up my humanity for money," he protested. "In the final analysis, *they're* the whores. Maybe they're looking for a political base or to call attention to themselves in their community." The problems of the South Bronx were not limited to that area alone, Newman continually asserted, arguing that the makers of the film were hoping that by showing the shocking reality, positive action would be taken.

As it turned out, only a minority was not persuaded. Following one press conference, a few members of the Committee Against Fort Apache said they would be able to gain more community support if they could learn the film's shooting schedule. But residents argued with the committee's public-relations representative. They were not offended by *Fort Apache,* nor were they persuaded to take a stand against the film. "I like having the movie here," asserted a young mother in a neighborhood playground. "It's very seldom anything happens up this way." Much later, tired by the drawn-out controversy apparently manufactured by a few dissidents and a news-hungry press, Newman shrugged off the film as "some good moments, I guess."

Despite the filmmakers' protests, some reviewers agreed with the criticism. David Denby in *New York* magazine commented, "Unfortunately, the people who've made *Fort Apache* don't seem to realize that a social situation of unparalleled chaos requires more than stock characters and TV-style filmmaking." Publicity surrounding the film focused on the charges of racism or emphasized Newman's apparently magical ability to defy the passage of years and tended to gloss over the excellence of his performance. Nathan Fain noted that Newman's silvering hair only further emphasized the glacial blueness of his famous eyes, adding that the legendary face had not changed. "It is a memorable piece of architecture, the face of America's impertinent cowboy. It is also the only face that ever challenged John Wayne for a special sort of national attention," he wrote in an article released about the same time as *Fort Apache.* In the same interview, Newman spoke of his alienation from his public image as sex symbol. "Well, I thought when I turned fifty, all that would cease. But I guess it hasn't. What can I tell you? It's always been bewildering, because what I see up there on the screen doesn't have anything to do with me."

The negative publicity surrounding the film obscured what is apparent now, years after the controversy has died down: *Fort Apache, the Bronx* is an exciting, well-made film in which Newman gracefully executes an assured, complex, generally terrific interpretation of a modern-day Quixote: Disillusioned, sardonic, alcoholic, perplexed, weary unto death of fighting what appears to be a losing battle against insurmountable forces of corruption, this career cop finally risks it all—friendship and financial security—to do the right thing.

Though Newman vociferously championed *Fort Apache* and his involvement in it, it was again time to take stock. He was about to turn fifty-five years old. The past two or three years had been perhaps the lowest point of his career, and, with the death of his son, the most painful of his life. "I'll tell you one thing I've been thinking about in my old age," he told the *Daily News*. "The corruption of the American actor. I always knew it happened to others, but I never knew until now that it could happen to me. It's not the money—I don't have to worry about money. It's that you start thinking of yourself as a movie star rather than as an actor."

Newman was the first to own up to his mistakes, and he admitted a few regrets to the *News*: "I made a couple of really bad ones back to back," he said referring to *When Time Ran Out* as "a terrible mistake" and *Quintet* as a "whimsical" career choice. "Probably I choose my films for a lot of the wrong reasons," he mused. "If I'm not working, I'll choose a script because it happens to be around, even though it might be worse than the one that came to me five months before, when I was working." Friends say he will often decide to participate in a project to help out a friend or because its shooting schedule fits in nicely with his racing plans. But it's not that his attitude toward acting is cavalier. "Of course I care! Listen, every actor alive wants to do critical blockbusters. Don't you think Marlon, Kirk . . . want good roles? Or Steve McQueen when he was alive? And how many films do the younger ones make? Think about it; how often do you see De Niro or Pacino? It must mean good roles aren't available. For five years, George Roy Hill, Redford and myself have been looking for something we can do together."

Though he was in a position to draw one to three million per picture, he vowed that if he found the right vehicle he would perform, if necessary, for free. "All I know," he says, "is twenty years ago I spent 15 percent of my time reading for the business and 85 percent of my time reading for my own pleasure, and now it's the reverse. Over a year, I'll read two hundred scripts. I keep turning them down, though. This must say something about what's going on in the business."

Elaborating on some of his poor choices, Newman admitted to having turned down parts that he later wished he hadn't. "I turned down *All That Jazz,* which I think was a great mistake. I didn't think the character was redeemable. And, of course, I didn't take Bob Fosse [the writer and director] into consideration. It was a dumb, *dumb* mistake." He also admitted to turning down the lead, played by Al Pacino, in *Bobby Deerfield.* He and Robert Redford have each turned down roles later played by the other, but in the end, Newman says, there must be no regrets.

At this point, Newman considered the height of his career to have been in the sixties, when he'd made three of his favorite films, *Hud, Cool Hand Luke,* and *The Hustler.* He said to a *Daily News* reporter,

> God, it doesn't *seem* that long ago. But there were really interesting films made in those days. The kind of pictures I want to do and enjoy doing aren't fashionable today. You know, if *Rachel, Rachel* came out today, I don't think it would have one-fiftieth of the potential it had then. I think more and more, people don't want to see the heavy stuff. They want to be entertained, they don't want to have to think. The main reason for this is TV. I don't think au-

diences today can focus on anything for more than the distance between commercials.

But another reason is the writing. The old writers have written themselves out and the young ones have a lot of viscera, but not a thread of intelligence in their work. There are obvious exceptions, of course. I saw *Raging Bull* the other night and it wiped me out. I sat down and wrote Scorsese and De Niro, and I never do that.

Newman also liked *Ordinary People,* which surprised him—when Redford first showed him the script, "I did not like it at all; I would have advised him not to touch it." He chafed at the restrictions the American propensity for typecasting has created. In Britain, he said, actors are expected to play a variety of roles. As an illustration of U.S. limitations he said he had optioned a novel, *The Front Runner,* with the idea of adapting it to film and playing the leading role of a homosexual coach, but in the final analysis, he had felt forced to back down. "I just don't know whether I would have been accepted in that role," he admitted.

But Newman does not shrink from offending those who cannot understand his motives. The furor over the blue language of *Slapshot* tickled rather than irritated him, and he remains proud of his work. "It may not have been the best movie I ever made, but it was the most original role I'd played in years," he said. "The funny thing is when I did it I knew I'd make a lot of enemies. I got one letter from a woman in Indianapolis who said I raced at *her* track in 1967 and that this was the high point of her life. 'But last night I saw *Slapshot,*' she wrote, 'And if you ever set foot on my property, I'll set the dogs on you!'"

Newman admitted that he had begun, unconsciously, to think of himself as "above going back" to the stage, a dangerous pattern of thought for any actor who takes his craft seriously. He hired a new agent to help rethink his career;

he also began to focus more energy on his own production company, which had just racked up a huge success with *The Shadow Box.* "In the last analysis," he said, "you have to develop your own projects, though I've never been good at that."

Newman claims that his primary interest, at least in the projects he directs, is to stimulate the deadened emotions of "this anesthetized society . . . I want to really get to an audience and wake them up." This, he says, is the reason he tends to select fairly grim material. "You can't deal with oral sex and get much emotion," he once said.

"As people feel more and more threatened, in order not to collapse, they have to anesthetize themselves. Do you realize that every American male is castrated, just like every Russian male, because you can't protect your family when the enemy is invisible." The enemy Newman was referring to was, of course, the looming threat of a nuclear holocaust.

Soon after completing *Fort Apache,* Newman headed down to Miami to costar with Sally Field in a film he felt he could be proud of, 1981's *Absence of Malice.* An intriguing story penned by Kurt Leudtke, an editor of the *Detroit Free Press,* it explores the theme of the freedom and responsibility of the press. Recalling recent scandals, particularly that of a *Washington Post* reporter who had won a Pulitzer for a story she had invented, Luedtke recalled a quote made by *Washington Post* publisher Ben Bradlee: "Truth? People think we print the truth? We don't print the truth, we print what people tell us." Leudtke wanted to pursue the implications of that statement, "to explore the question of press power and press responsibility, and the potential for abuse. To show the processes, some quite artificial, that create and make news, and how little relationship there sometimes is between truth—full-blown and developed— and the news that's being made."

In 1979 Leudtke had talked his story to an agent in the office of Ziegler Diskant, and the property was immediately grabbed for development by George Roy Hill. As so often happens in the hurry-up-and-wait movie business, the script languished until its 250 pages were passed on to Sydney Pollack who was able to detect the bones of a good story in the grossly inflated screenplay. "I felt *Absence of Malice* raised some interesting questions about journalism that hadn't been dealt with in recent films," the director said.

Pared down, the movie relates the story of Michael Gallagher (Newman), a Miami warehouse owner and son of a deceased mobster who kept his son out of the rackets. Despite his father's precautions, Gallagher is used by the cops to help solve the mysterious disappearance of a Jimmy Hoffa–type mobster. A Justice Department "strike force" leader (Bob Balaban) is being interviewed by news reporter Megan Carter (Sally Field). He leaves his office to allow her to peek at a bogus file on the investigation, left "carelessly" on his desk. The file falsely implicates Gallagher in the disappearance. The objective is to get Megan to write an article that will pressure Gallagher into persuading his Mafia relatives to talk. An ordinary guy who wakes up one morning to find himself smeared all over the front page of his local paper, Gallagher must call upon his latent heroism to disentangle himself from a snare of half-true newspaper headlines. He is besieged by the overly zealous Megan, who, out of an overriding ambition to make her mark as a crack reporter and a distorted sense of her own purpose, fails to realize she is being manipulated to write "accurate but untrue" exposés by the ruthless government investigators. A tentative romance between Gallagher and Megan barely gets off the ground before it is crushed by Megan's misguided integrity and plainly sloppy reporting. This leads her to expose in print the secret of Gallagher's friend, who could have provided the alibi that would have definitively cleared him. The friend, beautifully played by Melinda Dillon, is a Catholic schoolteacher whom Gallagher took out of town for an abortion on the day the mobster was abducted. When the woman sees her story on page one, she kills herself. In the end Gallagher, the ordinary citizen, turns the tables on the corrupt authorities by engineering his own leak and feeding it to the reporter, thereby using the corruption and weakness of his adversaries to best them at their own game.

The part of Gallagher is tailor-made for the imposing figure Newman now cut on the screen. Newman had finally come into his own as a masculine figure worthy of more than the quickened breath of his female fans. Above all, his name now elicited respect. With his lean torso and weighty, graying head, features chiseled down to a granitelike, heroic clarity, Newman had acquired another facet in his loner/hero persona without giving up the cocky feistiness of the underdog. He now projected the stability of majesty earned, a royalty not born into, accessible to the everyday guy who has lived an admirable, fearless, and honest life.

Melinda Dillon had played opposite Newman in *Slapshot* and been directed by him in *The Shadow Box*. She recalled for *On Cable* that she first got to know Newman during the seven hours it took to film a nude bed scene for *Slapshot*.

He was full of jokes and put me completely at ease. It was a breeze. He's [also] a wonderful director. In the twelve weeks it took to make *The Shadow Box* there wasn't one moment of waiting. We were always rehearsing. It was like being back at the Actor's Studio. He *is* a method actor, and that's not a dirty word. He develops his character, his and everybody else's—who they are, how they got there, what is going to happen to them.

He's fought that star thing so hard that he's remaining

alive and growing better and better. It shouldn't be so surprising.

But once again Newman's performance was over-
shadowed by the controversy of the movie. On the brink of
the film's release, Pollack talked about his intentions in
making *Absence of Malice:*

> I hope the film can raise questions or stimulate discussion
> about the obligations of a journalist. It's a very complicated
> process. What is truth? And what is represented as truth?
> Who believes it? Is it part of the responsibility of the read-
> ers'? When a journalist decides to write a story, just as
> when a director makes a film, it boils down to choices—
> what you leave *in* and what you take *out.* That changes
> everything. You can tell a story without telling a single fac-
> tual lie, but by virtue of what's not told, create an impres-
> sion that's quite different from the truth. I'm as guilty of
> that sin—directorially—as any journalist is. The difference
> is, a film is never intended to be the truth.

Like *Fort Apache, the Bronx, Absence of Malice* got
more attention for its attack on the newspaper establishment than for Newman's acting, which was exactly what the
marketing team at Columbia Pictures had schemed for, and
was the reason for opening the picture in New York and
Los Angeles, the nation's centers of communication, a full
month before the rest of the country. The film aimed to
raise questions about the collision between individual and
societal rights, between truth and accuracy in news reporting, and Columbia had few qualms about capitalizing on
any controversy *Absence of Malice* might provoke.

As expected, the film inspired a heated debate concerning ethics among irate print journalists in New York
and Los Angeles, who argued that they and their col-

leagues could not be duped as easily as was the Sally Field character, and that rather than being ambiguous as intended, the moral points attempted by the film were simply confused. "Grotesquely distorted," accused Lucinda Franks, a Pulitzer Prize–winning journalist in the *Columbia Journalism Review.* "There are legitimate reasons to criticize the press," wrote Seth Cagin in *SoHo News,* "its timidity and complacency are good starting points—but *Absence of Malice* simply uses the press for a scapegoat." Speaking of the movies' tendency to imply false generalizations from their portrayals of specific incidents, Vincent Canby in *The New York Times* wrote, "Why, we ask ourselves, would anyone make a film about a gullible reporter, a crooked cop or a venal congressman if the real point is not that *all* journalists, *all* cops, *all* congressmen aren't somehow suspect?" Michael Sragow in *Rolling Stone* reported that *Absence of Malice* strained his credulity and that he found it to be "part of a new trend in films: the nonmessage message movie." Jeffrey Wells in *Film Journal* wrote that the film "will not reach its true audience until it goes into 16 mm for high-school civics classes. It's that kind of movie: informative, high-minded, socially concerned and dramatically empty." Writing in the *Village Voice,* Carrie Rickey raised the issue of feminism:

> Here and there *Absence of Malice* raises a relevant question about journalistic ethics, but what it really does is question whether women are fit to step into the newsroom. There she is, poor Megan: Her feelings get in the way of what she does; she's flustered, incompetent, confused; she spills her coffee on her desk; she screws up people's lives and then, silly girl, attempts to help out, which only makes things worse. The movie pats her on the head and says, "If only you wouldn't try so hard, you might do better."

But Nat Hentoff, who devoted four *Voice* columns to dis-
cussing the issues rasied by the movie and the critics' reactions, found more truth than fiction in the most common
subject of attack on the film: the character and motivation
of the reporter. "Such reporters are not exactly hard to find
in real newsrooms," he wrote. Richard Schickel in *Time*
found the film's

> intelligence as entertainment is matched (and never over-
> whelmed) by the intelligence of its morality. And it is the
> presence of this latter quality that finally distinguishes it. It
> is not a blanket condemnation of investigative reporting. It
> simply says that unspeakable people can use the con-
> ventions of unnamed sources and unattributed quotes for
> ulterior motives, can twist them to make the journalist who
> thinks he is serving the public good actually serve private
> (or governmental) ends that are no good.

Clearly, *Absence of Malice* offered the socially-concerned
Newman more than a good role—as he put it, "a relatively
easy part for me and compatible with the image." Long
accustomed to misinterpretation and intrusions by the
press, *Malice* offered Newman a rare chance to get his own
back. In a press conference on the set of the movie, he
spoke of the press's propensity to see "turmoil where there
is no turmoil, protest where there is no protest, dissent
where there is no dissent." He was fed up, he said, with
"the arrogance in newspaper management . . . their ellip-
tical way of shucking responsibility," especially in the re-
traction of stories that prove false. He was fed up with the
way they close ranks and protect their own no matter what
the issue. "When I called a press conference to point out
what was *really* happening on *Fort Apache*," he complained, "the New York papers wouldn't even mention the
name of the paper [the *New York Post*] I was talking

about." Newman's career difficulties were exacerbated by personal loss. In 1982 his mother, Theresa Newman, died in her home of cancer at the age of eighty-three.

In his next film, 1983's *The Verdict,* Newman again aimed to make some points about an established institution of American life. It too stirred up a fair amount of controversy, but this time his brilliant performance could not be ignored. A singular determination and commitment attracted Newman to the character he played, a role rejected by Robert Redford. Less one-dimensionally noble than Gallagher in *Absence of Malice,* Frank Galvin, the embittered attorney with "his face down in a urinal," is unable to face his defeated idealism and his destroyed career; he insulates himself by maintaining a perpetual state of drunkenness.

From his first reading of the script, Newman's enthusiasm was based on the opportunity Frank Galvin offered to step down from the pedestal of invulnerability upon which his image had stranded him. "It's a very interesting character for me because he's unlike Cool Hand Luke, Butch Cassidy or some of the others who were the cool, collected types," Newman explained. "He's frightened. He's living on the edge and he's panicked. There are people who really do find their lives in a shambles and they decide they don't like it. Some just continue to degenerate and some, like Galvin, can pick themselves up."

For Newman, the part was "a relief," an opportunity finally "to let it all hang out—blemishes and all," and it stands as one of the few performances he feels unequivocably good about. "Parts like this don't come along very often," Newman said. "This guy accommodates almost any actor's invention, he's got a full spectrum of emotional colors that go under the microscope and that's very unusual. And he travels a long path, a really long path, so, I would like to think that I wouldn't have dodged this character if

I'd been asked to play him ten years ago. I probably wouldn't have done it quite as easily as I do now, but I certainly would like to think that I wouldn't violate the character in order to protect the actor."

Director Sidney Lumet, who had taken over after both Arthur Hiller and James Bridges were fired, had long been fascinated with the workings of our social systems, particularly the legal process. "The judicial process in this country," said Sidney Lumet, "is built to withstand corruption because of the brilliantly simple concept of placing the final decision in the hands of twelve ordinary citizens." Lumet's directorial debut in films had been made in 1957, with Reginald Rose's jury drama *Twelve Angry Men.* Twenty-five years later, Lumet was returning to the courtroom with a powerful suspense drama written by David Mamet as adapted from Barry Reed's novel and starring Paul Newman, Charlotte Rampling, Jack Warden, and James Mason.

Frank Galvin, a promising young Irish Catholic lawyer, was railroaded out of his firm by a corrupt senior partner for committing the sin of honesty. He spends most of his time hanging onto the bar rail in saloons and throwing up in hallways, when he isn't bribing funeral-parlor owners to let him pass his cards to the bereaved. In the past three years he has had five cases, of which he has lost four. The film concerns the fifth case, a suit for damages against the archdiocese of Boston. The charges were filed by the sister of a woman who, four years ago, was given the wrong anesthetic and was left in a coma by politically influential doctors at a Catholic hospital owned by the diocese. Galvin's ex-partner (Warden) brings him the case as a favor, a lawsuit no one is supposed to win, an open-and-shut case to be settled out of court. The attorneys for the archdiocese, headed by the reptilian senior partner (James Mason) of a prestigious firm, know the doctors are at fault. Their client is more than willing to settle with the victim's family for a payment of $210,000.

Galvin files the case somewhere out of memory, until he realizes his day in court is imminent. He hastily brushes up on the facts of his case, ready to go through the motions required of him, when he visits his half-alive, half-dead client to take some Polaroids. He then decides, without consulting her sister, that he can't go through with the deal. He must fight to expose the doctors who killed her. Galvin hasn't lost everything. He still has his integrity. "If I take the money I'm lost," he says. He will serve justice by trying the case, going up against the powerful law firm, the corrupt judge, and the diocese in order to punish the doctors, and, not incidentally, provide moviegoers with a rip snorting courtroom confrontation scene in which Galvin's final summation scores most of the film's major points.

Galvin's transformation is intended as a metaphor of the judicial system, an institution that, whatever its failings, has the capacity to be moved by the conscience and actions of a single individual and therefore always contains within its structure the possibility of serving justice. For Newman, *The Verdict* was "a story about the redemption of a human being. It's not an attack on the legal system or the Catholic church or hospitals. These institutions are a springboard for the development of his character. They're metaphors for what seem to be insurmountable obstacles all around him.

"There are a million ways Galvin can lose the case," Newman continued. "But whether he wins it or loses it isn't the point. His victory is that he fights it through all the way to the end. His emotional progression from a down-and-out alcoholic to a whole person again is tied in with his ability to find the strength to keep fighting. And he's battling more than just institutions: he's scratching and clawing to save his life."

But there were some who did think it mattered whether

or not Galvin won the case and how he won it, among them prominent lawyers and judges who wrote articles and letters questioning the tactics of an attorney who would refuse a settlement without first consulting his client, who would break into a mailbox to intercept a letter. "I was inflamed when I left the movie," said Judith S. Kaye, a member of the law firm Olwine, Connelly, Chase, O'Donell & Weyther. Kaye, who wrote an article in *The New York Law Journal,* told *The New York Times,* "It was partly because Paul Newman and James Mason were so good, but it was more the message of the movie: You have to go outside the law, outside the lawyers and judges to obtain justice." Judge Nat H. Hentel of civil court spoke for many in his objections to the character of the judge, who is blatantly aligned with the defense. "A judge like that would not last five minutes in any city with a bar association that did its job," he asserted to *The Times.* "He would be wiped out."

But lawyers who represent plaintiffs were more kindly disposed toward *The Verdict.* "On the law, the movie was a disaster," said Harry H. Lipsig, at age eighty-one one of New York's most respected attorneys. "But for the purpose of making clear to the public the whole subject of malpractice and its difficulties, the movie had a most beneficial function." Lipsig now questions jurors about *The Verdict* in order to identify those who would most likely be sympathetic to his clients. "If a juror says, 'I didn't like him,' you know you're on shaky grounds as a plaintiff's lawyer. I like Paul Newman and anyone who likes him is OK by me."

The Verdict may have its hokey and predictable moments—"the defeated idealist against the successful cynics," as critic David Denby wrote, but it works. By engaging head-on in the game he had refused to play, Galvin resurrects himself from a broken, defeated individual to a model of personal courage and conviction, and the audience floats out of the theater on a cloud of inspiration and renewed hope.

Despite the controversy concerning the film's point of view, this was undeniably one of Newman's finest performances in many years, controlled and totally believable, lean, clean, and stripped of the youthful lapses into self-consciousness and reliance on his native charm that had marred some of his earlier efforts. Newman had always been a master of the "acting is reacting" school. Even in his earliest film efforts one can see him listening, observing, and thinking, wholly and beautifully in character. Charlotte Rampling, who played Galvin's lover, echoed the sentiments of so many actors who have worked with Newman. "Paul is very even tempered and professional," she said. "He is a creative actor, always experimenting with new ways of doing scenes. Best of all, he listens well. It is terribly important for an actor to listen to what you're saying, not just go on with his lines once you've said yours. A lot of actors just don't open up enough to respond if you give them a change in a scene. Paul is not like that at all. He's very attentive." His awkward moments seemed to come in the middle of his longer speeches, as if the sound of his own voice had reached his ears and broken his concentration. At fifty-seven Newman was much easier on himself, more self-trusting. One could no longer speak of "great moments" in his performance, but rather of a beautifully sustained piece of work in a role that offered him the chance to further humanize his persona.

Milo O'Shea, who plays the corrupt judge, was impressed with Newman's concentration: "Sidney [Lumet] is a great theater man," he told *On Cable,* "and we all rehearsed for two weeks before shooting. I think Paul likes that sort of thing. He had obviously worked a great deal before the rehearsals started. It was not a question of just coming in at the door." O'Shea recalled that when Newman was about to film a scene with him in which he shows up late at the judge's chambers, Newman ran "around the studio twice so he would really be puffing and panting." O'Shea also thought that Newman's consistent hard work had paid off now that his physical image had matured. "He's found hidden depths that he hasn't plumbed before," O'Shea said. "He personally has been through a great deal. Losing his only son was a terrible blow both to him and Joanne. You can't push that off, not when you have a great wound like that. It has had a great effect on his work and his life. He really is feeling his way into a deeper part of himself, to a layer that has never been exposed before. Paul was 'sold' [to the public] on his looks. Now there are some lines and wrinkles on his face, giving him the character that perhaps he has been seeking."

Sidney Lumet always knew what Newman had sought to prove, that his versatility had been underappreciated and that "primarily, he is a character actor."

While they might not have been wholly enthusiastic about the movie, critics finally gave Newman the praise he deserved. "His acting in *The Verdict* is brilliant and solid and, what is more, brilliant in the right direction . . . utterly convincing, with enough restraint so that the audience does not get a hangover, and sympathetic enough so that he reaches out, shakily, and touches heroism," raved *Time*. "His voice has the breathy rasp of a drinker, his walk the uncertainty of a strong man going down." Janet Maslin in *The New York Times* called his performance "as shrewd and substantial . . . as he has ever given. . . . With his silvery hair framing his anguished face, Newman is an icon of wounded goodness. Once, in a seizure of desperation, he gets on the phone to try to make a deal with the opposition, his voice quivering between begging and bravado. In that moment, Newman creates real terror from nothing but a pure perception of character."

When asked how he would react if he were to win Best
Actor for his role in *The Verdict* after having been nominated five times only to lose, Newman admitted to mixed
feelings: "To say that I'm not interested would be hypo-
critical . . . I'm not competitive as an actor or a director,
but, by the same token, I'm enough of a pragmatist to realize that the Academy Awards are good for the industry,
they're good for a film. If you worked as hard as I did on
this film and with as much affection you will naturally want
the largest number of people to see it. So I would say that
it's very comforting to be recognized by your peers."

During the shooting of his next film, 1984's *Harry and
Son,* cast and crew agreed to let Newman and Woodward
take a day off to fly to California for the Academy Awards
presentation—a vote of confidence for the sixth Oscar-
nominated performance of Newman's career. But he made
the long trip from Florida only to applaud Ben Kingsley,
who won for *Gandhi.* As Peter W. Kaplan writing in *Life*
described it, though, the day off was worth it. As Newman
strode back onto the *Harry and Son* set, "the crowd of
spectators burst into cheers that went on and on, and Newman's red skin got redder than usual, and his white teeth
got wider, and his blues pointed straight at the ground."

Frank Galvin and other roles he has played since, notably Michael Gallagher in *Absence of Malice* and Eddie Felson in *The Color of Money,* are distinct from the cynical
loners and hot-tempered rebels he played in his earlier big
successes, such as *Cat on a Hot Tin Roof, Hud,* and *The
Hustler.* Yet these youthful malcontents are the "fathers"
of Newman's mature persona. Defeated by his own defiance yet a bit wiser for the gray hairs, in the final stretch
the older Newman hero is able to call upon a forgotten instinct for heroism prompted by the stirrings of his conscience. A Newman hero may appear to fall from grace,
but he'll never hit bottom. A last-minute surge of resiliency

and courage always sees him through, triumphant over adversity.

A lifetime of roles and off-screen activities had established Newman as a man who could do no wrong. He likes fast cars but not fast women. He may not cater to the demands of his fans, but he devotes his free time to worthy causes that benefit all humanity. He could have coasted on his masculine beauty, but he consistently resisted the studio's attempts to peddle him off as a sex symbol and sought out roles to stretch his gifts though they may have jeopardized his position at the box office. Though he embodied the ideal of traditional masculine heroism, Newman was able to satirize that stereotype and to illuminate its hidden dangers.

On January 29, 1983, Paul Newman celebrated his twenty-fifth anniversary with Joanne Woodward. The couple renewed their vows in an intimate ceremony at their home in Westport, Connecticut. At this stage in his life, the public and private Paul Newman had never been closer. He no longer had to work so hard to prove his worth as an actor or to deal with his fears of being turned into just another sex object. He had finally acquired the life experience and confidence to settle into a filmic acting style based on thinking as the character rather showing us what he knew as an actor. In his newfound ease, Newman was better able to play more subtle tones on the human emotional scale, and the public, more in love with this man of indomitable character than ever, willingly accepted this more naked version of his persona.

8

In 1984's *Harry and Son,* Newman overextended his reach in a mammoth effort that included co-writing (with buddy Ronald L. Buck, an L.A. lawyer and restaurateur), coproducing, directing and starring in the film suggested by the novel *A Lost King* by Raymond DeCapite, from which Buck had written a script a dozen years earlier. "It was rewritten twenty-five times in the last two and a half years," Buck told *On Cable* magazine. "Lots of things I liked were thrown out and lots of things I didn't like were put in. We were still writing on the eve of shooting." Overall, though Buck felt the script was "vastly improved," and praised Newman's ear for dialogue. "His credo is 'less is more,' in all aspects of life," said Buck. "He doesn't like spicy food or flashy clothes. He cut some funny lines out of the script, saying, 'Don't go for a laugh just for a laugh's sake.' Also with emotion—he'd say, 'We've got too much emotion;

when we really want to have emotion, people will be tired of it.'"

Despite the bankability of his name, Newman had difficulty convincing a studio that the project was viable. "I thought it was stage worthy, but a lot of people didn't. That pissed me off, and I find I work very well when I'm pissed off." Newman took on the challenge partially out of friendship for Ron Buck, who says of him, "Paul Newman is the most loyal friend I've ever had. It takes a lot to lose him and Joanne."

Initially Newman had hoped to cast actor Gene Hackman in the role of Harry, but "Joanne convinced me that I should play Harry myself," a notion not without its dangers. Newman's fear of heights had to be confronted in a scene where the character, a construction worker, walks on an exposed beam twenty stories high. Newman's evident terror in that scene was not faked. "Harry is a dynamic character role, and it's a wonderful part," Woodward opinioned. "That's why I urged him to take it. He had wanted only to direct, but Orion wanted Paul to play the lead. He didn't think he was right for it, but I convinced him he was. He didn't think he had the energy to do both. He hadn't done both since *Sometimes a Great Notion* and that was about twelve years ago. He says he'll never do it again either, not after *Harry and Son,* and I can't blame him, seeing what he's gone through for two and a half months. Paul worked like a fiend."

The plot concerns a widowed Florida construction worker who is laid off due to an ailment that renders him temporarily blind. The incident triggers off a middle-aged crisis in the macho blue collar man, provoked by his idleness and the time he has to reflect on uncomfortable life issues, particularly his troubled relationship with his sensitive, artistic son (Robby Benson) who lives at home, washes cars by day, and by night nurses a dream of becoming a writer. The second half of the film shifts focus to the son, who dabbles in assembly-line work and auto repossession in an attempt to settle down and please his father. Newman and his brother try to convince the kid to join his uncle's retail business, just as Newman in real life had thirty years ago felt pressured to work for Newman Sports.

Though many people read Newman's loss of his own son into the story of the construction worker struggling to understand his twenty-two-year-old, Newman denied he wrote the film in an attempt to resolve his feelings. "The name never came up," says Ronald Buck, although, as he acknowledged, "How could Paul not think of him? He had to be drawing on that experience. He never said so, but he had to have those feelings. Paul told me years ago, 'The kid's bigger than me. And I can't tell him what to do anymore.'" Though Newman refused to publicly acknowledge the connection to his son, he has stated at other times that he intended to make a film about Scott's death. "We were like rubber bands," he told a *Time* interviewer. "One minute close, the next separated by an enormous and unaccountable distance. I don't think I'll ever escape the guilt." To *People* he said, "I had lost the ability to help him . . . we both backed away." Speaking of his relationship with his five daughters, Newman said, "When they were growing up, I wasn't there much. I was very inconsistent with them. I was all over the place, too loving one minute, too distant the next. One day they were flying on the Concorde, and the next day they were expected to do their own laundry. It was very hard for them to get a balance. Maybe I could have behaved consistently with the kids if I had felt consistently good about myself. You've got to sit down with your lady and say, 'How do we want to raise these children?' Joanne and I never did that."

A subplot of *Harry and Son* involved Newman and a bizarre neighbor played by Joanne Woodward. "Lilly wasn't much in the script," explained Woodward. "We made Lilly up. *I* made Lilly up, because there was no Lilly. There was a small part, the part of Ellen's [Barkin] mother, a woman who originally owned an ice-cream shop. And she was hardly in it at all. A bit part." Woodward was to have accompanied her husband to the location to serve as a second director when he was in front of the camera. "I said to Paul that if I was going to go down to Florida and stand behind the camera, advising him, being his 'second eyes,' so to speak, I'd at least like to be doing something a little more creative," Woodward related. "I said I'd like to play a part. She had another name originally—Louise. I didn't like it. I said this woman would have a wonderful name. She would be a free spirit. She would be Lilly. I wanted her to look different. I wanted her to have an unusual wardrobe. I decided to make my physical Lilly a homage to my daughter Nell. Nell has the most exotic manner of dressing. She wears things in layers."

Woodward constructs her characters from bits and pieces of people she has known or observed, people who affect her. Unlike her Actors Studio–trained husband, Woodward "always works externally, which is exactly what I was taught at Neighborhood Playhouse not to do. Work internally, they tell you. Not me. I have to find out what the character looks like. With Lilly, when I first thought about her and what she would look like, I thought of a woman I'd met some years ago in Maine. The lady lived in a messy house and was a real earth mother—dirty feet, sandals, and she had long gray hair with a long pigtail. So I decided on a pigtail for Lilly, and Paul decided on my gray hair. He likes my gray hair and I guess it does go with my eyes. The funny thing is I never felt like Lilly until I got my pigtail on."

In the end, Woodward was occupied with her own character, and Newman shouldered the full directorial responsibilities. "Well, of course, that turned out to be a joke," she said. "What we discovered was you can't have two directors. I don't think it's possible, at least for me and Paul, because we work very, very differently." Newman explained: "Joanne's the opposite of what I am. Whereas I love to rehearse, she hates it. She'd much rather sit around and talk about it for a while, then shoot. Me, I have the actors on their feet, blocking a scene, immediately. I love to rehearse and develop everything and then my work is done."

Despite their differences in working methods, Joanne Woodward has found her husband to be her most sympathetic director. "When Paul directs me, he really has a sense of *how* to direct me, which is not surprising considering how long we've worked and lived together, even though we don't work the same way at all. He knows I don't like to be talked to. I can't stand it. I once walked off a picture because the director talked to me so much beforehand that by the time I got through talking to him I said, 'I'm sorry, I just left my performance in your office.' There was nothing left for me to discover. Paul doesn't do that. He will use a word, a phrase, and that's it."

With Woodward and some of his five daughters on the set, the atmosphere was as frenetic and jolly as the subject of the film was somber, even dreary. When it came time to film Newman's death scene, he asked Woodward to stand behind the camera during his most difficult scenes to make sure he was doing what he wanted to do and to keep an eye on the other actors. Woodward and one of her daughters stood by the camera, tears streaming down their faces. "Oh Paul," *Time* reports Woodward saying, "I'm so glad you didn't die."

After completing the film, an exhausted Newman vowed, "the last time, never again—you can't do both." On the set, however, he appeared jaunty and relaxed, popping half a dozen bags of popcorn every day at four o'clock for the crew. "It's incredible how cranky those guys would get if they didn't get their popcorn exactly at four o'clock," Newman joked in a plug for his product. But his carefree attitude masked an awesome inner concentration.

"We would work from 9:00 A.M. to 6:00 P.M. straight and he'd only break for popcorn," reported Ron Buck. "That ability to focus has been the key to his success in everything," he concluded. Michael Brockman, the young actor who plays the foreman forced to dismiss Harry, also marveled at Newman's "incredible" concentration. "I think he attacks his racing the way he approaches acting—very seriously, thoughtfully," the young man enthused. "It's as if he puts blinders on, seeing nothing peripheral to distract him from the job at hand. All the people that he races with say that. Also with Paul, the more adverse the track conditions are, the better he seems to be. Maybe it's the same with acting, especially when he's also directing," Brockman concluded.

But perhaps Newman was more interested in his racing, for despite Brockman's admiring words, the fabled concentration—the endless stares at meticulously planned camera setups, jaw grinding mercilessly on one kernel of very salty popcorn—failed to tie the disparate and confused doings of *Harry and Son* into dramatic focus. Newman was now fitting his film career around his obsession with racing rather than the other way around. The production was scheduled so that when he finished his acting on the movie, he could return to the racetrack and the Trans-Am races, which began on Sunday, May 1, at Moroso Motorsports Park in West Palm Beach, Florida, and would end in Phoenix on October 23.

This season he was scheduled to drive in all seventeen of the races while his partner and codriver, Mario Andretti, was scheduled to race in all fourteen of the CART races, beginning in Indianapolis on May 15 and ending in Phoenix on October 30. His careful scheduling was almost thrown askew when Robby Benson broke an ankle the day filming was to commence. Doctors predicted Benson would be incapacitated for at least one week, but the young actor delighted the race driver/director by healing sufficiently within twenty-four hours so that filming was only delayed one day. But the movie would have been better off without Benson's presence; one of the major flaws among the many that plagued this movie was his miscasting. Of all the current crop of young actors, Benson was probably the least likely candidate to impersonate Paul Newman's son. All in all, Newman was more successful on the race track in 1984 than with this film, which received disappointing notices and was scarcely noticed at the box office. Not even the formidable talents of editor Dede Allen could make any sense of a story construction built on a series of starts and stops, with few of the plot threads worked through to a logical conclusion and with little or no change in the situations or awarenesses of the characters. *Harry and Son* was especially disappointing given Newman's record in his brilliant, albeit limited directorial career, and given the generally fine talent he had gathered for the project.

Critics were understandably unreceptive. Writing in *Time,* Richard Schickel called the film "slow" and "predictable," citing the imbalance between Newman's "powerful presence" and Benson's "lack of one" as the film's major problem.

> Harry's boy should have been a mutt, the way his father must once have been, but Benson plays him like a doggy in a pet shop window, always hoping someone will scratch his tummy. All one can say in his defense is that his director makes a similar choice at every significant turn in the film.

Newman does not rage at the dying light; he keeps trying to cuddle up to it.

Vincent Canby in the *New York Times* was similarly unimpressed.

> *Harry and Son* looks like a first effort, partly because the screenplay has no focus and no particular tone of voice. Each of the actors, including Mr. Newman, must create his own character as he goes along, as if furnishing his own wardrobe. One is always aware of actors acting, sometimes quite well, but never for a moment does one become caught up in the film's circumstances.

Soon after completing the film, Newman and Woodward took a penthouse apartment in Manhattan with a breathtaking view of Central Park and a wraparound terrace so their one-year-old terrier, Harry, "would have a private place to poop." The children were grown, and the couple planned to spend three or four days a week in the city. In an interview with *People* magazine at the newly decorated apartment, Newman insisted he never reads reviews: "If they're good, you get a fat head, and if they're bad, you're depressed for three weeks." Clearly someone was reading the disastrous notices, for Newman hurriedly scheduled a clutch of network morning-program appearances for the day *Harry and Son* opened, in a vain attempt to promote some life into the film's distribution. "When he gets angry, he goes to war," said cowriter Buck. "I'm glad he's not taking this lying down."

Newman was definitely not ready to hang up his racing helmet, either, as rumors of the past few seasons had indicated. In 1984 it was reported that Newman had promised his wife he would quit racing after that season. He had just undergone a medical procedure to remove fat from his arteries, indications to the media that the star, who was then nearing sixty, might be slowing down. Budweiser, Newman's major sponsor, was reportedly looking for a new celeb racer and trying to reach the twenty-two-year-old reclusive truck racer John Clark Gable, son of Clark Gable, and Chad McQueen, the Formula-racing son of Steve McQueen. But Newman just couldn't bring himself to retire. "I guess those reports have to be discounted," Newman admitted, even though he had been their primary source. "I'd like to assume the role of elder statesman, taking walks in the woods and going fishing, but here I am, forever strapping myself into these machines."

"Sure, I've thought about quitting," he said. "But when you're not going well, you think 'I can't go out a loser.' And when you're going good, you tell yourself, 'This is no time to stop.' It's a double-edged sword. And now I want to defend my title. But I'll get out of it when I begin looking for a cushion—a cushion of safety. I'll start going slower, and I think I'll know when that time comes." The last time Newman had announced his retirement from racing, Woodward had taken him seriously. "She jumped for joy when she thought she wouldn't have to go to the track every weekend," Newman told *People,* "so when I changed my mind, she said, 'Do what you want, but I've finished my obligations.' In recent years, however, Woodward has not only accepted his racing but has come to enjoy the sport that so captivated her husband. "It's been a comfortable compromise," Newman added.

Too insecure about his driving skills to go by his full name, the movie star was first known on the track simply as P. L. Newman. But Newman had set about conquering racing as he had acting, with persistence, hard work, and intelligence. As good friend and former race driver Sam Posey once said, Newman may "not the greatest racing talent in the world, and, sure he's old to be doing this, but he has this incredible ability to focus, and he memorizes and knows a track inside out before he starts driving, and this makes him a fine driver." Newman also exhibits a determination to win that has sometimes carried him to extremes. Soon after winning a major stock car race driving a 280ZX for the Datsun factory team with his leg taped to the gas pedal because he had broken it several days before while jogging, Newman joked as he hobbled to the winner's circle: "I've gotta give up those dangerous sports like jogging." Though Newman clearly approaches everything in life with the same careful preparation, fierce concentration, and unswerving grit—a defense against his natural pessimism and critical inner voice—the race track allows him to be as competitive as his challenge-loving nature dictates. Acting, which requires the cooperation of a large group of people working as an ensemble, does not allow him that necessary outlet. "When you play a role, you never know if you succeeded or failed on your own, or was it the scriptwriter or the director or the makeup man who was responsible," Newman once explained. "In racing—given that the cars are usually about equal in equipment—it's you against the others behind the wheel, and you win or lose on your own merits."

"It's very hard to be competitive about acting," he said on another occasion, "and I'm a very competitive person. So that's why I like to race cars."

But Newman finds that acting and car racing do have something in common: Both require discipline and dedication, and he acknowledges that he learned both skills slowly. "In almost everything I do, it takes me awhile to get the hang of it." Even after college theater and his year at Yale, "it still took me about four years more to understand what acting was all about." Just as he learned acting from observing classes at the Actors Studio, in racing his model was Mario Andretti, now a close friend and part of the CART team sponsored by Newman and Carl Maas, a race-car owner from Chicago.

Newman's early years as a race driver were not easy. According to veteran driver Willy T. Ribbs in an interview with *The New York Times,* "He crashed a lot, raised a lot of hell because he was trying too hard." Willy added, "Now he's one of the best drivers, and one of the oldest. He drives with a lot of heart." Newman himself admitted, "At first I drove with a balloon foot [putting too little pressure on the accelerator because when he did come down hard, he couldn't control the car], until I learned better. It was a matter of developing experience and confidence and understanding what you can do and what the car can do."

Why this internationally known movie star wanted "so badly" to excel at racing mystifies even Newman himself. "Why? I don't know," he responded in his early racing years. "Who knows what goes on in the subterranean passages in your head. Guys race all their lives and never know why. Sometimes I think that the cars are better than the scripts. It's a joke, but it isn't. I mean, I've only done two movies in five years. The scripts often aren't that great. I've always been very competitive," he explains. "I played bad football, I played bad baseball, and I played bad tennis. I had the suicide crouch in skiing. I was pretty good on skates in hockey, but my stickwork was terrible. I was even a lousy dancer, unless we stayed with the box step.

"I remember being struck by a scene in *Cool Hand Luke.* I was walking down a road and there was this shambling, sticklike creature, and I said, 'My God, that's me!'

"I've thought about those things, and I've realized that the only time I've felt physically graceful was in a race car."

Though Newman was continuing to race full time, he was also campaigning in 1984 for Walter Mondale's bid to unseat Reagan's presidency, whose tenure Newman labeled a "tragedy." In addition, he was overseeing the work of the antidrug Scott Newman Foundation; talking about a *Rachel, Rachel* sequel to be filmed in Central Africa; and deciding how to divvy up the profits of his Newman's Own salad dressing, a business venture he "started as a joke" in 1982, and that quickly threatened to become a lucrative corporation. Joanne Woodward recalled for *Time* magazine that years earlier, at the fancy Hollywood restaurant Chasens—"It was one of our first stylish meals out"—Newman "took an already oiled salad to the men's room, washed it clean, dried it with towels, and returned to the table to do things right, with oil cut by a dash of water." From washing salads in restaurant men's rooms, Newman had progressed to marketing his recipe to local Connecticut gourmet shops, and from there to running a multi-million-dollar food corporation that, like almost every Newman-controlled project, is a family affair.

In 1985, the profits rolling in from his food business, Newman kept an appointment with Catholic Services in New York City, where he presented them with a check for $250,000 for emergency relief in drought-stricken Africa. Dismayed by the giggling crowd of female employees who had got wind of his visit, he whispered to Archbishop John J. O'Connor, "I thought this was supposed to be anonymous." O'Connor replied, "Your life just isn't like that."

Newman and his neighbor, writer A. E. Hotchner, had expanded their gourmet food line and were now producing Industrial Strength spaghetti sauce and Old Style Picture-Show popcorn in addition to their original product, Paul Newman's Own oil-and-vinegar salad dressing. The check to Catholic Relief Services was the largest the company had ever made out, as well as the most sizable corporate donation yet received by the African cause.

In 1985, Newman capitalized on his successful food company by publishing *Newman's Own Cookbook,* a collection of recipes compiled by his daughter Nell (a Joanne Woodward look-alike who races cars like her dad, but whose real interest is falconry) and A. E. Hotchner's daughter, Ursula. The book also includes anecdotes written by Hotchner, a spaghetti duet allegedly sung by Newman and Woodward, a photo of "P. Loquesto" Newman sprinkling salt on a live rooster, plus a sinful dessert recipe contributed by Ina Balin and a shrimp salad recipe concocted by Joan Rivers. All profits from book sales go to charity.

The labels on the Newman's Own food products and the cookbook attest to a sense of humor leaning toward limericks; their occasional raunchiness elicits groans from the Newman daughters and attests to a family tradition of affection with a bite. Since the death of Scott, and the family effort toward creating the food business, Newman has become more free in expressing his affection for his five daughters. The rough spots in their relationships seem to have healed. Eldest daughter Susan speaks with pride of her father: "Everyone tells my father what he cannot do, and he gets joy out of seeing the so-called experts with mud on their faces." But at home Newman doesn't receive the respectful awe he gets in public. Around the house, the man who has been described as Michelangelo's David come to life, goes by the monicker "old skinny legs."

While the food business continued at full throttle, in 1985 Paul Newman turned sixty and buckled himself into his Nissan 300ZX Turbo to fly past the finish line, first in the Sports Club of America's GT-1 national championships in Braselton, Georgia, and winner of the third national title of his career. During that 1985 season, Newman had won five of the fifteen races in which he had competed.

He had now been racing for fourteen years in amateur and professional competitions, racking up "seat time" by racing for five to seven months out of the year, determined, as always, to excel. Since beginning his second career at the age of forty-seven, Newman had totaled approximately fifty victories. As one would expect from this intensely private and modest man, Newman has never played the movie star on the track despite the guards that have to be posted to protect his racing suit and underwear when they are hanging out to dry by his trailer. Driver Jim Fitzgerald once asserted, "I mean, he was never, 'OK, I'm Paul Newman, give me room.' He's someone who genuinely cares about cars and racing, like the rest of us, and really doesn't like to have special attention paid him."

He and teammate Jim Fitzgerald were the doddering old men on the track until Fitzgerald's fatal crash in 1988. When Newman regaled his driving circle with stories about his penchant for practical joking, the fun began on the track. "He used to tell us about the practical jokes he and Robert Redford used to play on one another," said Wally Dallenbach, one of Newman's young driving buddies. "He would say, 'Nobody can beat me at practical jokes.' That's all we needed to hear."

Dallenbach, twenty-three, and another young driver, Chris Kneifel, twenty-five, sent the two senior racers gift certificates to Forest Lawn Cemetery. In June of the following year, Newman hired a plane to trail a banner over the track reading "Chris and Wally, call Mommy." The youngsters retaliated at Elkart Lake, Wisconsin, by filling a bus full of senior citizens sporting "Paul Newman Fan Club" T-shirts and leading them in a grand entrance onto the track, complete with police escort. The joking duel degenerated further with Newman's response—renting space on the younger pair's cars for signs saying "You Gobble." "Feeble," was the judgment of one of the young men. "I think he really is getting senile," they concluded and turned up at the track in Newman's Own olive-oil-and-vinegar salad dressing T-shirts, telling reporters that they had decided to consult for Newman, "at a lucrative fee, of course." "We'll coach him on driving," they added. "And in acting, so that maybe he can get either an Oscar or a Trans-Am win. Both seem to have sadly eluded him." Newman took the jokes with aplomb and played along. "Yes, I've hired them," he agreed. "These kids burn out so fast, I thought maybe I could give them a little something to fall back on—maybe a career in makeup or hair styling." He then proceeded to herd over one hundred fans through the younger drivers' camp, telling them to "touch anything you like." The ever-ready Kneifel greeted Newman, "Glad to see you up from your nap, Paul."

But the last laugh was Newman's, when he pulled into the winner's circle to win his second Trans-Am. As he told *USA Today,* "I suppose this does show that we're not quite ready to collect on our Forest Lawn certificates just yet."

Not all the denizens of the racing car circuit were enamored with their movie-star colleague. One driver, Doug Bethke, had been involved in a collision with Newman in 1983 at the track at Brazelton, Georgia. "He blames me," Bethke told the *New York Post,* "but I blame him. Suddenly, he slowed down more than I would have expected," Bethke alleged, "Of course Newman is mad but I was very much in contention." Bethke added that he and Newman had not talked since the accident. There had also been some grumblings about the advantage of the superior equipment Newman's money can buy, but Peter Slater, vice president of Bob Sharp Racing, the organization for whom Newman races, dismisses the validity of those complaints: "A few guys believed—and may still—that Paul had advantages. And that, 'Hey give me that same equipment and watch me go.' But when Paul was developing as a driver, he was losing with the same equipment that others had. And he's winning with virtually the same. The difference is in the driver."

Though Newman was now squeezing in his film commitments between races and visits to the Danbury, Connecticut, garage to check progress on maintaining and preparing his car for the next season beginning in April 1986, he was also devoting time to prepare for his next role, one worth waiting years for, a sequel to 1961's *The Hustler,* directed by the man to whom he had written a letter of appreciation for *Raging Bull,* Martin Scorsese, America's leading film-maker.

Speaking of his future as he moved into his sixties, Newman explained his increasing selectivity in choosing acting properties. "When you get to be my age, you realize that things are finite. It's like beachfront property. You can only get so many lots out of them, and I never thought I had very far as to how many movies I have left in me. When you are sixty-one, you think about how many movies you've got left." How many did he have left? "Two," was his conservative estimate.

In 1985, Newman and Woodward had been given the Screen Actor's Guild's highest honor—the annual achievement award in recognition for their "outstanding achievements in fostering the highest ideals of the acting profession," a reference not only to their work on the screen, but to their humanitarian works and political activism as well. For almost his entire adult life Newman had been involved: He'd been a longtime opponent of the nuclear arms buildup; a leader of PRO-Peace, the antinuke organization that planned a cross-country march for 1986; a vociferous foe of deregulation of natural gas; a champion of civil rights; a Democratic national delegate in 1968; a civilian delegate to the United Nation's special sessions on disarmament; and had devoted time and energy to innumerable other causes. Even the normally apolitical Woodward had become involved in the first national women's conference to prevent nuclear war.

In 1986 Newman was awarded an honorary Oscar "in recognition of his many memorable and compelling screen performances and for his personal integrity and dedication to his craft" in three decades of work. But the real recognition he craved from his peers—an Academy Award for the Best Actor of the Year for a specific role in a specific film—still eluded him. Accepting the lifetime achievement award via satellite in Chicago, where he was working on *The Color of Money* set, Newman thanked the Academy with typical equanimity. Recalling the practical joke played on him by his young track mates, he said, "I'm grateful this didn't come wrapped in a gift certificate to Forest Lawn." He continued, "Spencer Tracy, so the legend goes, was accosted by a young man who said, 'I'm going to be an actor.' To which he replied, 'That's terrific. Just don't let 'em catch you at it.'

"I don't know where I am on the learning curve," he added in a sly reference to the prematurity of the award, "but tonight has provided a lot of encouragement . . . my best work is down the pike."

According to his peers, official recognition was long overdue. "Paul is an actor who has more than made the most of his equipment," stated Martin Ritt, director of *Hud, Hombre,* and *The Long, Hot Summer.* "He's gotten better and better and better. There's a hell of a lot more to him than blue eyes."

"When I first met Paul, he was a very good-looking young man with those incredible baby blues," said Sydney Pollack. "A promising actor. But he was nowhere near the actor then that he is now. And that's come from commitment." Pollack labeled the award "well deserved. He's one of the nicest, most decent, best guys in the business."

Newman now had an Oscar perching on the mantelpiece alongside the one his wife had won years ago for *Three Faces of Eve,* but the award was clearly a look backward rather than forward to future successes, and the occasion must have given Newman pause to rethink his earlier esti-

mates of how much he did in fact have left in him. According to his friend and lawyer Irving I. Axelrad, he almost
refused the honor. "He said they'd always treated him as
second," Axelrad told Maureen Dowd in *The Times*, "and
now they were acting as if he was old and through." In
interviews he labeled the award "premature. I'd like to win
an award, I think, in my seventy-third year. Just so I could
get up there and say, 'Well, it's taken a long time.'" On
another occasion, he assured the public, "There's plenty of
mustard in this guy yet. Still, you don't kick people in the
butt who are trying to be nice to you." Newman would
have preferred the honor "for a specific piece of work."
The following year, his preference would be honored.

Paul was not the only Newman to have come into his
own in the past few years. Now that the children had flown
the nest and the parents had settled in their new Manhattan
penthouse, Joanne Woodward was enjoying her revitalized
career, working only when she liked in projects she liked,
with whom she liked. In 1981 she had starred in a production of George Bernard Shaw's *Candida* at the nonprofit
Circle in the Square off-Broadway theater, where she
serves on the board of directors. Directed by Michael
Cristofer, the actor and playwright who'd won a Pulitzer
Prize for *The Shadow Box*, the *Candida* production had
originated under Woodward's aegis and played the Kenyon
Festival Theater in Ohio in early summer. In New York it
enjoyed a limited run, from October 15 through November
22. "My husband was the one who got us all moving,"
Woodward told *The New York Times*. "Paul said, 'You've
got to do it in New York. It's the best Shavian production
I've seen.' I said, 'How many have you seen?'"

As ambivalent about stardom as her husband, Woodward
still chafed at being labeled the wife of a movie star, and
she described her marriage to Newman as "a tough fight. It
took many years of analysts, searching, finally getting out

and doing my own thinking," she told the *Daily News*. "I mean, from most people I still get, 'Oh my God, you're Paul Newman's wife, aren't you?'" Yet she was glad that, unlike her husband, she could shop at the supermarket without being descended upon by hordes of fans. "It must really be sad to be someone like Elizabeth Taylor, who hasn't been in a supermarket in ten years. I couldn't stand that. I do all my own shopping, and I have nothing to worry about whenever I go out in public."

Woodward recalled for *The New York Times* that

> initially, I probably had a real movie-star dream. It faded somewhere in my mid-thirties, when I realized I wasn't going to be that kind of actor. It was painful. Also, I curtailed my career because of my children. Quite a bit. I resented it at the time, which was not a good way to be around the children. Paul was away on location a lot. I wouldn't go on location because of the children. I did once, and felt overwhelmed with guilt.

In the late spring of 1985, Woodward starred in what she vowed "is probably the last movie I will ever do," playing a woman with Alzheimer's Disease in *Do You Remember Love*. In the May 21 *Family Circle* magazine, Woodward revealed that her mother is a victim of the disease. "They didn't make any real attempt to diagnose her. She is eighty-two now, and the doctors say that all the symptoms suggest Alzheimer's. The sadness to me is that had I realized the possibility of this disease, I could have reacted to her behavior in a different way." One of Woodward's reasons for doing the project was to call attention to the disease and its symptoms. The depressing effect the project had on her was clear—hence all the threats to retire from her acting career. "The older you get, the more you realize that life is, after all, finite. And that you should get on with doing the things you care about. I like the perspective that maturity gives me . . . I would hardly call it retirement, but I have no strong career ambitions. Before the age of forty-five, my life was a disaster," Woodward concluded. "I'm the only person I know who enjoys growing old." At the close of 1986, Paul Newman and Joanne Woodward celebrated growing old together on their twenty-eighth wedding anniversary. Their homes in Westport and Manhattan were filled with quiet dinners at home or with friends. Their daily lives were filled with his politics, the food business and the charities it supported, car racing, and her ballet, horseback riding, and needlepoint. Despite their gloomy predictions for their acting and directing careers, they continued to look for worthy projects on which to collaborate.

Around this time, Newman broke ground in Ashford, Connecticut, on a three-hundred-acre camp for seriously or terminally ill children. The idea for the camp generated from the many requests for individual help the food company had received, as well as from Newman's loss of both parents and several friends to cancer. The camp accommodates approximately three hundred children, from ages seven to seventeen, with Yale New Haven Hospital running the on-site hospital in cooperation with other area hospitals. "The whole foundation is basically a network of people working together," Newman said. And included in that network are some of the Newman daughters, notably the eldest, Susan, who said, "This project has been a sort of bonding. It has made him more aware of my capabilities, and I'm like any other kid who's looking for approval from her parents."

"From salad dressings all blessings flow," half-joked Newman at the ceremony, whose Newman's Own company had raised nine million dollars for charities, of which four million would go toward the camp's eight-million-dollar costs. The other four had to be matched by private charitable donations in order to comply with IRS regulations. One gift made in 1987 was by a twenty-five-year-old Saudi, Khaled Alhegelan, who suffers from thalassemia, an inherited chronic anemia that requires him to be hospitalized for blood transfusions every three weeks. When Alhegelan learned about the Hole in the Wall Gang Summer Camp (named after the gang Newman and Redford led in *Butch Cassidy and the Sundance Kid,* and modeled on an Old West town complete with log cabins, music halls, corrals, canoes, and a frontier-styled hospital, with no fee charged to the campers), he immediately got in touch with Newman and made plans to visit him. "We talked together for two hours," the young Arab recalled, "and he told me he appreciated hearing what it was like growing up with a disease which could kill me. I told him kids give up if they have nothing to look forward to but hospitals and that his idea of a camp would put vitality into children's lives. I know it because I have lived through it." Mr. Alhegelan, the son of a diplomat, made an appointment with the king of Saudi Arabia and persuaded his government to make a five-million-dollar contribution.

"It's ironic that the motivation for this would come from something as tacky as the food business," Newman joked with typical self-deprecating modesty. "I am actively hustling," he further admitted. "This is a dream being fulfilled." But his wife was unabashedly proud: "This was the best idea he's had in a long time," she asserted. "And he's had many." According to A. E. Hotchner, "I've never seen Paul as dedicated to an idea as he is to this. For him, it has really been a dream."

In the midst of all this worthwhile activity, there had to be a note of absurdity. In 1986, the *New York Post* was able to sell a record number of papers over what would otherwise have been a "slow news year" with a series of pieces on the controversial issue of Newman's height. In response to their promise to pay one thousand dollars for every inch Newman measured over five feet, eight inches, Newman challenged the paper to put real money where their headlines were. The paper then published a copy of the letter Newman sent them, putting in writing his accusation that "you guys turned chicken when it got to the big time." On television's *Live at Five,* the man who thought little of sawing a friend's expensive sports car in half and then paying for the replacement, told Liz Smith that he wanted to up the ante offered by the *Post.* "For a newspaper that loses ten million a year, a thousand-dollar bet is irrelevant," he told viewers. "I'll write a check to the *New York Post* for a half-million dollars. If they are wrong, though, then it's time to start playing some hardball. It's not one thousand an inch. It's one hundred thousand an inch, or one hundred twenty-five thousand a quarter-inch for anything above five feet, eight inches.

"These guys threw down the gauntlet, but it has the moral force of a powder puff," Newman added, when the paper refused to up the ante beyond the original one-thousand-dollar bet.

The tabloid also dug up people who claimed to have stood next to Newman and who insisted his height could not exceed the *Post*'s estimate. Not to be outscooped, the *Star* found an extra who claimed she'd worked with Newman in the early sixties. According to Sandi Burton,

> I and another girl posed next to him in promotional pictures for *A New Kind of Love,* which he made with his wife, Joanne Woodward.
>
> "I stood right next to him and distinctly remember looking down—much to my surprise. I was five feet, nine inches then—and still am—so there's no way Paul could be anywhere near five feet, eleven inches. Unless you grew some after your forties. Pay up, Paul!

Half a year later, on March 7, 1987, the *Post* wrote,

> Fanciers of devastating repartee may recall an extended dis-
> cussion the *Post* had last fall with Paul Newman concerning
> his height. The star is officially purported to stand five feet,
> eleven inches. We—while never actually suggesting that he
> sue the city for building the sidewalks too close to his der-
> riere—took the view that Paul really measured more like
> five feet, eight inches.

The paper then went on to protest that they attempted,
in vain, to invoke a moratorium on the subject, but the
burning issue had spread even as far as Europe, where the
Mail, a British equivalent to the *Post,* hit upon an ingenious
plan so impressive that its machinations were also published in an Italian paper, *Oggi.* The *Mail* put a crack po-
licewoman, an expert in body measure, to work on a
photograph of Newman strolling down a London street.
Using an intricate trigonometric formula, she arrived at the
conclusion that Paul Newman stands five feet, seven inches
tall.

More interesting than how tall or short Newman stood was the stature of his acting career. His next film performance, a brilliant turn rivaling his work in *The Verdict,* proved unequivocally that Newman had many more than two films left in him. He was only just entering his prime. *The Color of Money* would earn him his seventh Best Acting Oscar nomination, and at long last carry him to the finish line. Newman was a longtime admirer of maverick director Martin Scorsese, and had called *Raging Bull* "the best movie I've seen in a long, long time," with a leading role he would have liked to have played himself.

Scorsese is well known for his empathy with actors and his method of working with them as a collaborator, even sharing with them the emotions of their characters. It was Newman's call to Scorsese in September 1984 that initiated the project. Scorsese was in London, where he was resting after shooting *After Hours*. "When I first spoke to Newman on the phone, he said, 'Eddie Felson,'" Scorsese told *American Film* magazine. "I said, 'I love that character.' He said, 'Eddie Felson reminds me of the characters you've dealt with in your pictures and I thought more ought to be heard from him.'"

Newman still felt a personal connection to Fast Eddie Felson. As with Hud, his usual painstaking research had not been needed to unlock the character. "Ultimately it became a very personal feeling about the character," he said. Eddie was another familiar alter ego, a shadow side of Newman's own noble character.

The notion of a sequel to 1961's *The Hustler* had been in development for about a year before Scorsese was brought in, initiated when writer Walter Tevis showed producer Irving Axelrad an early manuscript of the sequel to his original novel. Axelrad showed the manuscript to Newman. "I had wanted to do the project as soon as I read Walter Tevis's new book," Newman told the *Times*.

> It reminded me that Eddie wasn't completed at the end of the first film like some other people I had played. Now Butch Cassidy was *seriously* completed. But Eddie's life wasn't. And I began wondering what he would be doing now. Eddie's thrust in life was taken away from him at the end of *The Hustler*. The character was left uncompleted. He left the tournament knowing that his skill for his occupation would never be tapped because he was being forced away from playing. We knew if we picked him up twenty-five years later, he'd still be hustling, and the situation was rich with dramatic possibilities.

While Scorsese liked Tevis's sequel, he thought the character of Eddie had become dull. Rather than make a sequel to *The Hustler*, Scorsese preferred to build a whole new story around the same character twenty-five years later. "We wanted this movie to stand on its own," said Scorsese. "The movie's only link to *The Hustler* is the character of Felson. He's no longer a pool player. He's now on the outside of the game looking in and with a whole new perspective.

."*The Color of Money* is about a man who goes on a journey toward self-awareness. It concerns a man who changes his ways of living, changes his values. The arena happens to be pool, but it could be anything else. The movie is about a deception and then a clarity, a perversion and then a purity."

As a man whose considerable gifts are equal only to his talent for self-destruction, Fast Eddie is a prototypical part of Scorsese's bleak gallery of anti-heros who characteristically *do not* redeem themselves at the last minute—although in *The Color of Money,* Newman's influence did give us a final moment of awakening. Scorsese's notion was to show us a mature Eddie who has "turned into everything he hates—a slick guy." He meets with a younger version of himself and feels compelled to corrupt him. "But then," Scorsese notes, "at a certain point, the two roles cross."

Richard Price, a novelist who had been working on another project with Scorsese, was asked to write the screenplay. At the initial meeting, the three men seemed, stylistically at least, to be worlds apart. Price described himself and Scorsese to the *Times* as

> the two New York guys on the beach. Marty's sitting there with his jacket and his nasal spray and I was smoking a cigarette, hunched over coughing. And then Newman comes out, all tanned up, Mister Sea and Ski, eating a grapefruit. It was the two New York clowns with the Hollywood platinum.

"We kind of hammered together a plot line that day," Newman recalled, "and we committed to it." That was the first of a lengthy series of brainstorming sessions held in restaurants, apartments, and offices across the country, during which, according to Price, "We not only went over every word. We went over every punctuation mark."

Price would write, Scorsese would look at Price's work and make suggestions, then Newman would read it and offer his ideas, and the process would begin again. One early draft called for Newman to shoot pool nude, Richard Price told *USA Today*. But Newman refused, "saying 'You don't want to see a sixty-year-old man nude.'"

Despite Price's rather fanciful description of the gulf in life-style that separated the scruffy New Yorkers from the Hollywood movie star, the collaboration was one of Newman's most enjoyable. "There was a feeling of camaraderie about this film that was very special," said Newman. "There was a sense of generosity and selflessness on the part of all the people connected with it; an enthusiasm to try new things, to not be stifled by preconceived ideas."

One reason the project was so satisfying to Newman was that Scorsese instructed Price to write specifically for the actor, who had the final say. "I told Richard, 'We're making a suit for the man—in a way,'" he recalled for *The New York Times*. "'The words you're writing have to come through Paul Newman's lips. So if at times you write stuff and we hear him say it and it doesn't sound right, we have to change your stuff.'" According to Price, he and Scorsese pushed to make the character meaner, while Newman was constantly pulling to humanize Eddie. Newman "loves playing the antihero . . . the Outrider, but the Outrider that you just can't bring yourself to hate," Price theorized. "You see, Marty and I like mean things—the meaner the better because the greater the shaft of light in the end. And while Newman wanted to explore aging in this, his forty-fifth screen role—the fear of losing it—he just thought the character was too hard."

"Sometimes Newman would say, 'Guys, I think we're missing an opportunity here.' And the minute I heard that I would groan, 'Oh no, here we go again.' Unfortunately, he was rarely wrong. But there were points when I thought, if I hear 'we're missing an opportunity' one more time, you're going to be missing a writer."

"Remarkable meetings," was Scorsese's terse description to *American Film*. "Four o'clock. 'Why does this guy have to play pool, anyhow?' Paul says, 'Guys, I don't know, I have to go race, so I'll see you in about a million years.' He'd come back with a big steel bowl of popcorn," was Price's half-joking description.

In its final form, *The Color of Money* picks up the character of Eddie Felson some twenty-five years of hustling later. Disillusioned and cynical, Eddie learned a bitter lesson over two decades ago when he beat Minnesota Fats and won a lifetime blackball from the game. He has permanently hung up his cue stick. Now in his sixties, Eddie is still touring the dives of the American underworld, this time as the owner of a lucrative liquor distributorship, traveling in a shiny white Caddy, dressed in a cashmere coat, and flashing a diamond ring. Eddie keeps a hand in the game by playing stake horse on the side to a stable of promising young pool hustlers, but as the movie eventually reveals, a few embers of his former passion for the pool hustle still glow deep within what is left of Eddie's heart. The sight of a talented nine baller, Vince Laura, a "natural character" who in his cocky innocence aims to be the best, provokes Eddie's remark, "It's like watching a home movie." Eddie stakes the flamboyant young showboater to a big nine-ball tournament in Atlantic City for 60 percent of his winnings. Eddie, Vince, and Vince's tough, sexy girlfriend, played by Mary Elizabeth Mastrantonio, form a business partnership and set off on an odyssey of initiation into pool sharkdom that is, for Eddie, a voyage into his past, through the sleazy halls that mark the route between Chicago and Atlantic City. The cocky young protegé balks initially at throwing an occasional game to up the hustle because he loves to show what he can do. But Vince gradually takes to his master's lessons in "human character," which translate as instruction in the fine arts of cheating and manipulation. "It ain't about pool . . . it's about money," Eddie tells the boy.

But it's Eddie who has the real lesson to learn. Watching Vince's joy in the game fans those dying embers into a full-out passion for the game. Eddie's instinct for competition returns, and he undergoes a moral rejuvenation. He wants to play for the sheer beauty of the game. He realizes he has become a slightly more palatable version of the George C. Scott character who corrupted him so many years ago. *"The Color of Money* is about rediscovering what makes you happy," Newman said. "Felson has been compromising all his life and has become the very thing that he hated. In the final analysis, that's what he liberates himself from."

The sucker games climax with a *mano a mano* confrontation at the table between the mentor and his protegé. This time Eddie comes out the winner in an upbeat, ending-at-a-new-beginning finale that did not sit well with many critics, who praised the rest of the film for the complexity of the relationships.

As with Newman's next project, a collaboration with his wife on *The Glass Menagerie,* the Tennessee Williams play in which they had both performed as novice actors on the brink of their careers, *The Color of Money* carried with it the satisfying extratextual meaning that the Paul Newman cannon had arrived at the zenith of a full circle. There's a noticeable shock in the audience when Tom Cruise calls Fast Eddie, who was not *that* long ago the quintessential

young man on the make, "Gramps." He may have resented
the confusion of his screen image with his real self, but how
could Paul Newman not have relished meeting his cinematic doppelgängger once more? It was as if Eddie had
been living and aging alongside Newman these twenty-five
years—an invisible but almost palpable twin, the "bad
brother." Playing Eddie once again gave the actor a chance
to "comment" on his earlier performance, as well as an
opportunity to see how much his craft had matured over
those long years.

Newman often criticizes his early efforts, for the actor's
cardinal sin of "demonstrating"—showing the audience
what he wants to convey instead of simply being the character and *allowing* that to show. To illustrate his point, Newman told a typically Newmanesque bawdy joke to a
Newsweek interviewer. "There's an old bull and a young
bull and they're walking together on a ridge. Down below
there's a herd of cows. The young bull says, 'Let's run
down and jump one of them cows!' 'Naw,' says the old
bull. 'Let's *walk* down and jump 'em all.'"

An older, wiser, more confident Newman simply didn't
need to push as hard. His newfound restraint, more subtly
suggestive than a pull-out-the-stops operatic display of
emotion, took him infinitely further than his earlier Academy Award–nominated performance in *The Hustler*. Newman could indeed thumb his nose at the Academy that had
pronounced his career on the wane with that lifetime
achievement Oscar they'd given him the year before.

The Color of Money was rewarding for Newman for another reason as well. Not only did he reacquaint himself
with Eddie Felson, but he found in Tom Cruise a new
friend, one with whom he would enjoy the closeness he had
hoped for but had achieved only sporadically with his son.
Scorsese had wanted an ethnic actor for the role of Vince,
and Vincent Spano, who'd starred in *Creator* and *Alphabet*

City, was almost given the part. Newman had met Cruise when he read for *Harry and Son;* Cruise was then too young for the role. Scorsese had shared a pizza one sunny California day in 1983 with Cruise; he'd been favorably impressed with his performance in *All the Right Moves,* and when Newman brought up Cruise's name in one of their writing sessions, his desire to work with the young actor won out. Even with Newman playing the leading role and the involvement of this hot new star, the project still went in search of financing, wandering from Fox to Columbia. It finally found a home at Disney's Touchstone Pictures, astute enough to see that the pairing of these box-office giants with over a generation separating them had great appeal, enough to make them cover boys for the November, 1986 *Life* magazine.

Cruise called his costar "Mister Newman" for the first month. Despite this formal address, Cruise was able to overcome much of his awe during the two-week rehearsal period, and the two men formed a close relationship. A. E. Hotchner described the relationship to *US:* "They are genuinely fond of each other. They had a wonderful time working together, and it's patently the cliché thing of the father and son. That really was what underscored the movie relationship, and it's become quite like that. They have a nice, jokey, kind of rapport, and I think it's one of those good, solid exchanges that's going to go on."

There is a trace of paternal pride in Newman's insistence that Cruise quickly became a better pool hustler than Newman, who wields a mean stick himself. When Newman made *The Hustler,* he said on TV's "Today Show," "I had a pool table in my dining room about four months before we started shooting. . . . And Cruise had a pool cue in his hand for about three weeks before we started shooting this film. And by the time we started shooting, he was better in three weeks than I was in four months. He's a gifted athlete and he's got wonderful coordination. Surprised a lot of people, including the hustlers.''

Cruise described Newman to *US* as

> very easy. Very down-to-earth. Really open. We would go over and eat at his place; he'd cook. We all got so fat— oh, yeah, I had to eat his salad dressing. He says, 'You gotta put a little mustard in it.' I would go over to his trailer, and we would have lunch every day, dinner every night. It was like this family working together. Gained about a hundred pounds. We had a blast. He is an extremely bright man, very eloquent, gracious, generous, knows how to tell a good joke.

During the shooting of the film Newman celebrated his sixty-first birthday with a noisy party hosted by the producers. Cruise presented his friend with a garter belt and bra from a sex shop, one of the many jokes, of the type generally preferred by pimply faced boys, that were traded between the two.

But for all the fun the work was intense and serious. Scorsese created a creative conspiracy on the set, an environment in which the actors felt safe enough to expose themselves without risk of embarrassment. Like Newman, Scorsese always insists on a substantial rehearsal period before the cameras roll. In this case, "the most preplanned film I had ever made," Scorsese told *American Film*, "the writing sessions eventually took on the aspect of rehearsals."

Nevertheless, while rehearsing for *The Color of Money* Newman found time to take care of his many interests, particularly his food company that just kept expanding even though Newman and company persisted in treating it like a good joke. When the company introduced Newman's Own Oldstyle Picture Show microwave popcorn, he delivered a mock spiel extolling the virtues of this latest product. "The good news is our microwave contains an aphrodisiac," sang a sailor-suited chorus at the press conference Newman and Hotchner called at Hanratty's, an East Side pub. "This is so tacky," Newman shuddered on the sidelines as he sipped a beer with his partner, but he forged ahead anyway. "In 1952, we had microwave popcorn," lectured Newman, pointing to mock drawings of various corn-popping machinery through the ages. "What we didn't have was an oven— we had to find the machinery." Among the defective machinery Newman demonstrated were the Ford ("It could not add butter and salt at the same time") and the Reagan ("It only works three hours a day").

In addition to his filming and food-business chores, Newman always found time for car racing. In August 1986, prior to *The Color of Money*'s Christmas release and before beginning production on a new film version of Tennessee Williams's *The Glass Menagerie,* the sixty-one-year-old Newman won an eleven-thousand-dollar purse for his second 100.98-mile Bendix Trans-Am at Lime Rock in his home state of Connecticut. Typically self-effacing, Newman labeled his win an "inherited victory," because the two front-running cars had been forced to drop out. "Clint Eastwood wouldn't have done it this way," Newman responded to a comment from a *USA Today* reporter that his win was "a made-to-order role for Paul Newman." But his cohorts at the track thought differently. "He's paid his dues," said driver Les Lindley.

"He's here to race, which is a lot different than some other celebrities, who are out there just getting in everybody's way," commented last year's winner and the frequent butt of Newman's practical jokes, Wally Dallenbach, Jr.

By early fall, near the close of the racing season, the first screening of *The Color of Money* was celebrated by a benefit party at Manhattan's Palladium, for Newman's beloved alma mater, the Actors Studio. One thousand two hundred guests, among them Helen Shaver, Mary Elizabeth Mastrantonio, Martin Scorsese, Ellen Burstyn, Emilio Estevez, Mariel Hemingway, Jennifer Beals, Aidan Quinn, Danny DeVito, Bianca Jagger, Shelley Winters, Michael Douglas, Calvin Klein, and Gay Talese jammed the chic night spot that had been done up for the occasion to look like a New York pool hall. Guests received chits to play roulette, blackjack and craps, and if they were lucky, won *Color of Money* sweatshirts, suspenders, and pool cues. Decked out uncharacteristically in a blue suit and red tie, Newman greeted Tom Cruise's grand entrance in plaid suit and gray cowboy boots with a whistle and a "Nice boots, cowboy."

A week later, Newman went down to Georgia for the October 19 Valvoline Road Racing Classic, where he was joined by Cruise and his girlfriend, Mimi Rogers. They'd sent Newman a good luck floral arrangement with a card reading, "These are for your garden. Go get them. Love, Tom and Mimi." Encouraged by Newman, Cruise took a one-day driving seminar at the Chestnut Mountain, Georgia, racetrack, with Newman's Nissan teammate and Road Atlanta's chief driving instructor, Jim Fitzgerald. Newman also rented a half-mile track to do a little coaching himself. "He took me out and spent a lot of time talking about it," Cruise recalled for *US*. "I've always loved cars and motorcycles and stuff. Racing is one thing I said that I wanted him to get me into." According to the proud Newman, Cruise has "star status. He just likes to race. He sees it as a lot of fun." Janet Upchurch, operations manager for Road Atlanta, told *USA Today,* "As far as Tom is concerned, he shows a lot of ability and potential as a racer. He's a smart young man and we're hoping he gets into road racing. He seems to enjoy it very much."

"I hope he continues," Newman said, clearly seeing something of himself in his young friend. "He's a good athlete, and I think actors need something besides acting as a release. Acting isn't competitive—it can't be competitive! You need another release if you're a competitive person."

Cruise has continued to race. He entered his first pro race with Newman in 1987, at Road Atlanta. The actors had hoped to race without drawing undue attention to themselves, but the local publicist preferred to ignore Newman's statement that "We're here as racers, not actors."

"The biggest names in entertainment have taken the challenge!" screamed a local ad for the event. One driver with a sense of humor posted a sign: "See Tom Cruise: $.50. Paul Newman: $1. Tammy Faye Bakker: $4.5 million. Tax deductible."

Despite the silliness, Newman finished seventh out of a field of forty-four entries in the feature event, the 300-kilometer Road Atlanta Kuppenheimer Camel GT Challenge, and won a purse of four thousand dollars. During practice Cruise had bounced off a railing, forcing him to borrow another Nissan 300ZX from a driving school so he could compete in a three-hour endurance race against forty-three other drivers. Despite a few mishaps, Cruise was cheered on by Newman and Mimi Rogers, now Cruise's bride of two months, as he and his teammate came in fourteenth.

Though Newman's friendship with Cruise may have started as a kind of substitute for Newman's deceased son, the camaraderie was also based on simple compatibility. These two men would have become close friends no matter what their relative ages. "I've been around the two of them together," Jim Fitzgerald said. "I don't know whether a father-son relationship would be like this. It's more professional, though. It's a friendship."

But Newman does seem to see his youthful self in Cruise, and he attributes to the younger man talents and abilities he has denied possessing himself. When asked about Cruise's potential for a lasting career, Newman answered with the formula for his own enduring success—hard work and perseverance: "I don't see why he can't last. He obviously has the motivation and the ability. You have to be able to keep the glitz in perspective, and that's tough to do at twenty-two. He does a good job of that. If he continues to work hard, I don't see why not."

Newman's next film project, *The Glass Menagerie,* was undertaken almost solely for the purpose of preserving a Long Wharf Theater production of Tennessee Williams's first and most produced play. It had been hailed as the advent of a new genre, the poetic memory play, when it premiered in a landmark production on Broadway in 1945 and is considered by many to be his finest work. Despite several attempts, *The Glass Menagerie* had yet to receive its definitive treatment on the screen. It had won for the young playwright a Tony and a Pulitzer Award. For its hitherto unknown author, the work was a case of "emotion recollected in tranquillity." The characters of Amanda, Laura, and Tom were based on Williams's mother, a faded southern belle who tried to live out her dreams through her frail daughter; his sister, Rose, who eventually succumbed to mental illness; and Tennessee himself, who had undergone a struggle similar to his leading character's in order to break free of his mother's entangled web of half-truths and fantasies. In 1950, Hollywood attempted a disastrous adaptation starring the wonderful Gertrude Lawrence—who was more at home in a Noel Coward drawing room—Kirk Douglas, Jane Wyman, and Arthur Kennedy. Williams complained that the production "opened up" the play needlessly with a scene of Laura at the typing school, and that it tacked on a typically happy ending. In general, he thought, it cheapened his work. A more reasonable television production aired in 1973, starring Katharine Hepburn,

Michael Moriarity, Sam Waterston, and Joanna Miles. But of all the screen adaptations of his plays, Williams approved only of the film version of *The Roman Spring of Mrs. Stone,* starring Katharine Hepburn and Warren Beatty.

The challenge of coming up with a film adaptation worthy of this American theater classic had to be at least part of the project's appeal. Newman would be the first director to do Williams's play justice. Everyone involved was united in their desire not only to preserve a fine theatrical production, but to remain faithful to the letter and spirit of the text. Newman had initially been reluctant to take on filming the production originally mounted at the Williamstown and Long Wharf theaters in 1982 by Nikos Psacharopoulos. "I said no because I wasn't sure I could bring anything to the piece," he admitted. When he realized it would not get backing without his name, he agreed, thinking of his role as that of an archivist. Though Newman did not dwell on the point, it was clear that this attempt "to give the best rendering of a Tennessee work ever put on film," was almost an act of atonement for the Newman who had twice found himself in movies (*Cat on a Hot Tin Roof* and *Sweet Bird of Youth*) that had performed a fair degree of butchery on Williams's original work. Newman also felt that the truth of the play, its complex and vivid emotions, countered the dangerous state of narcolepsy that seemed to him to be paralyzing modern society.

Admittedly the project was hardly a shoo-in for commercial success, but Newman was unconcerned. "Obviously a good deal of it is dated, but, hell, that's its charm. I never even had a screenplay. I just took the play as Tennessee Williams wrote it. I've added some stuff to it." But Newman was careful to avoid the mistakes of the 1950 film version, which "considerably altered [the play] with significant additions and subtractions." Newman joked that his role of director was limited to serving "popcorn every day at four o'clock." He did add, however, that "the contribution of the actors had to find its own focus. My job was to keep the integrity of the actors' intentions, bring them from the six-teenth row into the proximity of the camera. It's not a quick process, but the actors came down from the moun-taintop quite peacefully, and without complaint."

Despite the restriction of the action to one cramped set and the abandonment of his initial plan to use some outside shots, Newman felt the play could translate more easily to the screen than Williams's other works. "*The Glass Menag-erie* is Tennessee's most filmable play, even though it is re-stricted cinematically to an apartment in St. Louis during the Depression," said Newman. "*The Glass Menagerie* has language that is more speakable for actors and is less de-signed for the stage than his other plays."

Filming *The Glass Menagerie* was a project fraught with memories for Newman. Not only had he and Joanne sepa-rately performed in it in regional theaters, but Newman's first audition in New York had been in the same studio they were now rehearsing and filming in, the Astoria Studios in Queens. "When I came to New York in the summer of '52," he recalled for *USA Weekend,* "the first job I applied for was here. I didn't get it."

Woodward had played Laura, but making the transfer from the stage to a soundstage was not easy. "Working in films was always a difficult thing for me—it still is," she told *Show* magazine. "And it's probably one of the reasons I don't do them very often. I love being onstage," she con-tinued. "It's where I started as a kid." For the role of the overbearing yet touching mother, Woodward drew upon some of her own aunts' and her mother's mannerisms, as she had for *Do You Remember Love.* She recalled for *Show* magazine that the parallel was not too farfetched. "When Tennessee met my mother years ago, he came over to me and said, 'Joanne, if I didn't know I'd written this play about my mama, I would've thought I'd written it about yours.'" Having played Amanda twice onstage over the previous two years and now on film, she added, "Amanda is much closer to me now than when I first played her at Williamstown. In a way, she *is* me. We are both from the South and I understand her. She is a real survivor in a matriarchal society."

For three weeks before the start of principal photography, the actors rehearsed with Newman on the empty soundstage. "The scenes were blocked out with tape on the floor," said production manager Joseph Caracciolo, "and the actors improvised the furniture." Immediately after the rehearsal period (during which workers constructed a set designed by Tony Walton), Newman broke away long enough to win his fourth national car-racing title.

For the shoot, Newman characteristically supported himself and his cast (Karen Allen, John Malkovich, and James Naughton) with a fine crew. Cinematographer Michale Balhaus, who was director of photography on fifteen of Rainer Werner Fassbinder's films, including *The Marriage of Maria Braun*, had connections of his own to the play, though his were more familial. Raised in a small acting troupe in Germany, he had seen over twenty-five productions of *The Glass Menagerie*. "My mother has played Amanda and my wife played Laura," he said with a laugh.

A reporter from *USA Weekend* visited the set and described the fabled Newman concentration at work on directing a dance scene:

> Newman has the scene redone five times, though it will constitute about ten seconds of screen time. "Let's slow down, guys," he tells the crew. "We're relying too much on the technological stuff. It's the actors that hold me up"— make his directing look good. Later, viewing the scene with

the editor, he explains why he bucks yet another Hollywood trend that says keep it moving. "My instinct is to let that silence sit like a painting."

Well prepared by the three weeks of rehearsals and allowed the luxury of filming the action in sequence, the cast had little trouble with the ten-hour workdays. Newman gave his actors a good deal of freedom to move around inside their characters and then gently assisted them in chiseling away the excess to allow the final performance to emerge. He also instructed Balhaus to film in long takes, to allow the actors to set the film's rhythm rather than relying on short takes and fast cutting, and he asked for many close-ups in order to bring the audience out of the set right into the characters' thoughts and emotions. "It's great to be directed by him," enthused Malkovich. "He's so supportive. He knows so much about film acting. And he's also very open and smart." Karen Allen concurred. "I've been just as happy as I can be while working with Paul. He's such a joy. He knows what tasks are difficult for actors to do, and he is always protecting us by making these things less difficult. Paul holds everyone together, and grants us the luxury of allowing us to do two or three takes in a row. . . . I think I did my best work on Laura in the film because of the rehearsal period and then having it shot in sequence."

The cast reported that filming was a lot of fun despite the notable drop in the Newman practical-joke quotient at the request of Woodward, who prefers a bit more seriousness on the set. "We shot a lot of pool," said James Naughton, who plays the Gentleman Caller and who lives "down the road" from the Newmans in Westport. He added that Newman is a "generous and patient" director. "We went to a race in Miami to see Mario Andretti. We took a jet, a helicopter and a golf cart—all in one day." Naughton said of the Newman concentration, "Whether he's driving, or fishing, or directing, there's that commitment that's noticeable and terrific."

Newman did play one practical joke, but he had a serious point to make. John Malkovich had arrived late on the set the first day of the shoot. "They were fine about it," he reported, "But when we wrapped, Paul had bought about eighteen alarm clocks, all of which went off. So I said, 'You realize that if I'm late tomorrow because the car didn't pick me up—you've set a precedent here. You'll have to buy me a Lotus or something.' He said, 'Try me.' But I didn't."

In February of 1987, while Newman was editing *The Glass Menagerie,* newspapers carried a report that he had refused a White House request to tape a public-service announcement with Nancy Reagan about drug abuse, despite his active work in that area since his son's death. Rumors flew that a reliable source had told the producer of the spot, Jerry Weintraub, that Newman had declined because of his disagreement with the Reagan administration policies. Warren Cowan, Newman's press agent, maintained that his busy schedule had been the deciding factor: "He just couldn't find the time."

Newman was busy. He was putting in overtime at the editing table, polishing his production so that it would be ready for viewing by the Cannes Film Festival screening committee well before it began in May. He was so busy, in fact, that for the first time Newman did not appear at an Academy Awards ceremony in which he was a nominee— this time for *The Color of Money*—despite the fact that he was the odds-on favorite to win. Janet Maslin in *The New York Times* rhapsodized,

> Mr. Newman, during the course of his career, has progressed from the brash, sexy confidence that made him a star in the first place to the terse, introspective, more

guarded manner of his best recent performances. Here, as
in *The Verdict*, he brings the weight of a moral victory to a
man's struggle to regain his faith and proficiency. This time,
the enemy is within.

People magazine raved that

> Paul Newman makes everything he's learned in three de-
> cades of screen acting pay off in this forceful follow-up to
> his 1961 role. . . . At sixty-one, Newman hasn't lost his
> looks; he's improved upon them. And his acting isn't lazy;
> it's eager, feral. He's in full maturity and he's never been
> better. An Oscar nominee and no win would stick it smartly
> to the Academy for sending him prematurely out to pasture
> last year with one of those honorary-gold-watch awards.

According to Newman's publicist, Newman's no-show
was not a case of "sticking it smartly to the Academy." But
Newman did not take the evening off because he was too
busy. "He feels he's jinxed himself by being present" for
previous nominations, Cowan explained. Perhaps he was
right, for the night of March 30, 1987, after James Woods,
Bob Hoskins, and Dexter Gordon had toasted their absent
conominee in the lounge during a break in the interminable
show, Paul Newman won the Best Actor Oscar for his performance as Fast Eddie Felson. Martin Scorsese commented, "Paul gave a special performance that was
controlled yet emotional. His Oscar was no consolation
prize."
As for Newman, he tried to play it as cool as Eddie at the
pool table. "It's like chasing a beautiful woman for eighty
years," he commented. "Finally she relents and you say, 'I
am terribly sorry. I'm tired.'" But nobody had swallowed
those tall tales about being too busy or being long past caring. After seven nominations and a brush-off in the form of

an honorary award, Newman had finally got what he'd always wanted, official recognition of his abilities from the beast of Babylon that had once tried to swallow him whole in order to regurgitate a patented image of fifties Hollywood glamour. "I was always a character actor," he had once commented. "I just looked like Little Red Riding Hood." Newman celebrated the occasion with a double date—Joanne Woodward and he with Tom Cruise and Mimi Rogers—for dinner at a trendy New York restaurant, Wilkinson's Seafood Cafe on York Avenue.

From there it was onto the south of France, where the distributors for *Menagerie,* who were banking on a positive response, put the Newmans up in a palatial $650-a-night—meals *not* included—hotel suite in Beaulieu, a few miles outside Cannes.

Unaccustomed to international gatherings of cinema celebs such as Cannes, Newman admitted his discomfort: "I'm not all that public a person, but I want the film to be seen. I want it to get the widest circulation it can and I would like to see the actors get paid something. I suppose that's crass commercialism, but I would like that." In order to finance the film, the cast and director had worked essentially for love, receiving scale and a cut of possible future profits. While Newman struggled to maintain his cool amid the blinding flashbulbs of shoving paparazzi and the crowds of star-struck French tourists, Woodward was mugged by thieves who took her money, identification, and passport. She was physically unharmed, though understandably shaken. Attending film festivals, Newman concluded, is as much fun "as walking down the street with a revolver in my mouth."

Though the critics were generally admiring of the integrity of Newman's production, some faulted him for having too much respect for Williams's play; Newman had wanted to avoid just that. "You take it too seriously, and create this sepulcher-type thing, it's really dangerous," he had told *USA Today.* But a few thought he had fallen into that very trap. Janet Maslin wrote in *The New York Times,*

> It's a serious and respectful adaptation, but never an incendiary one, perhaps because the odds against its capturing the play's real genius are simply too great. In any case, this *Glass Menagerie* catches more of the drama's closeness and narrowness than its fire.

Scott Haler, writing in *People,* had a similar reaction:

> Paul Newman seems content to play preservationist to this memory play. . . . Newman seems overpowered by Williams's poetry. To showcase the heightened language, he has staged a compulsively faithful production that functions more as a play than as a movie. . . . Newman treats Williams too much in the manner Laura treats her glass animal collection—like a fragile curiosity that would shatter if it were touched.

But one wonders what other choices Newman could have made without violating Williams's intentions. Newman decided, and rightly so, to serve the play rather than use it as a vehicle for his own individual artistic expression. This was a homage and payment of a debt to Tennessee Williams, not Paul Newman's movie. As Newman had noted, despite the confinements of the single set, the poetic language, and Tom's narration, the play was inherently cinematic. Newman was justifiably proud of the film, particularly of his wife's performance. "She's the best there is," director Newman assessed, "and getting better."

Back in New York for the opening, Newman arrived in a celebrity bus after a special screening at another benefit for the Actors Studio, this time at Sam's, Mariel Hemingway's

Manhattan café. The restaurant was crowded with celebrities: Patti Lupone; Sargent Shriver and his wife, Eunice; their daughter, Maria Shriver Schwarzenegger; Sally Jessy Raphael; Polly Bergen; and Elizabeth Ray, the celebrated Washington typist. Newman sat next to his racing buddy Mario Andretti and talked racing.

Clearly Newman had found one activity that kept him from becoming emotionally anesthetized, car racing, and if he had begun to be immured to the thrills of that sport, his headline crash at California's Riverside International Speedway in May 1987, right after his return from Cannes, must have reminded him of just how exciting his second profession was. Earlier in the race, Newman's Nissan had spun out into the middle of the track as the other cars rushed by. Not too long after, at a speed of 100 mph, he slammed his vehicle into a wall. A long, tense moment passed before a tight-lipped Newman unbuckled himself, climbed out of the window, and walked away from the destroyed car. "He's just upset because he was in contention to win the race—he was in the top ten," raceway spokesman Jim Hyneman said. "And when you are in the top ten, you're always in contention. Newman is a professional driver before he is an actor," Hyneman stressed. "The public may not understand that, but he's full time." Tom Cruise was in the sidelines to cheer his friend on, but Joanne Woodward was not present. Though Woodward had no comment about the incident, she had made it clear that she "wouldn't think of asking him to stop. It is an interesting sport for a grown man who is doing what he chooses." Having made her peace with car racing, Woodward remained cool even after his worst crash. "I talked with her the day after the accident," said a friend, "and she didn't mention it once."

For his part, Newman promised to be back in the driver's seat within a week. "I'm not sure what happened," he said.

"The brakes seemed to give at the entrance to Turn Nine. The car lurched and I went into the wall. I can't even recall how many times I felt I was off the track. The car was capable of winning, but it just wasn't our day," he concluded. In any event, he soon treated the accident in his usual laconic manner. "Oh that," he shrugged upon being queried by a *Daily News* reporter. "Well, the rumors of my death were greatly exaggerated. I did love one headline after an accident in Atlanta. The headline was 'Newman Almost Killed Though Uninjured.' I thought that one had a certain flair," he laughed.

Newman's racing team director, Gene Crowe, commented on Newman's assumption of responsibility for the accident. "A lot of drivers will find all kinds of fault with the car when they're not going as fast as they should be. But Paul tends to blame himself, even when there is something wrong with the car." Witnesses to the accident agreed that Newman could not have handled the situation better. Course photographer Frank Mormillo said, "The course workers all had a great deal of praise that he was able to keep the car against the wall. The natural tendency is to bounce back on the track, which is a greater hazard, but in addition to saving himself from the impact, he saved the other drivers as well."

This was not the first brush with death Newman had experienced since pursuing car racing full time. When his brakes failed one time when he was doing 140 mph, he "picked out an escape route that quickly sloughed off 60 mph. Then I slammed into a wall and pretzeled the car." When he and a partner crashed after hitting a rut on a dirt track in New Orleans, "We hardly had our hair mussed," he said. "But as I stood by the car, somebody slammed the door on my hand." In 1980, at Lime Rock, Connecticut, Newman again walked away intact from a series of rear-end collisions. Three years later, in Braselton, Georgia, he hit a guardrail after another car clipped the back of his car.

On November 8, 1987, Newman's racing crony sixty-five-year-old Jim Fitzgerald met his death from a broken neck, when his Nissan 300ZX crashed broadside into a concrete wall as he entered the first turn on the third lap at the GTE St. Petersburg Grand Prix. "The aging Butch and Sundance of the Trans Am racing circuit," *People* had labeled them. The Newman-Fitzgerald friendship had begun fifteen years earlier at Road Atlanta, a major racing and teaching complex. "I had the beer cooler, he had the beer," Fitzgerald once joked. Dubbed "the Geritol Gang" by the younger drivers with whom the older men exchanged an endless series of elaborate practical jokes, driver Deborah Gregg recalls Newman and Fitzgerald as a "perfect match. They shared the same sense of humor. They'd have dinner together. Jim would help with Paul's driving, and Paul would help Jim."

Newman watched from his own car as Fitzgerald's crashed and his friend was instantly killed. And he waited with everyone else for the forty-nine minutes it took for the race to resume. During that interminable period Newman gripped his wheel tightly, eyes closed. When the race resumed he was unable to go on. He left immediately and flew home the next morning, but to this date Newman is still racing.

He hasn't slowed down his political activity, either. An active member of the Center for Defense Information, a research group that opposes many Pentagon policies, Newman stays abreast of what's happening and lets everyone else know as well. "Paul calls me at least once a week with ideas," the center's director, retired Admiral Gene LaRocque told *USA Weekend*.

He suggested we take out full-page ads listing Nobel laureates who want a ban on nuclear weapons, which we did. He's done far more than just be incredibly generous financially. He's gone with me on programs like "Donahue" and "Good Morning, America," and Paul always says the only thing he hates more than bureaucracy is live television.

A more rich and active life could hardly be imagined, yet Newman remains modest to the point of self-disparagement. Ron Buck, his friend and coauthor of *Harry and Son,* recalled to *USA Weekend* that he once visited Newman, carrying a copy of *Time* with the actor on the cover. "We worked for eight days straight at his house before he even picked it up," Buck marvels.

Newman has come a long way from the miserably self-conscious young actor moping through *The Silver Chalice* in a Grecian "cocktail gown." Yet one could see clearly, even in his younger days, all the qualities of the mature version that was to come. At sixty-four, the essential Newman has changed very little. He has developed a newfound trust in himself, an ease with who he is that has allowed him to become even more fully himself, but at the same time what actually has happened is that *we* have changed. Paul Newman stuck to his principles and finally forced us to see the real him.

10

CONCLUSION

From the very beginning of his career, Paul Newman fought to be accepted on his own terms. He refused to play Hollywood, to allow himself to be poured into the mold that would have turned him into another disposable sex symbol, by nature doomed to a short life and an anonymous death. Sidney Lumet managed to build a long and venerable career in New York City during the heyday of the Hollywood studio system; he fully understands Newman's maverick status. "Paul's done it without their rules. And in Hollywood, they love labels and they love people who are beholden to them."

Though his screen image incorporates elements of the macho male cut along somewhat old-fashioned lines, Newman has never been easy to figure out. Guided by an unspoken motto that might read, "If I didn't sweat for it, it isn't valuable," Newman projects an intense combination of courage, sexual charisma, and statesmanship.

He embodies our image of a real hero, one with a true sense of purpose—to right the wrongs of the world. Newman also has the even greater bravery to show us the vulnerability often cowering in the giant shadow cast by the archetype. He is us, only bigger than life. Outwardly Paul Newman is a wonderful image of a man—what we all want a man to be—but inwardly he feels blemished, flawed somehow, as we know all men really are, and it is that inner dissatisfaction that is Newman's greatest challenge. It provides the driving force to show us a perfect exterior at the same time as it creates his need to show us his weaker, darker self.

Well into his sixties, Newman is still physically gorgeous. His looks have purified, and as the flesh recedes the underlying facial structure emerges, along with inner reserves of character we often missed, captivated as we were by the voluptuous mouth, and the wide, azure eyes. "There's a stillness in his acting now that is quite magnificent," notes Sydney Pollack, director of *Absence of Malice.* "You can see him thinking. He has the depth of a clear pool of water, not rippling or churning or tumbling."

Newman will speak of an actor he admires, such as Brando, as an artist, but when he talks of his own work, he often disparages acting as an occupation unsuitable for a grown man. "To be a good actor," he once told *People,* "you have to be a child. But who wants to take a lot of credit for being a child when you're nearly sixty?"

Part of that devaluation of his craft might be attributable to his dissatisfaction with the film industry, particularly in the seventies. "I couldn't take a great deal of pride in my craft when the biggest stars were a shark and two robots."

But he also admits to personal disappointment in his own work. "I felt restless," he told *The Aquarian*. I was duplicating myself on screen. I suppose that's one of my great regrets. I don't see variety in my past films. I'm envious of guys like Olivier and Guinness who seem to have an almost inexhaustible supply of characters in them—all different."

While he may have occasionally scoffed at acting as child's play, Newman's fear of playing the fool spurred him earlier in his career into a frenzy of preparation for every role. As Joanne Woodward pointed out some years ago, "Paul spends the first month of every movie convinced that his characterization is so inept that people will laugh at him."

But Newman can feel some pride in his development as an actor. "I'm just now beginning to learn a little something about acting," he told Maureen Dowd in *The New York Times*. "I don't say that as a joke and I don't say it because I'm being modest. I don't think I ever had an immediate gift to do anything right."

Newman doesn't like to view his earlier films, even the more successful roles, because he claims he could see himself working at the character, "indicating" what he wanted the audience to know. "In the scene in *Hud* when I was talking to my nephew and I said, 'My Mamma loved me but she died,' I was working too hard to find the emotions," Newman told *The New York Times*. "I compare that to the summation scene at the end of *The Verdict*. The emotions are there, but you couldn't see the machinery."

Newman no longer needs to spend lengthy periods of time in preparation for a role. "My imagination appears to be more fertile," he told the *Times*. "I don't really have to get down on my hands and knees and look under the rocks. I remember for *Hombre* I went down to an Indian reservation for five days and brought back one thing. I drove past a general store and there was a guy standing there in front with one foot up and his arms crossed. He was in exactly the same position when I drove back four hours later. That whole character came out of that."

Now Newman says he discovers a character "by finding his nerves." In the scene in *The Verdict* where Frank Galvin follows a doctor down the street desperately trying to get him to testify for his client, Newman played it "the way a dog follows somebody that has a bone in his hand—sideways." For the role of Michael Gallagher in *Absence of Malice,* Newman drew on his own physical characteristics but pared down to a minimalist performance that told the audience everything. "He knew a lot," Newman told the *Times.* "And people who know a lot don't do very much with their bodies."

Director Martin Scorsese recalled for the *Times* that when he was editing *The Color of Money, The Hustler* came on the television set that was always left on in the corner. Scorsese watched the thirty-three-year-old Newman at the same time as he watched the sixty-one-year-old on his editing screen. "I like him better now," said Scorsese. "He looks like he's been there and survived but taken something with him. There's so much information in his eyes about what they're seeing."

Though he's always resented the confusion of Paul Newman private citizen with Paul Newman movie star, he does admit the irony that the influence has often been reciprocal. Over the years, bits and pieces, little telling traits or points of view of Hud, Fast Eddie, or Frank, have found their temporary and even permanent niches in the crevices of his own personality. "There's a hangover from characters sometimes," he once admitted. "There are things that stick. Since *Slapshot,* my language is right out of the locker room. And ever since I played Rocky Graziano, I spit on the street. I think you can be fined for that in New York, can't you?" And acting techniques have crept their way into his everyday behavior. "I can listen better than any-body without hearing a thing," he has said. "I can be com-pleting a bridge hand in my head and be bidding four no trump at the moment that the other guy is saying, 'My god, he really listens quite attentively.'"

Newman has worked hard at his craft over the years, as the steadily enriched quality of his work testifies. He has viewed his looks as a kind of handicap, something he didn't earn by the sweat of his own brow. As one would expect, Newman has little respect for anyone who doesn't make use of whatever talents they do possess. "I resent people who have big talents and don't work at it," he commented on "The Today Show," "because I have a tiny little talent and I squeeze the tube about as dry as it is going to get."

As he moves toward the fifth decade of his career, the man with "a tiny little talent" remains way ahead of the game, playing characters at least ten years younger than himself, always getting the girl who is often twenty or thirty years younger, successfully challenging the system, and ending the film as he is about to embark on a promising new life. In fact, his recent acting successes undoubtedly result partially from the double-edged blessing of age. Lib-erated from the glamour of his youth, Newman can now tackle roles without that distraction. "Paul's always been one of the best actors we've got, but there was that great stone face and those gorgeous blue eyes and a lot of people assumed he couldn't act," said Sidney Lumet. "He got rele-gated to leading-man parts and he wasn't using a quarter of his talent. Now he's able to cut loose and do sensational work."

No one has determined whether or not the daily immer-sions in ice water are fiction or reality, but he did suffer a hernia recently from overexercising, so he now maintains his washboard stomach by doing his sit-ups on a slant board, and by daily workouts on his exercise bike and weight machines while he monitors world happenings via television news reports. Ever the paradox, an inside tip led to a report in one newspaper that at least three times in one month, Newman followed his thrice-weekly work out at a Westport gym with stops at Serendipity 3 for a frozen hot chocolate, a snifter filled with forty-five different kinds of chocolate. His wardrobe is informal to say the least, comprised mainly of jeans, T-shirts, and the like, including a favorite beat-up navy orange flight suit. His jewelry consists of a large, diamond-studded ring and a silver neck chain with a beer tab presented by Budweiser. "Fashion bores the bejesus out of me," he told *New York Times* reporter Maureen Dowd. Pointing to a small, battered leather satchel he uses for weekends, he asked the writer, "Would Sylvester Stallone have luggage like that?"

Despite his recent successes, the greatest of his career, Newman seems unconcerned with acting, finding the challenges he craves in directing, producing, automobile racing, and, more than ever, humanitarian causes. As an active member of SEA (Seaside Environmental Alliance), he has put in his time walking up and down beaches collecting signatures protesting the methods of oil companies. The profits from his food company have made him one of the world's most generous philanthropists. "Once you allow your face to adorn a bottle of salad dressing, there's no way you can take yourself seriously," he told *USA Today*. "It's been wonderfully humbling."

The many millions in profits from Newman's Own have gone to a long list of medical, cultural, social, and environmental, international as well as American, organizations. Some of the groups to receive substantial funds have been the Scott Newman Center; Catholic Relief Services, dedicated to alleviating famine in Ethiopia; *The New York Times* Neediest Fund; the Fresh Air Fund; Habitat for Humanity, which builds homes for those in need; Flying Doctors; African Medical Researchers; Children of the Night, a Los Angeles group aiding street children; Hospital for Sick Children in Toronto; New York Hospital Burn Center; CLASP Homes for the Retarded; Hope Rural School in Indiantown, Florida, for children of migrant workers; the College of the Atlantic's new science laboratory, where his daughter Nell pursued her interest in falcons; New York's Channel 13, which is dedicated to developing innovative programming; and, of course, Newman's beloved Actors Studio. In 1986 the company brought in enough profits to begin building the Hole in the Wall Gang Summer Camp.

The company that started by bottling Newman's favorite salad dressing grew to include a tart, English-style lemonade that he claims "restored Joan Collins to virginity," and that his partner says is "the official drink of Planned Parenthood." One reason for the success of the all-natural-food line is its uniform high quality. "Quality control?" Newman exclaims. "Are you kidding! We have them send jars from *Australia,* randomly off the shelves, so we can test it."

But the main offices remain characteristically humble, reflecting Newman's dismissal of the whole enterprise as a "tacky" joke that suddenly got very serious. Located in the Newman Westport home, the offices are furnished with lounge chairs from Newman's pool, a president's desk sporting an attached striped umbrella, and a ping-pong table that serves as board table. The staff consists of a part-time bookkeeper, and a part-time secretary whose activities often include a game of darts or ping pong with the company officers. Newman's favorite job is writing the Joycean stream-of-consciousness labels adorning the jars, such as the one on the spaghetti sauce, which reads, "Working 12 hour days . . . wrecked . . . hungry . . . arrive home, deserted by wife and children . . . cursing! Cook—junk! YUCK! Lie down, snooze . . . yum, yum . . . slurp,

slurp . . . Terrifico! Magnifico! Bottle the sauce . . . share with guys on the streetcar . . . ah, me, finally immortal!''

He is particularly tickled when he receives praises for his food from people who don't have a taste for either his politics or his acting. On the wall of the office is a letter from Michael Sullivan of Rancho Cordova, California, praising Newman's spaghetti sauce: "My girlfriend mentioned that you were a movie star and I would be interested to know what you've made. If you act as well as you cook, your movies would be worth watching. P.S. Are any of your movies in VCR?"

Newman's Own's great success has been tempting bait for the large corporations. "We have been offered countless millions to be bought out," Hotchner told the *Times*. "Beatrice Foods inquired about our availability. We won't meet with them. It's more fun to have a couple of bumbling idiots running the company."

Because of his longtime political activism and his pattern of looking for new fields to conquer even as he is riding high on the success of yet another venture, many people have anticipated Newman's official entry into the political ring, just as several other actors, most notably Ronald Reagan and Clint Eastwood, have done before him. One tabloid ran an "I want to run for President" story, which purported to quote Newman directly, claiming that he and Joanne Woodward "never see each other." Three weeks later they printed another story maintaining that "they are closer than ever." Newman was enraged with both stories, saying the fiction made him "look like an ass." He talked of consulting his attorney and publicly denied once again that he would ever run for office. "I am a very private person and have enough troubles as it is." When he is asked about his political ambitions, he usually responds, "As Joe Biden. Ask Gary Hart."

That Newman would subject himself to the minute public

scrutiny a political career necessitates is unimaginable. "It would drive me *wild*. It would blow my marriage and drive me crazy," he once said.

Periodically, Newman has threatened to retire from public life altogether to become, of all things, a gentleman farmer of the future, an aquafarmer. In the meantime, he continues voraciously reading scripts and books, planning his acting schedule around the months when he races and finding causes guaranteed to keep him on the "hit list" of any right-wing president. "I just hope when my mind goes, or when my body does, I have the guts to end it the way Hemingway did," he told a *Life* reporter. "I don't want anybody wiping drool off my chin." That statement sounds very much like the Newman movie star persona, worthy of Hud, Eddie, and others. The real Newman is, in fact, a man who keeps his distance from all but a very select few. On January 29, 1988, the Newmans celebrated their thirtieth wedding anniversary. "I've never seen a man as devoted to his wife," says Ron Buck.

But Newman admits the marriage hasn't always been smooth-running. "I've been packing a few times, but we're not quitters," he avows. Compromises have been made. Early in their marriage Woodward described her new husband as "victorian," but added that "I like that about him." With the years, Woodward came to feel more of a need to establish an identity other than that of the wife of a movie star, and, with her time freed from raising their daughters, pursued her interests more fully.

Among Newman's less-publicized interests are poetry and painting. "So you wound up with Apollo/If he's sometimes hard to swallow/Use this," reads the Newman-penned verse inscribed on a silver sherry cup he gave his wife for a wedding anniversary. In her *New York Times* profile of Paul Newman, Maureen Dowd described a paint-

ing in the bathroom of the Newman Manhattan penthouse
as

> a framed picture of a delicate flower, inked in shades of
> brown, violet, and yellow. It is signed "Paul Newman,
> 1982" and labeled "Self Portrait." However, when a friend
> arrives with a restored oil painting that Newman bought
> downtown for $200, the actor decides that this should be his
> self-portrait. It shows a Dutch nobleman looking out at the
> world with dark, watchful eyes. "I've been accused of being
> aloof," he says. "I'm not. I'm just wary."

Although Newman was roundly criticized for explaining
his fidelity to his wife by saying, "I have steak at home,
why go out for hamburger?" he now likens his wife to "a
classy '62 Bordeaux. "No, make it '59. That's a year that
ages well in the bottle. Will I get into trouble for that?"

"He's enjoyed the last three years enormously," Susan
Newman told *USA Weekend* in March of 1987. "His professional experiences have been good ones; his marriage is
strong and his children have grown . . . and that relieves
responsibility."

In the mid eighties the *New York Post* announced that
Newman was cooperating with an unidentified man to write
an authorized biography. The story was confirmed by his
press agent, Warren Cowan. When a publishing house got
wind of the project, however, Newman wrote them that he
had no plans to actually publish the work. "I'm just gather-
ing information that I am going to pass on to my children."

He had once talked of writing a film about his son and
their relationship, but he later thought better of it. "You
can't fictionalize grief," he said.

"There are liabilities and assets," he has said concerning
his children's role as Paul Newman's kids. "Some of my

children have focused more on the liabilities and others have been able to enjoy the assets."

Gore Vidal says Paul Newman "has a good character, and not many people do. I think he would rather not do anything wrong, whether on a moral or an artistic level. He is what you would call a man of conscience—not necessarily of judgment, but of conscience. I don't know any actors like that."

The fact that Newman is preeminently a man of decency is echoed by his many friends and working associates. Professional and always helpful on the set, Newman is not plagued by typical movie-star concerns such as flattering angles or the size of his trailer. "Flattery will get you nowhere with Paul," Sidney Lumet told the *Times*. "He doesn't want to hear what's good because, first of all, he knows, and second, if there's trouble he wants to know about it." "Charm is not one of Paul's big points," said George Roy Hill, director of *Butch Cassidy and the Sundance Kid* and *The Sting*. But professionalism is. Hill recalled for *The New York Times* that when the stuntman hired to perform bicycle tricks for *Butch Cassidy* refused on the grounds that they were too dangerous, Newman suddenly appeared coasting down the road, standing on the seat of the bike with one leg extended behind him. "I said two more words to the stuntman—'You're fired,'" says Hill. Sally Fields recalled Newman's difficulty in playing a scene in which he was supposed to knock her down and rip her blouse. He couldn't bring himself to hurt her. "He kept trying to fake it," she told the *Times*. Newman consistently refuses parts that promote what he considers senseless violence; he turned down *Romancing the Stone* for that reason.

Newman continues to be a regular on the East Coast car-racing circuit, roaring down the track in his red, white, and blue monster of a 869 horsepower Nissan. Though he has been accused of having a death wish by those who confuse his early reckless-rebel image with the real man, the truth is probably the opposite—what looks like daring is probably the admirable bravery of an innately cautious man. A friend has said of him, "Paul loves life, and he will get the last gallon of gas out of it, to the end."

Challenge, physical demands, knowing his limits and perpetually testing those boundaries "beyond which you cannot go" have been key themes in Newman's life. He loves a challenge, but not certain failure. With racing and acting, Newman has found the perfect balance to express his complex personality.

Paul Newman would like to fix the world, but he is also a man who "loves to have a good time," as his pal Robert Redford says. Unlike most of us, Newman has used to the fullest his natural gifts and turned his head firmly away from misguided advice. Ultimately the voice he listened to was his own. How did he do it, and why? His daughter Susan responds, "Who knows? None of us in the family has a handle on how Old Skinny Legs made it." And none of us has a handle on what he will do next.

FILMOGRAPHY

1955   *The Silver Chalice*   Warner Brothers
1956   *The Rack*   MGM
1957   *Somebody Up There Likes Me*   MGM
1957   *The Helen Morgan Story*   Warner Brothers
1957   *Until They Sail*   MGM
1958   *The Long Hot Summer*   Twentieth Century-Fox
1958   *The Left-Handed Gun*   Warner Brothers
1958   *Cat on a Hot Tin Roof*   MGM
1959   *Rally 'Round the Flag, Boys!*   Twentieth Century-Fox
1959   *The Young Philadelphians*   Warner Brothers
1960   *Exodus*   United Artists
1961   *The Hustler*   Twentieth Century-Fox
1961   *Paris Blues*   United Artists
1962   *Sweet Bird of Youth*   MGM
1962   *Hemingway's Adventures of a Young Man*   Twentieth Century-Fox
1963   *Hud*   Paramount
1963   *The Prize*   MGM
1964   *The Outrage*   MGM
1964   *What a Way to Go*   Twentieth Century-Fox
1966   *Lady L*   MGM
1967   *The Moving Target (Harper)*   Warner Brothers
1967   *Torn Curtain*   Universal
1967   *Hombre*   Twentieth Century-Fox

1967   *Cool Hand Luke*   Warner Brothers
1968   *Rachel, Rachel,* (director only)   Warner Brothers
1968   *The Secret War of Harry Frigg*   Universal
1968   *Winning*   Universal
1968   *Butch Cassidy and the Sundance Kid*   Twentieth Century-Fox
1969   *W.U.S.A.*   Paramount
1970   *Sometimes a Great Notion* (star and director)   Universal
1971   *Pocket Money*   National General
1971   *The Life and Times of George Roy Bean*   National General
1972   *The Effect of Marigolds on Man-in-the-Moon Marigolds* (director only)   Universal
1973   *The Mackintosh Man*   Warner Brothers
1973   *The Sting*   Universal
1974   *Towering Inferno*   Twentieth Century-Fox
1976   *Buffalo Bill and the Indians or Sitting Bull's History Lesson*   EMI
1976   *Silent Movie*   Twentieth Century-Fox
1977   *Slapshot*   Universal
1979   *Quintet*   Warner Brothers
1980   *When Time Ran Out*   Warner Brothers
1981   *Fort Apache, the Bronx*   Twentieth Century-Fox
1982   *Absence of Malice*   Columbia
1983   *The Verdict*   Twentieth Century-Fox
1984   *Harry and Son* (directed, cowrote, starred)   Orion
1986   *The Color of Money*   Touchstone Pictures
1987   *The Glass Menagerie* (directed only)   Cineplex Odeon
1990   *Blaze*   Warner Brothers

INDEX